PROFLIGATE SON

BRANWELL BRONTË
AND HIS SISTERS

Profligate Son

BRANWELL BRONTË
AND HIS SISTERS

JOAN REES

ROBERT HALE · LONDON

© *Joan Rees 1986*
First published in Great Britain 1986

ISBN 0 7090 2788 5

Robert Hale Limited
Clerkenwell House
Clerkenwell Green
London EC1R OHT

British Library Cataloguing in Publication Data

Rees, Joan
    Profligate son : Branwell Brontë and his
    sisters.
    1. Brontë (*Family*)   2. Novelist, English
    — 19th century — Biography
    I. Title
    823'.8'09   PR4168

ISBN 0-7090-2788-5

Set in Ehrhardt by Derek Doyle & Associates, Mold, Clwyd.
Printed in Great Britain by
St Edmundsbury Press, Bury St Edmunds, Suffolk.
Bound by WBC Bookbinders Ltd.

Contents

For my dear Yorkshireman
Cedric Day

Acknowledgements

Everyone who writes about the Brontë family must be grateful for all the enthusiastic and dedicated work that has gone before from Elizabeth Gaskell onwards, as is shown here in the source notes and lists of works consulted.

The detailed biographies of Winifred Gérin who, together with her husband, so immersed herself in the life of Haworth, must be noted in particular, and I am grateful to the Oxford University Press for permission to quote from them. I also acknowledge with thanks the permission of the British Museum to quote from the letters of Charlotte Brontë to M. Heger, and of Messrs Routledge and Kegan Paul to quote from *The Powys Brothers*. The quotations from the Brontë novels have been taken from Messrs J. M. Dent's easily available Everyman paperback edition.

My thanks are due to John Gibson for suggesting this book, and as always to the most efficient and helpful service of the London Library.

Above all, I would like to thank Dr Juliet Barker, Curator and Librarian, and the staff at the Brontë Parsonage Museum for their ready help and warmth of welcome. It is an inspiration to work there and I only wish I could have stayed much longer. Generous permission has been given by the Council of the Brontë Society for quotations from manuscripts held in the Museum, from articles in the *Brontë Society Transactions*, and for permission to reproduce illustrations.

Finally, I am sure that everyone who goes there for whatever reason would like to thank the people of Haworth in the inns, cottages, and shops, for their good humour and courtesy during each year's invasion of visitors, and in our particular case for a most delightful stay in Mrs Sandra Ogden's Bramble Cottage.

JR

List of illustrations

Acknowledgements

The author would like to thank the following for permission to reproduce the illustrations: Brontë Parsonage Museum: 1, 2, 3, 4, 7, 8, 10, 11, 12, 17, 18, 20, 21, 23; National Portrait Gallery: 5, 9, 14, 22; Cedric Day: 6; M. René Pechère, The Readers' Digest, and the Hamlyn Publishing Group Ltd.: 13; The Walsall Health Authority (with thanks to Peter Allen) and George Farnham of Quorn House: 15, 16; The Brotherton Library, University of Leeds: 19.

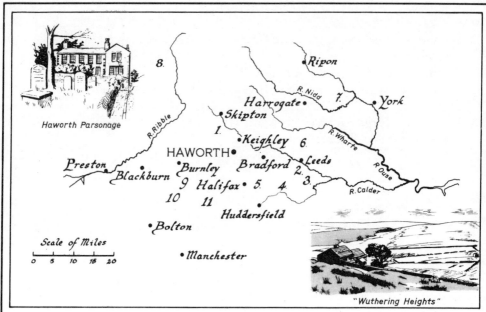

Haworth Parsonage

"Wuthering Heights"

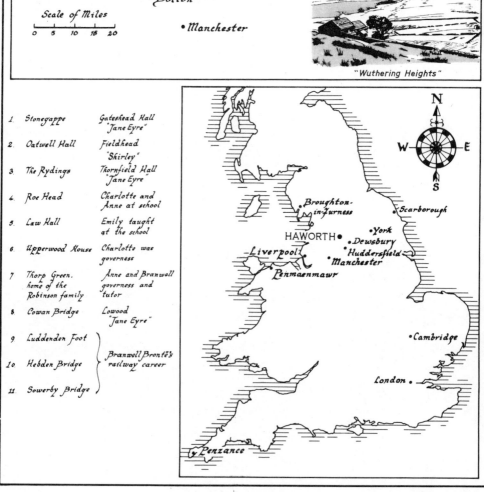

1. Stonegappe   Gateshead Hall
                 "Jane Eyre"

2. Oatwell Hall   Fieldhead
                 "Shirley"

3. The Rydings   Thornfield Hall
                 "Jane Eyre"

4. Roe Head   Charlotte and
                 Anne at school

5. Law Hall   Emily taught
                 at the school

6. Upperwood House   Charlotte was
                 governess

7. Thorp Green.   Anne and Branwell
   home of the   governess and
   Robinson family   tutor

8. Cowan Bridge   Lowood
                 "Jane Eyre"

9. Luddenden Foot

10. Hebden Bridge   Branwell Brontë's
                 railway career

11. Sowerby Bridge

The Brontë Country

Introduction

The story of any one of the Brontës must, at the same time, tell the story of the whole family. To a certain extent, this is always true of any members of a family, but never more so than in the case of these four surviving motherless children, brought up in an isolated village, without suitable local playmates, by a father and aunt who valued above all things their own privacy. That privacy must have been difficult to preserve in the confines of Haworth Parsonage, where four highly intelligent children were left together for many hours of each day, but otherwise alone.

Alone, it must be said, apart from the vivid creatures of their own creation with whom they peopled the world in which they most truly lived: the world of their imagination.

When they grew up, Charlotte, the eldest, made the most conscious effort to renounce this world which had begun to make her feel guilty; Branwell's immersion in it, talented, clever, even diligent though he was, made him practically incapable of sustaining any role in real life; Emily and, to a lesser extent, Anne continued to enjoy 'playing at' their chronicles of Gondal, at the same time as they were writing their novels, without any qualms of conscience. Emily's only qualms were about letting any of her writing go before the public. Once she had, and then only because of the vehemence of Charlotte's insistence, she apparently became inhibited from writing any more. It can only be hoped that almost until the end, when she and Anne were on their own, the Gondals still flourished 'bright as ever'.

The works they have left speak for themselves, but most of what is known of the lives and characters of the three younger Brontës has been shaped and influenced by Charlotte, the sister who survived to become a figure on the literary scene and who provided Mrs Gaskell with the information for her great biography of Charlotte, which gave at the same

time what became the definitive picture of the rest of the family. Most of
Mrs Gaskell's additional and invaluable material came from Charlotte's
friends, and it seems that Charlotte was something of a chameleon,
presenting herself to them in the way she felt they would like her best.
The letters she wrote to kind, conventional, religious Ellen Nussey, which
were preserved, were clearly in a very different vein from those she wrote
to the forthright, outspoken, adventurous Mary Taylor, which were not.

In the beautiful memoirs prepared for the 1850 edition of *Wuthering
Heights*, *Agnes Grey* and *Selected Poems*, Charlotte put her own
interpretative gloss on her sisters' works and presented her own picture of
their characters. Invaluable though these are, they were subjective and
were greatly influenced by Charlotte's tragic loss and her grief at the time.
Most unfortunate of all was her decision to destroy many of her sisters' –
and no doubt her brother's – letters and papers after their deaths. It
cannot be known what was lost, but Emily and Anne must have written
at least some letters during their long periods of separation both to each
other and to Charlotte, and with their aid a much fuller account would
now be possible of certain sketchy passages of their lives, as well as that
impact, immediacy and feeling that come from personal letters not
written for publication, and in particular to and from people who enjoyed
the intimacy and rare rapport granted to Emily and Anne.

The letters which must have been written by Anne during the period of
her stay with the Robinson family would surely have thrown some light
on the mystery of what really happened to Branwell Brontë at Thorp
Green, and the effect on the Brontë sisters of their only brother's final
disintegration and death, which followed this episode, can hardly be
over-estimated.

This study concentrates principally on Anne and Branwell, with special
emphasis on their time together at Thorp Green; on the changing
relationships which occurred within the family unit; and on Charlotte's
ultimate rejection of Branwell which, understandable though it was,
tragically contributed to his final self-destruction.

1. Origins: from Dewsbury to Cowan Bridge, 1812–24

For most readers, the Brontës and Yorkshire are indivisibly linked. Many make their way to the harshly beautiful northern county solely to see where the children of Haworth parsonage lived and wrote their poems and novels. Yet the strange fact is that they were alien transplants. They did not belong to the landscape in which they were reared. Only Emily found there her spiritual home – a home which it was spiritual death for her to leave.

As for Patrick Branwell, their only brother, he began life with every promise of brilliance, then withered and died like a sprig of bright shamrock perishing among the heather.

The Brontë family, with an Irish father and Cornish mother, was Celtic on both sides. Their father, Patrick Brunty, as his name was then, was born in 1777 in a tiny thatched cottage at Emdale, Loughbrickland, in the parish of Drumballyroney-cum-Drumgooland in County Down. His parents, the handsome Protestant Hugh and the beautiful Catholic Eleanor McClory, who renounced her faith on marriage, had made a runaway love match, and Patrick was the eldest of their ten children. In practical terms, their family life was a perpetual struggle for survival, and in later life Patrick was to suffer from dyspepsia due to his poor and frugal diet, and from weak eyes aggravated by his fine linen weaving, one of the ways in which he added to the family's income, and by perpetual reading in a dim, flickering light.

Patrick Brontë's escape from his background is one of the most striking achievements in the Brontë story. The hard work and perseverance required for this poor Irish boy to gain admission to St John's College, Cambridge, at that time, can hardly be imagined today. From his earliest boyhood, the various odd jobs he worked at were designed to advance his ambitions, and he soon saw that his best hopes of gaining an education were through his involvement with the Church.

He was fortunate in securing the help first of the Reverend Andrew Harshaw and then of the Reverend Thomas Tighe, who had been a friend of John Wesley. In due course, the bright pupil was promoted to teacher and in fact tutored Thomas Tighe's young sons. It was with Tighe's help that, at the age of twenty-five, Patrick Brontë was admitted to Cambridge University under the designation of a sizar, which permitted him to study as an undergraduate and to earn a small but indispensable allowance, later supplemented by a Hare scholarship.

Even so, life at Cambridge must have been a financial struggle for Patrick, who was also to send what little he could spare home to his mother, but he managed to keep his head above water, graduated in 1806 and was accepted as a candidate for Holy Orders. He had worked with energy and dedication, fulfilling his own hopes and those of his patrons, exhibiting the concentration and tenacity of purpose that his own talented son was so disastrously to lack.

Patrick's first appointment was as curate to the parish of Weatherfield in Essex in 1806. A year later, shortly after one final visit to Ireland, he was ordained at St James's, Westminster. By this time his name had been transmuted to the more romantic Brontë, no doubt inspired by the tribute conferred on Nelson of his Sicilian dukedom. Perhaps there can be discerned here a vein of hero-worship, similar to his daughter Charlotte's lifelong devotion to the Duke of Wellington.

Because he was not portrayed in print until he was a sad and elderly gentleman, Patrick Brontë has acquired the character of a curmudgeonly eccentric, but in the days when he first went to Essex, he was a gallant young man who had inherited his parents' good looks, with all the well-known charm of his race, including an appealing voice and beguiling Irish accent. He was photographed in later life when he was a craggily handsome old man.

He lost no time in setting these advantages to good effect in his courtship of a well-placed local girl, the niece of his landlady, Miss Mary Burder. In spite of her parents' disapproval, she let it be known that she was attracted to the dashing curate. When Patrick moved to Wellington in Shropshire, the romance was continued by correspondence. Apparently it was he who finally let it languish, so that the disappointed Mary was embittered by the feeling that she had been jilted. Whether this was a failure of affection or passion, or simply the effect of distance and the blight of parental discouragement, is not clear.

At Wellington, Patrick's fellow curate was the Reverend William Morgan, who became a loyal friend; neither young man stayed there long, both moving north in 1809 to Yorkshire, which county Patrick was never again to leave. His first appointment was at Dewsbury, later to become of importance in the life of his daughter Charlotte, where he was popular and appreciated for his compassion and courage in dealing with some of the more belligerent of his parishoners.

His next move, in March 1811, was to the nearby village of Hartshead, where the church was much neglected, and the parishoners so far flung that to visit them conscientiously meant long, tiring and frequently wet walks over the moors. Patrick Brontë was long remembered there for his zeal and tirelessness in carrying out his duties. It was during his stay that the discontented workpeople, who became known as the Luddites, began rioting. These poor people, frightened of the consequences of the mechanization of the Industrial Revolution, seeing only unemployment following the introduction of machines to take the place of handwork, set out to break the new weaving frames – a penalty of progress such as is being experienced today. A poor man himself, in his heart, Patrick Brontë was on their side, but at the same time he could not bring himself to condone brute force and lawlessness. It was a violent and disturbing time, during which for safety's sake he began his lifelong practice of keeping his firearms near at hand, in working order and loaded.

In 1812, at Woodhouse Grove, Airedale, a Wesleyan school was started by John Fennell who, like his wife, formerly Miss Jane Branwell, had come from Penzance in Cornwall. Patrick's old friend William Morgan, now in Bradford, had suggested that he should be appointed examiner there, to assess how the boys had progressed in their Latin and Scripture. Patrick was pleased to accept the post, and when he went to the school to carry out these duties, he saw again his friend Morgan, now engaged to the Fennells' daughter Jane, and met her cousin, Miss Maria Branwell, also of Penzance, who had been helping as an assistant.

Perhaps William Morgan's love affair put romance into Patrick's mind once more and, in any case, he was now thirty-five years of age and feeling it was time to take a wife and settle down. Maria Branwell was a tiny, elegant woman some five years younger than Patrick. She was a Wesleyan Methodist from a very respected family, her brother was

Mayor of Penzance, and she had a small private income of £50 a year. Marriage between these two was a practical and sensible proposition, but this apart, there is no doubt they both fell deeply in love.

Maria was not used to love, and she was both unsure of how far it would be correct to go in declaring her affection, and nervous of being hurtful to her sweetheart if she held back. But their courtship was not to be a long and teasing one, and after having been virtually her own mistress for several years, it seems Maria was pleased to give her life into a husband's hands 'in circumstances of uncertainty and doubt, I have deeply felt the want of a guide and an instructor',[1] she wrote, when describing her former state to her future husband.

Just before their wedding, Maria wrote to Patrick – her 'saucy Pat' she calls him revealingly – about the shipwreck of some of the precious possessions she had asked to be sent to her: 'Having then received a letter from my sister giving me an account of the vessel in which she had sent my box being stranded on the coast of Devonshire, in consequence of which the box was dashed to pieces with the violence of the sea, and all my little property, with the exception of a very few articles, being swallowed up in the mighty deep; if this should not prove the prelude to something worse I shall think little of it, as it is the first disastrous circumstance which had occurred since I left my home.'[2] These were to be sadly prophetic words.

In a letter written soon afterwards, there is news of the preparation of the wedding cake, and then on 29 December 1812 there took place what must have been a joyous double wedding ceremony. Maria and Patrick were married by William Morgan, with Jane Fennell as bridesmaid, and then Jane and William were married by Patrick, with Maria by then a matron of honour. In spite of the tragedies lying in wait for them, that Maria and Patrick Brontë were and remained an extremely happily married couple.

By now, they had both proved to be writers. Maria's letters show her direct and unselfconscious style, and she had also written a little treatise with the rather intimidating title *The Advantages of Poverty in Religious Concerns*. Patrick himself had ventured into print with a book of verse, *Cottage Poems* – a modest venture with the worthy aim of appealing to the less educated classes of society. These productions would probably no longer be remembered had it not been for the brilliance of the children who followed. But they pointed the way.

Mr and Mrs Brontë began their married life in the little parsonage at Dewsbury, from whence Patrick sent forth his second book of verse, the *Rural Minstrel*, followed by more verse and some prose tales. It was here that in 1814 their first baby was born, a little girl called Maria after her mother, who from the first proved an unusually calm and forward child. She was soon followed by a second daughter, Elizabeth, and then in 1815 Patrick Brontë moved to his next curacy, in Thornton, near Bradford.

The Brontës were to spend five years in their little house in Market Street, Thornton, which Patrick was always to look back on as the happiest time of his life. He continued his writing, and both he and his wife joined in the social life of the neighbourhood, with visits and tea parties. At this time, friendships were made which became an integral part of the Brontës' later life, especially with Miss Elizabeth Firth of Kipping House, who was godmother to Elizabeth, Charlotte and Anne.

Before long, Maria became somewhat withdrawn from all this socializing, simply because of her continual pregnancies. Elizabeth had been followed by Charlotte in 1816; her only son, Patrick Branwell, was born on 26 June 1817, Emily Jane in 1818 and finally frail little Anne on 17 January 1820. Maria had always been slight, never robust, was not in her first youth, and the wonder is that she survived so long in those days of elementary gynaecology to produce six living children in seven years. Not surprisingly, the effort was too much for her. By the time her husband made his next and final move, she was already seriously ill.

The latest baby, Anne, was only a month old when her father was licensed as perpetual curate to Haworth. This was a new challenge for Patrick Brontë, to follow in the steps of the famous and terrifying Wesleyan preacher William Grimshaw. It was not a distant move, being only six miles to the north-west from Thornton, and the family made the journey in a light hooded waggon, with their possessions following behind in seven carts. Their young servants, Nancy and Sarah Garrs, went with them. Thus on 20 April 1820 the Brontë family entered the home which now enshrines it, the parsonage of Haworth.

'This living ... is mine for life, no-one can take it from me ... my salary is not large, it is only about 200 a year, I have a good house, which is mine for life, also, and is rent free.'[3]

Clearly, Patrick Brontë was pleased and relieved by the security of his new situation. As was to be expected from his record, he was to prove a hard-working and caring pastor, deeply involved in every aspect of the lives of his parishioners throughout the long years he was to spend there.

The family, then totally obscure, now forever famous, consisted of a vigorous Irish, Tory, Church of England clergyman, an ailing, intelligent, loving mother and wife, five little girls, aged between six years and a few months, and one bright, red-headed little boy. His name was Patrick Branwell and, no doubt to distinguish him from his father, at home he was always known as Branwell.

After her congenial life among friends at Thornton, it can be imagined that the ailing Maria approached her more beautiful but isolated new home with some dismay.

Mrs Gaskell's account of her own arrival there, although some thirty years later, probably gives a more accurate picture of what Maria saw than any that can be gained today.

> The soil in the valley (or 'bottom' to use the local term) is rich; but as the road begins to ascend, the vegetation becomes poorer; it does not flourish; it merely exists; and, instead of trees, there are only bushes and shrubs about the dwellings. Stone dykes are everywhere used in place of hedges; and what crops there are, on patches of arable land, consist of pale, hungry looking, grey-green oats. Right before the traveller on this road rises Haworth village ... The flag-stones with which it is paved are placed end-ways, in order to give a better hold to the horses' feet; and, even with this help, they seem to be in constant danger of slipping backwards. The old stone houses are high compared to the width of the street, which makes an abrupt turn before reaching the more level ground at the head of the village, so that the steep aspect of the place, in one part, is almost like that of a wall ... The parsonage stands at right angles to the road, facing down upon the church; so that, in fact, parsonage, church, and belfried school-house, form three sides of an irregular oblong, of which the fourth is open to the fields and moors that lie beyond. The area of this oblong is filled up by a crowded churchyard, and a small garden or court in front of the clergyman's house.[4]

To the young woman from the favoured and fertile Cornish coast, her new home must have appeared bleak. The village was almost like a fortress against the wildness of the moors and her home was encroached upon by the headstones, the grim reminders of death that came all too often in Haworth, with its low life-expectancy for its population of mainly weavers' families and appallingly high infant mortality. The graveyard itself, with its seepage into the supply of drinking water, made a notable contribution to the population's general debility and high death-rate.

At the same time, this dirty, rugged village had its own beauty, with its mingling of old houses of the Tudor, Jacobean and Georgian periods set against the rise and sweep of the landscape. Always described as bleak, in the spring sunshine, with the ewes and young lambs wandering over the moors, the sun shining, the trees coming into bright leaf, and the birds calling and singing, Haworth appears an attractive, cheerful place.

But arriving as she did in the depths of winter, it is unlikely that poor Maria would have been able to appreciate the more pleasing aspects of her new home.

The parsonage, now extended from its original square shape, was a dignified and comfortable dwelling, built in 1778 of local stone. There were four bedrooms and a sliproom, the width of the landing between the two front bedrooms, which hardly deserved the name of 'nursery' accorded it and which was later Emily's bedroom, a kitchen and three rooms on the ground floor, with an attractive stone-flagged hall leading to the handsome staircase and spacious landing. In the backyard were some outhouses, a well and a privy.

The windows are large, extending almost to the floor, so that in bright weather the house must have been light and cheerful. But it must have been a tight fit for the husband and wife, six children, two lively and affectionate young servants, Nancy and Sarah Garrs, and before long Maria's nurse and her sister Elizabeth, always known as Aunt Branwell. Later, Charlotte made some alterations and the north wing seen today was added ·by the Reverend John Wade after Mr Brontë's death. Although, naturally, the house now opened to the public has been adapted to suit its new functions, every effort has been made to recapture the impression of the family home, particularly as it struck Mrs Gaskell:

> I don't know that I ever saw a place more exquisitely clean; the most dainty place for that I ever saw ... The door-steps are spotless; the small old-fashioned window panes glitter like looking glass ... All the table arrangements had the same dainty simplicity about them. Then we rested and talked over the clear, bright fire; it is a cold country, and the fires were a pretty warm light dancing over the house. Everything fits into, and is in

harmony with the idea of a country parsonage, possessed by people of very
moderate means. The prevailing colour of the parlour is crimson, to make
a warm setting for the cold grey landscape without.[5]

If their mother had survived, the story of the Brontë family might have
been very different, but her health, poor when she arrived, soon
deteriorated. Before long, she was confined to her bedroom, and the
sadness of illness and approaching death descended upon the house.

It can hardly be doubted that the cramped sleeping accommodation in
the parsonage and the appalling lack of sanitation of Haworth were to
have a terrible effect on the constitutions of all the Brontë children, but
Mrs Brontë herself did not die of consumption, and it has been suggested
her death was due not to cancer but more probably to 'chronic pelvic
sepsis together with increasing anaemia'.[6] Mr Brontë took the best advice
available to him at the time, but the case was pronounced hopeless.

On January 1821, it was believed she was dying, but perhaps her
will-power and the thoughts of her six little children helped her pull
through.

Only a few months of painful suffering were left, and these must have
placed a most unnatural burden on the six-year-old Maria, already an
exceptionally intelligent and capable child. From the moment her mother
ceased to move about the house, little Maria tried in many ways to take
her place, to exercise a motherly role over the children smaller than
herself. Although she was to die when he was so young, her brother
Branwell was never to forget her, and she remained an inspiration in his
poetry throughout his life.

In May 1821 Mrs Brontë's older sister arrived to take over the reins of
the household. Unfortunately, kind and well-intentioned though she was,
she was never able to provide the motherly love and affection that flowed
from that little girl to her sisters and brother.

Elizabeth Branwell was a good and conscientious, severe and
narrow-minded woman, an austere, unbending figure, unused to children
and difficult to love. She was never to be reconciled to spending her life in
Yorkshire, so far from the congenial life she had created for herself in
Cornwall. She did her duty but she was never happy, and she was totally
incapable of creating an atmosphere of happiness for others. This was
inevitable while her sister lay dying but was to have serious consequences
on the children she was to have charge of later. Paradoxically, the child

she affected the most adversely was the one she loved the best – the only one who was cast in the Branwell rather than the Brontë mould, the youngest and prettiest of the girls, Anne.

After much agony, on 15 September 1821 Maria died at last. By this time, her husband must have been bitterly reconciled to the inevitability of her loss. For the poor sufferer herself, it can only have been a relief.

At the age of forty-four, still a potent, vigorous man, with a young family to rear, from every point of view the most practical step was for Patrick Brontë to seek a second wife, although he had dearly loved and was always to mourn his Maria, for on both sides theirs had been a genuine love match.

Unfortunately, when he had had time to pull himself together enough to consider this, Patrick forgot that a poor but handsome bachelor in his thirties was a very different proposition from a saddened middle-aged man with six tiny children and very little money.

The first lady he approached must have seemed to him ideal. Not only was he fond of her but she was godmother to three of his girls, she was an affectionate, attractive, pious woman, and she possessed a useful fund of money. Above all, he had discerned that she was warmly disposed towards him. But Elizabeth Firth was only twenty-five, and her independent income made her an attractive marriage prospect. Fond though she was of Mr Brontë and his family, she was not prepared to burden herself with such a responsibility. She remained a lifelong caring friend, even after her marriage two years later to another clergyman, the Reverend James Clarke Franks of Huddersfield, but her cheerful, loving presence in the Brontë household would have made an inestimable difference to their lives.

Disappointed but not disheartened, Patrick looked back into the past and remembered his former sweetheart, Mary Burder. With masculine tactlessness, forgetting his own lack of constancy and the changes the years had wrought in his circumstances, and – worse – with no attempt at any preliminary sentimental renewal of the early joys of courtship, he made a blunt proposal of marriage to his old love which, understandably, was equally bluntly and with some bitterness refused. Probably that was as well. Mary Burder, unlike Elizabeth Firth, would hardly have made the Brontë children a sympathetic and understanding stepmother.

Perhaps trusting in the old saying 'third time lucky', Mr Brontë tried once more. This time, his choice lighted on a Miss Isabella Dury of

Keighley. Little is known of this lady, except that she was no more disposed to contemplate such a match than the formerly slighted Mary Burder had been.

'I should never be so silly,' she wrote to a friend, 'as to have the most distant idea of marrying anybody who had not some fortune and six children into the bargain.'[7]

After this refusal, as far as is known, Mr Brontë did not venture into the matrimonial lists again but accepted that the mother figure in his family would have to be his sister-in-law, 'Aunt Branwell'. Poor Mr Brontë, who had travelled so far from his deprived beginnings, was now fated to live the rest of his days in straitened circumstances and without a loving companion by his side. Clearly, celibacy was far from being his chosen way of life, and his frustration and need for wifely affection must certainly account for much of what seemed his eccentricity in later life.

Miss Elizabeth Branwell left Cornwall for good and made her home in Haworth early in 1824. As soon as her permanent role in the family life had been established, there were changes. First, and most important, it was decided that the little girls must go to school, except for Anne who was still far too young. The choice of school was not easy, for Mr Brontë wanted to give his girls the best education available for the small fees he could afford. With five girls to provide for on his income, as well as his son, there would be no dowries for them later, and unless they were lucky, when they were adults his daughters would have to fend for themselves – no easy matter for gentlewomen in the nineteenth century. For many reasons, the best available prospect seemed to be the Clergy Daughters' School at Cowan Bridge recently founded by the Reverend William Carus Wilson.

The two eldest girls, Maria and Elizabeth, were to have joined the school in January 1824, but they had been ill for months with one childish ailment after another, chickenpox, whooping cough and measles. Never robust, they had both been pulled down by these illnesses, and when they eventually arrived at Cowan Bridge in July, they were quite unfitted to withstand the harshness of its spartan regime, let alone any infection. Little Charlotte joined them three weeks later, and Mr Brontë was sufficiently impressed by what he was shown to determine to send Emily to join her sisters.

Ill-prepared for school in many ways (apparently their sewing left much to be desired), in others the three girls (being well read) were precocious. Maria, in particular, had been Mr Brontë's confidante and companion with whom he discussed on equal terms the affairs of the day as reported in the newspapers, all of which she afterwards related to her brother and sisters. Charlotte's memories of this motherly sister went into the creation in *Jane Eyre* of the almost too-good-to-be-true Helen Burns. Clearly, Maria was an exceedingly clever child, and Mr Brontë was always to believe she might have proved the most outstanding member of his brilliant family.

By now, Charlotte was eight years of age, but she was the youngest in the school, where most of the thirty pupils were in their teens. Perhaps not unfairly, her abilities were summarized as 'Reads tolerably – Writes indifferently – Ciphers a little and works neatly – Knows nothing of Grammar, Geography, History or Accomplishments – Altogether clever of her age but knows nothing systematically.'[8]

'Lowood' was easily identified as Cowan Bridge when *Jane Eyre* appeared, and Charlotte's condemnation of the school was the subject of much controversy. To a modern reader, Lowood cannot fail to seem to have much in common with Dotheboys Hall, but it must not be forgotten that the school at Cowan Bridge was founded on prevailing religious principles and good intentions, misguided though these may now seem. However the case was argued then or now, and although Charlotte's memories were darkened by the tragedy so soon to be enacted, from the child's point of view the regime was unloving, pitiless and harsh. The food was badly cooked and insufficient, the curriculum unimaginative and dull, the children were not clad warmly enough for the rigours of the weather to which they were all too often exposed, and few allowances were made for illness.

Emily, six years old, joined her sisters in November, so the four young girls, from the warmth of the Haworth kitchen and the affectionate care of Nancy and Sarah Garrs, the eldest two already frail and in a weakened state of health, had to face together the hardships of the Clergy Daughters' School and the onset of the Yorkshire winter.

For the first time in their lives, Anne and Branwell were the only two children together at the parsonage.

2. Only Four Left, 1824–31

For Aunt Branwell, it must have been a pleasant interlude to have only two children instead of six in the crowded home, and above all the two she was always to love best.

Shy, pretty, delicate little Anne was now nearly five years of age, and from the first her sweetness of nature was apt to disguise an essentially tough and brave character. As far as her aunt was concerned, she was always eager to please, and Miss Branwell took special pains over the upbringing of her favourite niece. Unfortunately, Anne was to suffer much spiritual agony later from her indoctrination since early childhood into her aunt's form of Methodism; nor was her chronic asthma improved by the long hours she was forced to spend by night and day in Miss Branwell's stuffy bedroom. For years Anne was to share with her aunt the room in which her mother had died, which Aunt Branwell turned into her own domain and where she gave the girls lessons in needlework and instructed them in the Bible. On Anne was bent the whole force of her own view of religion, in which fear of sin, not love of God, predominated.

Branwell, who naturally spent a great deal more time alone with his father than any of the girls, was also to suffer from his aunt's narrow teaching, which may well have been responsible for his retreat from any form of religion later in life.

Another reason for Aunt Branwell's added comfort at that time was that the lively, cheeky young Garrs sisters had been replaced by the fifty-four-year-old Tabby Ackroyd, dour and sharp-tongued, hard-working, with the proverbial heart of gold and, particularly as far as Aunt Branwell was concerned, altogether more suitable.

Nancy had left to get married and Sarah had gone with her, but Nancy's description of Miss Branwell many years later makes it clear that under her supervision harmony had not reigned: 'So crosslike an' fault finding' and so close, she ga'e us, my sister Sarah an' me, but a gill o' beer a day, an' she gi'e it to us hersel', did Miss Branwell, to our dinner, she wouldn't let us go to draw it oursel' in t'cellar.' In fact, to quote Nancy again, Miss Branwell was 'a bit of a tike'.[1]

Later, Charlotte's school and lifelong friend Ellen Nussey described Miss Branwell clicking about the house in pattens, with a front of auburn curls before her caps, which were 'large enough for half a dozen of the present fashion', dressed all in silk and forever talking about the past.[2] But with all her faults and gloominess, Miss Branwell, according to her own principles, was dutifully doing the best she could for her charges, living frugally, as far as she herself was concerned, and setting aside much of her own small income to help them later in life.

Just as Mr Brontë was looking ahead to his daughters' future when deciding on their education, so he was concerned about the prospects for his only son. In many respects, Branwell was a bright and many-talented boy, and it would be natural for his father, who had done so much to help himself when he was young, to expect that, in his far easier circumstances, Branwell would not only forge ahead but be in a position at some time in his career to aid his sisters.

His father was coaching him at home and, well pleased with his boy's progress, although there is no record of it in the register, it has been said he entered him for some months as a pupil at Haworth Grammar School. Mr Brontë may well have thought that it would benefit his only son to mix with other boys. If this is so, it was now that Branwell must have met his first failure – perhaps because he was very small for his age, and for the first time he realized that physically he was always to stand low among his contemporaries, however superior were his intellectual accomplishments; perhaps because he was teased on account of his bright red hair; or even because his delicate constitution made the rough $1\frac{1}{2}$ mile walk to get there too difficult a trial in bad weather. Whatever the cause, if he did indeed attend the school, Branwell was removed after a very short while and resumed his more congenial lessons with his father.

While life went on evenly at Haworth, tragic events were taking place at Cowan Bridge.

Predictably, Maria had proved a brilliant misfit. She could not conform to the school's conventional expectations. Clever though she was, she was also disconcertingly forgetful and untidy. Pathetically, her teachers failed to recognize that, although she was bravely battling on, she was a very sick girl. As Mrs Gaskell describes,

> The dormitory in which Maria slept was a long room, holding a row of narrow little beds on each side, occupied by the pupils: and at the end of this dormitory there was a small bed-chamber opening out of it, appropriated to the use of Miss Scatcherd [actually a Miss Andrews]. Maria's bed stood nearest to the door of this room. One morning, after she had become so seriously unwell as to have had a blister applied to her side (the sore from which was not perfectly healed) ... the sick child began to dress, shivering with cold, as, without leaving her bed, she slowly put on her black worsted stockings over her thin white legs ... Miss Scatcherd issued from her room ... took her by the arm, on the side to which the blister had been applied, and by one vigorous movement whirled her out into the middle of the floor, abusing her all the time for dirty and untidy habits. There she left her ... Maria hardly spoke ... but in slow trembling movements, with many a pause, she went downstairs at last – and was punished for being late.[3]

Not surprisingly, soon after this episode Mr Brontë was requested to remove Maria from the school. He collected her from Cowan Bridge on 14 February 1824 and took his dying daughter home.

Branwell and Anne saw the arrival of the wasted little body. Anne was perhaps too young to understand, Branwell was not. Maria, his sister and almost mother, died on 6 May and was buried six days later. Branwell was never to forget her death and funeral. They were perhaps the most significant and certainly the most moving experiences of his life.

While Maria was dying at home, her sister Elizabeth was growing steadily weaker at school. She too was already stricken by the consumption which was to kill her. But this was hardly noticed in the general panic which took place when an outbreak of typhoid fever swept through the school. With the prevailing dampness, the poor food prepared by a dirty and unhygienic cook, and totally inadequate sanitary arrangements for a community of more than seventy, the school proved a fertile breeding-ground for infection. Not until several girls had died and pupils began leaving was a healthier regime introduced. Under this, the girls were encouraged to spend long hours out of doors (it was by now May), a new cook was engaged and the food became more plentiful and nutritious. These measures saved the lives of Charlotte, Emily and many others. But it was too late for Elizabeth, who, on 31 May, like her sister before her, was sent home to die. She survived a fortnight.

When this sad news came, understandably alarmed about the two surviving Brontë girls, the school despatched them immediately to the home of the founder at Silverdale on Morecambe Bay. From there, a sad Mr Brontë brought them back to the rest of the family at Haworth on 1 June. On that date, the remaining young members of the Brontë family were reunited: Charlotte and Branwell, Emily and Anne. Now the eldest of the children, young though she was, and perhaps as Maria had done, feeling herself the children's leader, Charlotte somewhat resented Aunt Branwell's authority. From the very beginning a law unto herself, in any spiritual sense, Emily simply ignored it.

An often quoted but revealing picture of his six children, recalled for Mrs Gaskell by Mr Brontë, was an occasion when, before the deaths of the two eldest girls, seeking unselfconscious answers, he questioned them while they each wore a mask he happened to have in the house.

> I began with the youngest (Anne) and asked what a child like her most wanted; she answered 'Age and experience.' I asked the next (Emily) what I had best to do with her brother Branwell who was sometimes a naughty boy; she answered, 'Reason with him, and when he won't listen to reason, whip him.' I asked Branwell what was the best way of knowing the difference between the intellects of men and women; he answered, 'By considering the difference between them as to their bodies.' I then asked Charlotte what was the best book in the world; she answered, 'The Bible.' And what was the next best; she answered 'The book of Nature.' I then asked the next (Elizabeth) what was the best mode of education for a woman; she answered 'That which would make her rule her house well.' Lastly, I asked the eldest (Maria) what was the best mode of spending time; she answered 'By laying it out in preparation for a happy eternity.'[4]

Maria was about ten years of age when she gave this sadly prophetic reply. Elizabeth was to have no chance of ruling her house.

Unperturbed by his eccentricity, or perhaps unaware of it, the children shared with their father an intellectual companionship and deep affection. His habit of eating apart from them, perhaps due to the indigestion from which he suffered – for those prone to them, nothing is better calculated to bring on dyspeptic attacks than the lively table talk of children – did not disturb them, and they always enjoyed the long evenings they spent together.

No doubt some form of fantasy world would have been invented by the four surviving imaginative and isolated children in any case, but their famous childhood sagas seem to have sprung from Mr Brontë's gift to Branwell of a box of simple wooden toy soldiers.

'When I first saw them in the morning after they were bought, I carried them to Emily, Charlotte and Anne. They each took up a soldier, gave them names, which I consented to, and I gave Charlotte Twemy (Wellington), to Emily, Pare (Parry), to Anne, Trott (Ross), to take care of them, though they were to be mine and I to have the disposal of them as I would – shortly after this I gave them to them as their own.'

The account forms part of Branwell's *History of the Young Men* which was 'a statement of what myself, Charlotte, Emily and Anne really pretended did happen among the "Young Men" (that being the same we gave them) during the period of nearly six years'.[5] As can be detected from the tone, perhaps because he was the only boy or because he was the owner of the soldiers, at this time Branwell was taking the lead.

Over the years, the soldiers were added to and the cast of characters increased. What no doubt originally began as a childish game became established and extended when the children began writing their fantasies down in minute print in tiny booklets which they made themselves and sometimes illustrated. Most likely, this apparently innocent pursuit was welcomed by their elders. It was educational, allowing them to make use of their extensive reading and the news of the day they invariably discussed with their father, and when the weather did not allow them to go out onto the moors, it kept them happily and quietly occupied during the long afternoons and evenings.

As Charlotte describes, at first there was no concealment practised about these games, but as time went by and the subject matter was heightened and extended with a wealth of uninhibited romance and emotion, the children became more secretive. Not surprisingly, later Charlotte grew to regard her departure into her overcharged world with an element of guilt.

'Our plays were established; "Young Men", June 1826; "Our Fellows", July, 1827; "Islanders", December, 1827. These are three great plays, that are not kept secret. Emily's, and my bed plays, were established 1st

December, 1827: the others March, 1828. Bed plays mean secret plays; they are very nice ones .... All our plays are very strange ones. Their nature I need not write on paper, for I think I shall always remember them.'[6] Charlotte always did.

She gives a strikingly natural picture in the following passage of the children actually at play.

The play of the Islanders was formed in December 1827, in the following manner.

One night about the time when the cold sleet and dreary fogs of November are succeeded by the snow storms and high piercing night winds of confirmed winter, we were all sitting round the warm blazing kitchen fire having just concluded a quarrel with Taby concerning the propriety of lighting a candle from which she came off victorious, no candle having been produced, a long pause succeeded, which was at last broken by Bany saying in a lazy manner, I don't know what to do. This was re-echoed by E & A.

T: Wha ya may go t'bed.

B: I'd rather do anything than that.

C: Why are you so glum tonight? suppose we each had an island.

B: If we had I would choose the Isle of Man.

C: And I would choose the Isle of Wight.

E: The Isle of Aran for me.

A: And mine should be Guernsey.

We then chose who should be chief men in our islands: Branwell chose John Bull, Astley Cooper, and Leigh Hunt; Emily, Walter Scott, Mr Lockhart, Johnny Lockhart; Anne, Michael Sadler, Lord Bentinck, Sir Henry Halford. I chose the Duke of Wellington and sons, Christopher North and Co Mr Abernathy. Here our conversation was interrupted by the, to us, dismal sound of the clock striking seven, and we were summoned of to bed.[7]

Branwell's *History of the Young Men* was his first substantial piece of writing, and it provided the basis for the saga of Glasstown, later Verdopolis, and the Angrian wars, which, growing more and more complex occupied both him and Charlotte for a period of some nine years. At first Emily and Anne were also involved in the game, but in 1831, when Charlotte went away to school, they broke away on their own and began imagining and writing *The Gondal Chronicles*. The epic sequences of stories and, more importantly, poems were the most absorbing aspect of the two younger girls' lives until about fourteen years later, when they began writing their published works. Although there is an erotic content in *The Gondal Chronicles*, it is not of the self-involved, deeply subjective type that Charlotte infused into her Angrian stories and, most probably for that reason, neither Anne nor Emily suffered from the same guilt about their writing. It was never in that particular sense for them an escape or a compensation.

Fascinating though these juvenile productions are, it is only Brontë scholars and students who are likely to gain any useful integrated picture of them particularly since much of the Gondal material has been lost. For the more general reader, their greatest interest is that they provided the mine from which so much of the published work was extracted: the influences, the characters, the themes and, above all, the poems. Since they were, in fact, basically children's 'plays', it is probably misleading to try to impose too much pattern and logic upon them.[8]

Many talented groups of children invent similar fantasies. For example, John Cooper Powys involved his brothers in a country called Volentia, appointing himself commander-in-chief of the army. In a letter from school he asked, 'Are the Volentias prospering? I hope they are.'[9] This is a distinct echo of Emily's cheerful assertion, 'The Gondals still flourish bright as ever.'[10] Quite on her own, Jane Austen wrote an impressive and characteristic body of juvenilia.

What is unique about the Brontë's productions is that they wrote in collaboration, they sustained an unusually wide, almost epic vision, embodying a diversity of integrated themes and a very large cast of characters, and they continued creating and extending them from childhood, through adolescence into adult life.

It seems likely that once the Brontë children had become adjusted to the tragedies of the deaths of their mother and two elder sisters, the next five years – until Charlotte went away to Roe Head school – were among the most settled and happy of their lives.

Since the children were so young when their mother died, only Charlotte and Branwell remembered her at all; in fact, Branwell's imagination was much more affected by the loss of Maria and his lasting memories of her death and funeral. Charlotte too was never to forget her sister's dying days at Cowan Bridge, which were to reappear many years later to such poignant effect in *Jane Eyre*. These memories united in friendship Charlotte and Branwell, and the lack of them Emily and Anne.

They had soon established a routine fitted in with the rather strange lives of their father and aunt, with Tabby in the kitchen, sensible, scolding and affectionate, to keep them earthbound. They worked and wandered over the moors, Branwell played with the village lads, and in the evenings they were children no longer but the Genii Tallii, Brannii, Emmi and Annii who manipulated the characters and happenings in the world of their own creation.

Branwell had early established an unstable temperament, which his father hoped that time, his own good example and hard work would extirpate. He was prone to go into temper tantrums which almost amounted to fits, and it is possible that he suffered from some degree of *petit mal*. Because of this weakness, he was protected and indulged more than was good for him – added to which he enjoyed the privileged position of an only boy with three sisters. Although all his life he was easily diverted he was never lazy and made great strides under his father's tuition:

> By the time Branwell was ten, as his first manuscripts show, he had assimilated the Homeric and Virgilian epics; Greek and Latin history; contemporary history, with special reference to the French Revolution, Napoleon's and Wellington's campaigns; the exploits of the late eighteenth century and early nineteenth century explorers ... Contemporary politics, Continental as well as English, and the whole field of English literature, from the Elizabethan dramatists to the living 'romantic' poets of the day, from all of which Branwell could freely and not incorrectly quote like household words, made up his pasture.[11]

Both Mr Brontë and Aunt Branwell gave lessons to the sisters, and all four children were allowed to read what they liked and what they could obtain from the various sources available to them, such as the Keighley Mechanics Institute, in which Mr Brontë took a lifelong interest, and Mr Heaton's library at Ponden Hall, the Tudor manor which was possibly Emily's model later for Thrushcross Grange in *Wuthering Heights*. Robert Heaton was a church trustee with a young family of four boys. The children often walked over the moors to Ponden Hall when the weather was fine, through Sladen Valley and past the falls they named 'the Meeting of the Waters'. Because of his friendship with the Heaton boys,

Branwell was able to 'go out with the guns' – a privilege he much enjoyed. Frail though he was, he was truculent and, unexpectedly, pugilism was to become another of his passions.

Much of their wide reading influenced the writing of the Brontës, but in particular the minds of the three eldest were stimulated by the novels of Sir Walter Scott and the poems of Lord Byron, descendants of whose heroes stride through all their works; in Anne's, the gentle melancholy realism of William Cowper was always to hold sway.

Besides literature, the children were captivated by art and music. All four of them had a more than average ability to draw and were much influenced during these years by the Annuals of the Swiss engraver Rudolph Ackermann which featured illustrations by many of the leading artists of the day, principal among them John Martin, who drew vigorous and detailed representations of such subjects as the destruction of Babylon, Nineveh and Pompeii and made visible many of the scenes the children had read described in the Bible. Charlotte, in particular, was to spend many hours making exact copies of some of the illustrations that moved her especially, probably to the detriment of her already weak eyesight, a defect she shared with her brother.

Later, her poor eyesight was to make it difficult for Charlotte to see the notes of the music when she studied the piano, but the other three in their various ways were competent musicians, Branwell performing grandly on the organ; Emily later displaying pianistic gifts that might well have been developed to the standard of concert performance; and Anne singing with a small but remarkably true and sweet voice.

It was Branwell's career which, for practical reasons, most preoccupied Mr Brontë, and gradually it seemed to emerge that his greatest talent was for art. Probably this was a mistake. Branwell was one of those, perhaps unfortunate, people talented in several directions but unable to develop any one of their gifts in a specialized way.

It is not surprising that Mrs Gaskell's great biography has conveyed the lasting impression that life in the parsonage was always prevailingly gloomy. By the time she and Charlotte became acquainted, she visited Haworth and began recording her friend's reminiscences, what might be termed the second period of the Brontë family tragedy was drawing towards its close.

But the contemporary records contained in various of the children's diary papers paint a more lively picture. In 1829, when she was thirteen,

Charlotte wrote, 'I am in the kitchen of the Parsonage, Haworth; Tabby, the servant, is washing up the breakfast things, and Anne, my youngest sister (Maria was my eldest) is kneeling on a chair, looking at some cakes which Tabby has been baking for us. Emily is in the parlour, brushing the carpet. Papa and Branwell are gone to Keighley. Aunt is upstairs in her room, and I am sitting by the table writing this in the kitchen.'[12]

Emily, the most reserved, untamed and mystical of the girls, was at the same time in the domestic sphere the most practical, and, until her fatal illness, much the sturdiest. In a similar scene in a diary paper, she writes five years later,

> Anne and I have been peeling apples for Charlotte to make an apple pudding ... Aunt has come into the kitchen just now and said where are your feet Anne Anne answered On the floor Aunt papa opened the parlour door and gave Branwell a letter saying here Branwell read this and show it to your Aunt and Charlotte ... It is past Twelve o'clock Anne and I have not tidied ourselves, done our bed work or done our lessons and we want to go out to play we are going to have for Dinner Boiled Beef Turnips, potatoes and applepudding The kitchin is in a very untidy state ... Tabby said on my putting a pen in her face Ya pitter pottering there instead of pilling a potate I answered O Dear, O Dear, O dear I will directly with that I get up, take a knife and begin pilling ...[13]

These on-the-spot, hastily written little notes take us back to the scene, almost like snapshots.

This halcyon period when all the children were at home together was broken in January 1831 by Charlotte's going away to school. This was probably decided on because of Mr Brontë's serious illness the previous summer and the realization that their very home was endangered. In the event of Mr Brontë's death, the parsonage would have to be vacated for his successor. Life was precarious indeed and, as the eldest, Charlotte, it was felt, should begin to prepare herself to earn a living.

Well aware of the situation, her conscientious godparents, the Reverend and Mrs Thomas Atkinson, offered to pay Charlotte's fees to attend a new school, recently opened in their own district of Mirfield by the Misses Wooler, sisters well known to them, in the pleasant house named Roe Head.

The whole plan was kindly and entirely suitable, but it is not difficult to imagine the chill and terror that struck Charlotte's heart as she contemplated her departure. Her last memories of school were of Cowan Bridge and the tragic deaths of her sisters. She was happy as she was; she did not want to leave her brother and sisters, nor the wonderful imaginative life they shared. She was self-conscious about her appearance and aware that she would probably be deficient not in ability but in the formal learning already acquired by the other girls there. The very thought of meeting a group of unknown girls, accustomed as she was to the company of only her own family, appalled her. But Charlotte was dutiful and good and accepted that to Roe Head she must go.

Roe Head was a very different establishment from Cowan Bridge but at first Charlotte was miserable.

Mary Taylor, who was to become one of Charlotte's two closest friends, well recalled the first time she saw her,

> ... coming out of a covered cart, in very old fashioned clothes, and looking very cold and miserable. She was coming to school at Miss Wooler's. When she appeared in the schoolroom, her dress was changed, but just as old. She looked a little old woman, so short-sighted that she always appeared to be seeking something, and moving her head from side to side to catch a sight of it. She was very shy and nervous, and spoke with a strong Irish accent. When a book was given her, she dropped her head over it till her nose nearly touched it, and when she was told to hold her head up, up went the book after it, still close to her nose, so that it was not possible to help laughing.[14]

In later years, Mrs Gaskell was to describe

> ... her limbs and head ... in just proportion to the slight, fragile body ... with soft, thick, brown hair, and peculiar eyes, of which I find it difficult to give a description ... They were large and well shaped; their colour a reddish brown; but if the iris was closely examined, it appeared to be composed of a great variety of tints. The usual expression was of quiet, listening intelligence; but now and then, on some just occasion for vivid interest or wholesome indignation, a light would shine out, as if some spiritual lamp had been kindled, which glowed behind those expressive orbs ... As for the rest of her features, they were plain, large, and ill set: but, unless you began to catalogue them, you were hardly aware of the fact, for the eyes and power of the countenance overbalanced every physical defect; the crooked mouth and the large nose were forgotten, and

the whole face arrested the attention, and presently attracted all those whom she herself would have cared to attract.[15]

It is a great loss that Mrs Gaskell did not have the opportunity of painting similar pictures for posterity of the rest of the family.

Apart from her appearance, Charlotte feared, with justice, that she would fall short of the other girls in her attainments. Luckily Miss Wooler was kind and intelligent and quick to understand the quality of her unusual pupil. Her original plan – that Charlotte should be placed in the second class until she had caught up with the girls of her own age – was greeted by such a storm of tears that she immediately agreed that the new girl would join the first class and work hard at her private studies to make up for the lost time. Far from merely catching up, Charlotte soon surpassed her fellows and gained three prizes at the end of her first term.

She was never able to compete at games nor even join in the fun of playtime with the other girls. Apart from the fact that she could never see the ball, she preferred simply to stand apart under the trees, looking at the pleasant views surrounding the house, not so grand as those at Haworth but softer and gentler, watching 'the shadows and the peeps of sky'.[16]

Mary Taylor was a forthright, intelligent girl from a radical family, all of whom were to make a great impression on Charlotte. The second friend she made there was the quiet, gentler, more conventional Ellen Nussey.

The school was run by the four unmarried Wooler sisters; a fifth, Susanna, had recently left to become the wife of the Reverend Edward Nicholl Carter, the curate of Mirfield church, where the girls walked to the service every Sunday. The head of the school, Miss Margaret Wooler, was also to become, with some ups and downs, Charlotte's lifelong friend. Ellen Nussey recalled their teacher as 'short and stout, but graceful in her movements, very fluent in conversation and with a very sweet voice ... She wore white, well-fitting dresses, embroidered. Her long hair, plaited, formed a coronet, and long large ringlets fell from her head to shoulders. She was not pretty or handsome, but her quiet dignity made her presence imposing. She was nobly scrupulous and conscientious – a woman of great self-denial. Her income was small. She lived on half of it, and gave the remainder to charitable objects.'[17]

Still under forty at this time, Margaret Wooler was a well-educated and compassionate woman, with a special gift for languages, and

Charlotte was fortunate in her godparents' choice of school. Far from suffering the seering experience she had anticipated, after the painful beginning Charlotte made her own special mark on the life of the school; she profited from the channelling of her wide and indiscriminate reading into more disciplined methods of study, she enjoyed and made the best use of her opportunities, and she made friendships which valuably extended her previously precious but limited world.

While their sister was away, Emily and Anne, always devoted to each other, grew ever closer, and perhaps feeling a little out of things, Branwell sadly missed his own particular companion and collaborator.

Charlotte, whose greatest joy in life it was to escape from the everyday reality of school routine to her infinitely more exciting daydreams of Angria, was touched and thrilled when Branwell walked the twenty miles from home to spend the day with her. The letter she wrote to him afterwards does not do full justice to this wonderful day, when brother and sister were reunited and when they no doubt spent much of their time getting up to date with Angrian affairs, but it shows clearly enough how united in understanding and loving friendship were Charlotte and Branwell at this time in their lives.

Dear Branwell, – As usual I address my weekly letter to you, because to you I find the most to say. I feel exceedingly anxious to know how and in what state you arrived home after your long and (I should think) very fatiguing journey. I could perceive when you arrived at Roe Head that you were very much tired, though you refused to acknowledge it. After you were gone, many questions and subjects of conversation recurred to me which I had intended to mention to you, but quite forgot them in the agitation which I felt at the totally unexpected pleasure of seeing you ...[18]

3. Into the World, 1832–5

His forty-miles walk, just for a few hours with Charlotte, gives some indication of how much Branwell was missing his favourite sister. In her absence, his *History of the Young Men* had begun to take on a more military and practical note. He felt Emily and Anne too young to collaborate on an equal basis with him, while they soon grew tired of his businesslike dispositions and lists and somewhat dictatorial editorial approach.

The two younger girls – with Emily providing most of the inspiration and Anne not just an admiring and enthusiastic audience but a worthy participant – struck out to develop a more romantic, increasingly feminine sphere of their own. They began now to live and write the chronicles of Gondal. Gondal became their great play, the private world in which both girls in their different but complementary ways explored the world around and inside them, the physical and the mystical, and learned how to express the drama of their imaginary creations and their keen awareness of the natural and the spiritual in both poetry and prose.

All four children lived a life within a life but, as will be seen, although their relationships to one another shifted and changed, that between Emily and Anne remained until the time when Emily had moved beyond all human contact. If Anne had no other qualities or achievements to commend her – which she had – she would have deserved some special recognition in that Emily Brontë, one of the great solitary figures of English literature, chose this sister to be her most intimate companion and loving friend.

The reading and instruction of all three children proceeded as before while Charlotte was away at Roe Head. Branwell continued his studies to his father's satisfaction but now, at the age of fourteen, he was perhaps allowed a little too much dangerous freedom. In some ways wisely, Mr

Brontë did not debar his only son from making contacts in the village, but perhaps these should have been, from the start, supervised more closely. Throughout his life, lack of any ready cash, of the smallest kind, was one of Branwell's perpetual embarrassments, and perhaps even at this early age he was using his persuasive tongue to cadge and beg small favours. He was certainly the only member of the family with the Irish gift of the Blarney. In some ways his eloquence was the greatest of his many talents and, for himself, the most perilous. Small and unimpressive though he was, he had only to speak to charm and dazzle.

His great confidant was always to be his father's sexton and general Man Friday, John Brown, who lived with his wife and six daughters only a few paces away from the parsonage in Church Lane. As Branwell's portrait of him shows, John Brown was a striking man, some twenty years older than his young friend, intelligent and surprisingly well read, a stonemason of skill and talent. Several of his girls went to work at the parsonage, his daughter Martha spending twenty-three years there working alongside the faithful Tabby.

With Charlotte away, no doubt Branwell began to see more of this interesting, pithy character than formerly. Grave-digging, which was among John Brown's duties and had to be performed only too regularly, is thirsty work and he was a drinking man. It was perhaps thus early that Branwell was introduced to the delights of Haworth's now famous Black Bull, the comfortable little world in which he always shone and where he was welcomed and loved.

Writing much later, Francis Leyland describes an account he had heard of a visit Branwell paid, whether with or without paternal permission, to Keighley Fair, a colourful scene of noise and merriment, which illustrates his capacity to live life to the full.

> 'Branwell's excitement, hilarity, and extravagance knew no bounds: he would see everything and try everything. Into a rocking boat he and his friend gaily stepped. The rise of the boat when it reached its full height, gave Branwell a pleasant view of the fair beneath; but, when it descended, he screamed out at the top of his voice, "Oh! my nerves! my nerves! Oh! my nerves!" On each descent, every nerve thrilled, tingled, and vibrated with overwhelming effect through the overwrought and delicate frame of the boy.'[1]

In June 1832 Branwell completed his *Ode to the Polar Star*; the following is the final stanza:

Blesser of Mortals! Glorious Guide!
Nor turning ever from thy course aside,
Eternal pilot, while Time passes by,
While earthly guides decay and die,
　　Thou holdst thy throne
　　Fixed and alone,
In the vast concave of the nightly sky.
Kingdoms and states may droop and fail,
　　Nor ever still abide:
The mighty moon may wax and wane,
But thou dost silent there remain, –
　　An everlasting guide![2]

A creditable effort for a boy of fifteen.

Charlotte spent three half-year terms at Roe Head and returned home in May 1832. Their reunion was a time of great happiness for all four young people. The deep bond between Emily and Anne in no way lessened their affection for their older sister, and as for Branwell, he was delighted to bring Charlotte up to date with all the progress he had been making in Glasstown affairs in her absence and to resume their collaboration.

While Branwell's instruction by his father went on and a certain amount of time was spent each day by the girls with their aunt, Charlotte's duties now included imparting what she had learned at school to her younger sisters. This task must have given her a false impression about the normal life of a governess or schoolteacher which, for all three girls, seemed the only possible career open to them, apart from marriage. Not only were Emily and Anne far above average ability and intelligence, they were eager to learn. So hungry for education themselves, it was some time before the Brontë girls realized that for young people in the great world outside this was far from being the usual case. Later, in varying degrees, all three were to find that teaching those with no inclination to learn was an uphill, unrewarding battle.

Although she had been so agreeably surprised by her sojourn at Roe Head and particularly valued the friends she had made there, Charlotte's chief delight at being home again was that she was able to be her true self. There was no more need for concealment about the inner life she had secretly tried to maintain and which she could now lead without contrivance and with the eager aid of Branwell, who, in the course of growing from a boy to a young man, had introduced many new elements into their plays.

Charlotte, in the tumult of her adolescence, tended to leave the military and political elements of their sagas to her brother, and more and more her own deeply felt contributions dealt with their characters' complex, passionate and often very far from what could then have been considered proper love affairs.

At this time. Emily and Anne were aged fourteen and twelve. More high-spirited and athletic than Charlotte, whenever they could be out they were roaming the moors, which were of the greatest significance to Emily but almost equally loved by Anne.

Fortunately, Charlotte's friendships with the Taylors and Ellen Nussey both survived her schooldays. While at Roe Head, she had frequently visited the nearby Taylor home at Gomersal, getting to know the family, listening to their lively chatter which she found 'one of the most rousing pleasures I have ever known'.[3]

Her friendship with Ellen Nussey was on a more minor key but, in its way, equally precious. Both girls' acute and careful observation of their unusual friend were invaluable to Mrs Gaskell and later biographers. Ellen Nussey kept all the many letters Charlotte was to write to her. Unfortunately, Mary, who became an adventurous, independent-minded but discreet woman, did not.

Ellen's mother was a widow living with three other daughters and three sons at the pleasant house known as 'Rydings' in Birstall. It was Ellen who suggested that she and Charlotte should maintain a correspondence when they left school, sometimes conducted in French, and in the autumn of 1832 she invited her friend on her first visit to her home.

Here Ellen looks back on this first visit, remembering after many years how things then were:

Mr Brontë sent Branwell as an escort; he was then a very dear brother, as dear to Charlotte as her own soul: they were in perfect accord of taste and feeling, and it was mutual delight to be together. Branwell had probably never been far from home before! He was in wild ecstacy with everything. He walked about in unrestrained boyish enjoyment, taking views in every direction of the old turret-roofed house, the fine chestnut trees on the lawn

... a large rookery, which gave to the house a good background – all these he noted and commented upon with perfect enthusiasm. He told his sister he was leaving her in Paradise, and if she were not intensely happy she never would be! Happy, indeed, she then was *in himself*, for she, with her own enthusiasm, looked forward to what her brother's great promise and talent might effect ...[4]

This visit was returned in the summer of 1833, when Ellen first came to Haworth. Although Charlotte's circumstances were poorer than her own, Ellen noticed the elegance and refinement of the home and was particularly struck by the family's great love of their pets, ranging from dogs and cats to ponies, donkeys and birds, tamed and wild. (Such a love of animals was not only unshared but scarcely tolerated by Aunt Branwell.) Ellen's memories of this time are invaluable.

In fine and suitable weather, delightful rambles were made over the moors and down into the glens and ravines that here and there broke the monotony of the moorland ... Emily, Anne and Branwell used to ford the streams, and sometimes placed stepping stones for the other two; there was always a lingering delight in these spots – every moss, every flower, every tint and form were noted and enjoyed. Emily especially had a gleesome delight in these nooks of beauty – her reserve for the time vanished. One long ramble made in these early days was far away over the moors to a spot familiar to Emily and Anne, which they called 'The Meeting of the Waters' ... seated here, we were hidden from all the world, nothing appearing in view but miles and miles of heather, a glorious blue sky, and brightening sun ... Emily, half reclining on a slab of stone, played like a young girl with the tadpoles in the water, making them swim about, and then fell to moralizing on the strong and the weak, the brave and the cowardly, as she chased them with her hand.

Emily had by this time acquired a lithesome graceful figure. She was the tallest person in the house except her father. Her hair, which was naturally as beautiful as Charlotte's, was in the same unbecoming tight curl and frizz, and there was the same want of complexion. She had very beautiful eyes; but she did not often look at you; she was too reserved. Their colours might be said to be dark grey, at other times dark blue, they varied so. She talked very little ...[5]

Anne, dear gentle Anne, was quite different in appearance from the others ... Her hair was a very pretty light brown, and fell on her neck in graceful curls. She had lovely violet blue eyes, fine pencilled eyebrows, and clear, almost transparent complexion.[6]

But it is to Charlotte that we owe the liveliest picture of Branwell at this time, in his fictional role of Patrick Benjamin Wiggins:

> ... a low slightly built man attired in a black coat and raven grey trousers, his hat placed nearly at the back of his head, revealing a bush of carroty hair so arranged that at the sides it projected almost like two spread hands, a pair of spectacles placed across a prominent Roman nose, black neckerchief adjusted with no great attention to precision, and, to complete the picture, a little black rattan flourished in the hand. His bearing as he walked was tolerably upright and marked with that indescribable swing always assumed by those who pride themselves on being good pedestrians.[7]

At this point in his life everyone, not least himself, predicted a great future for Branwell. He wrote well, he could draw and paint, he was musical, he was a brilliant talker and, because his circle had been so confined, he was full of confidence.

By this time there was a piano in the house, and the children were being taught by Abraham Stansfield Sunderland, the organist at Keighley church. Branwell was also studying the organ, which he continued to play occasionally in Haworth church up to Christmas 1839. In the 1834 diary paper already quoted, Emily wrote, 'Anne and I have not done our music exercise which consists of b major ... Mr Sunderland expected.' Like many children before and since, the young Brontës evidently sometimes hastily scrambled through their scales and practice just before their teacher's arrival.

Probably the children's first art teacher, who came to their home as early as 1829, was Thomas Plummer of Keighley. They all enjoyed drawing and devoted many hours to it, but Branwell's talent in this direction was taken more seriously. For the successful practitioner in the days before the invention and then the later increase of photography, an artist, especially one adept at securing a good likeness, without being a genius, but with industry and useful contacts, could soon build up a profitable connection and earn a comfortable living. Given so much evidence of facility, Branwell's projected career as a portrait painter was not then the impractical dream it might seem today.

In 1834 Mr Brontë took his children to Leeds to an exhibition where two flourishing Yorkshire artists were represented, Joseph Bentley Leyland, the sculptor, and William Robinson, the portrait painter. Clearly impressed by Robinson's paintings and his success in this field, Mr Brontë engaged him at a fee of 2 guineas a visit, which must have seemed to him at the time a small fortune invested in his son's future, to teach the children, and Branwell in particular, to paint.

William Robinson had studied painting in London under Sir Thomas Lawrence and at the Academy schools, where he became a well-known and sought-after portraitist, gaining important commissions to depict such celebrities as the Duke of Wellington and the Princess Sophia. By the time he returned to Leeds, his reputation was established, but he was to die in 1839 of consumption at the age of only forty. Unfortunately Robinson's opinion of Branwell's talent has not been recorded, but it seems likely that he went on teaching him until he left for London. In view of his own prospering career at the time, he would hardly have devoted so much time to a pupil unless he felt there was at least a good chance of his achieving some success.

Various good old friends, Mrs Franks, Miss Outhwaite, Aunt Branwell and others, contributed to a fund for Branwell's expenses. A draft letter outlined Branwell's intentions:

> Having an earnest desire to enter as a probationary student in the Royal Academy, but not being possessed of information as to the means of obtaining my desire, I presume to request from you, the Secretary to the Institution, an answer to the question –
> Where am I to present my drawings?
> At what time?
> and especially,
> Can I do it in August or September?[8]

According to the records of the Academy Schools, this draft does not appear to have been copied and sent, certainly not received. But armed with some letters of introduction and the precious hoard of money his friends had collected for him, it seems certain that some time in the late summer of 1835 – no doubt with the confident feeling that he was about to repeat the success story of his teacher – the short, slight, red-haired, bespectacled provincial youth of just eighteen set off hopefully for London.

Possibly life might have proceeded better for Branwell if only his father had gone with him to direct his first faltering steps, as he was to do later, perhaps with the benefit of hindsight or merely because they were young ladies, when Charlotte and Emily travelled to Brussels.

These ambitious plans for Branwell could not proceed without necessary changes.

Charlotte had been home for three years now, giving her younger sisters the benefit of the education she had gained at Roe Head. She had been happy both in the day-to-day family life and in the unbounded world of her imagination, but all along she had known that sooner or later she would have to begin earning her own living.

When her first opportunity came to do so, it was both well-timed and congenial. Miss Wooler had written to offer Charlotte a teaching post in her school, plus a free place for one of her sisters in part payment for her services. From all points of view, this was a chance not to be missed and was certainly easier for the shy Charlotte to contemplate than taking a leap into the dark with strangers. The obvious choice for her companion was Emily, the elder of her sisters and the next who would need to earn a living. How Emily felt about this at the beginning is not known. The two girls made their preparations and left home before Branwell, on 29th July.

For a short space of time again, Branwell and Anne were alone, Anne now more able to be a companion to this sometimes bewildering brother. '... my dear little Anne,' Mr Brontë had written, 'I intend to keep home for another year under her aunt's tuition and my own.'[9] But this was not to be.

Charlotte had found and overcome certain difficulties in her first lonely sojourn at Roe Head School. Fresh from her life of freedom and imagination, now just seventeen, Emily proved quite incapable of settling down to what she found a totally irksome and repressive routine. Hers was not a mind or nature to be regimented. Genius as she was, she did not work systematically, she could not conform. She was wildly out of her element, quite unable to form relationships with the other girls she found there, she missed Anne miserably, and with Charlotte busy and absorbed by her new duties, she saw all too little of her. Before many weeks had passed, all too clearly Emily was growing ill. As Charlotte was to write later,

Liberty was the breath of Emily's nostrils; without it, she perished. The change from her own home to a school, and from her own very noiseless, very secluded, but unrestricted and inartifical mode of life, to one of disciplined routine (though under the kindliest auspices) was what she failed in enduring. Her nature proved here too strong for her fortitude. Every morning when she woke, the vision of home and the moors rushed on her, and darkened and saddened the day that lay before her. Nobody knew what ailed her but me – I knew only too well. In this struggle her health was quickly broken; her white face, attenuated form, and failing strength threatened rapid decline. I felt in my heart she would die, if she did not go home, and with this conviction obtained her recall.[10]

It was fortunate that Charlotte was on hand to make this decision and act on it in time. No doubt she had those terrible memories of Cowan Bridge to guide her.

But the offer of the free place was too valuable to be given up, and Emily's happy release was Anne's sentence. However, just as shy and attached to home life, there was in Anne an uncomplaining streak of stoicism which enabled her to soldier on when Emily had given way. She arrived at Roe Head some time in October 1835, presumably after Branwell's departure and before his return home. She was no happier at the school than Emily had been, but she stayed.

Like so many episodes in his later life, the story of Branwell's first great adventure, his journey to London, is hazy and mysterious.

To start with, it was the first long journey he had taken alone, travelling by coach via Keighley and Bradford. Most probably he would have booked in, as his father had in his youth and was to do when revisiting London later, at the Chapter Coffee House in Paternoster Row, once the haunt of literary men but by this time patronized mostly by provincial clergymen.

It seems that the vast world of Branwell's imagination had ill prepared him for the great noisy bustle of the reality that was London. He felt himself small and insignificant, and he was very lonely.

Most of the evidence of what he did during his stay comes from the fifth part of his *History of Angria*, virtually transformed into the musings of his character Charles Wentworth a year later when he had had time to recollect and shape his miserable memories.

He threaded the dense and bustling crowds and walked for hours, never staying to eat or drink, never calling a coach or attending to personal appearance, but with a wildish dejected look of poverty-stricken abstraction. His mind was too restless to stop and fully examine anything ... He was going about striking sparks from his mind by a contact with scenes connected with glorious events, associations, persons ... then he turned, passing through many noble streets without hardly turning his eyes to look at them. He entered his hotel, stretched himself on a sofa, and listlessly dreamed away his time till dark ... Next day found him still unknown and unvisited, without participating in the splendours of wealth, no more than if he had not a pound in his pocket. Nor was he bent studiously on ransacking the great libraries or studying in the picture galleries. He was restlessly, aimlessly, and with the same anxious face feeding his feeling with 'little squibs of rum', as he called them to himself, since he was perfectly aware they would only the more depress him afterwards.[11]

Branwell Brontë did not take up any of the useful introductions he had been given, nor did he present himself to the Academy Schools at Somerset House. His confidence at this time appears to have totally failed him. Perhaps the little squibs of rum were designed to boost his spirits to the point when he could put himself to the test for which he had come. But evidently they did not succeed. In fact, according to his later reminiscences to his friends in Bradford, apart from the Chapter Coffee House there was only one place in London that Branwell came to know very well. This was the Castle Tavern in High Holborn to which he was irresistibly drawn by the fame of its landlord, Tom Spring, the retired boxer. The tavern was patronized by both sporting and artistic customers and, finding himself at last in the congenial friendly atmosphere where he could begin to feel at home, no doubt Branwell's generosity became liberal. It is easy to picture his alternations between inebriated joy and apprehensive remorse as he watched his little fund of other people's hard-earned money, representing their faith in him, draining away. Before much time had passed, he had run through an amount which, laid out frugally, would have kept him in London for a considerable while. Having frittered his assets away, he could think of no other course but to hurry home.

In one way, it must be said, this ignominious retreat took quite a deal of courage. He had been expected to return home months later as a conquering hero. As it was, he had thrown away a great opportunity in a remarkably short time. Not only did he have to excuse this failure to his family but he had to explain it away to William Robinson, the teacher who had been so kind and had devoted so much time to him.

There was only one way the imaginative Branwell could see of overcoming these problems, and that was to concoct a plausible tale which would absolve him from any guilt in the matter. No doubt he told his tale well, and his disappointed father and aunt apparently accepted at face value his account of having been set upon by sharpers and robbed of most of his money. They received him back with critical kindness, for two such shrewd people must have had reservations. So much was always to remain unexplained. From then on, Branwell's golden future could never again seem so bright, and his own golden image was tarnished.

No doubt he and Emily, the two young Brontës at home at this time, were able to console each other. Emily was always able to accept people as she found them, without censure. They had both set out on enterprises that had failed. For both of them, these experiments had started a repeating pattern. Emily could never thrive nor be contented away from her life-giving moors: Branwell, although he fretted against the chain, was never able to live successfully for any length of time apart from his family. Now they both had to decide again what the future was to hold in store for them.

Once the bitterness and disappointment had receded, time began to pass pleasantly. Emily and Branwell, now it was their turn to be alone together, grew closer than they had ever been before and must have spent many hours in fruitful and stimulating companionship, reading, writing and chatting. Emily Brontë's unique genius enabled her to create without direct experience, but it is important to remember when considering both her life and her brother's that, apart from their father, Branwell was practically the only man she was ever to know with any degree of closeness and intimacy.

Emily always enjoyed helping in the house, and she was famous in the village for her skill in breadmaking. There were the moors and her animals, and the music she and Branwell could enjoy together. She missed Anne constantly, but she was able to continue alone to immerse herself in her powerful Gondal creations in prose and verse.

It was not long before Branwell talked his way back into general favour and was able to hold his head up in the village and enjoy himself

regaling the regulars in the Black Bull with his London adventures in the
Castle Tavern. He was admitted to the Haworth Lodge of the
Freemasons, of which his staunch friend John Brown was Worshipful
Master, and he was regular in his attendance. He was also keeping up his
informed interest in local and national politics.

Temporarily disenchanted with painting, he plunged back into his
writing and was soon hard at work again on his Angrian chronicles,
writing out his disappointments and venturing into serious verse which
reflected his mood of depression and defeat.

Dated December 1835, the poem entitled 'Misery Part I' initiated a
series of poems in which he looked at his life philosophically in an
attempt to answer some of his self-questionings, returning as he was
always to do in times of stress to his memories of his sister Maria and the
sad difference her death had made to him. At the same time, it seems clear
that he was hoping that some of these poems at least might be accepted
for publication. Branwell was the first of the four young Brontës to get
into print, and when assessing his talent, it should be borne in mind that
some of his passages were for a long while attributed to Emily.

The following lines were published under Emily's name by Clement
Shorter:

> It seems as to the bleeding heart
>   With dying torments riven
> A quickened life in every part
>   By fancy's force was given;
> And all those dim disjointed dreams
>   Wherewith the failing memory teams
>   Are but the bright reflection
> Flashed upward from the scattered glass
> Of mirror broken on the grass,
>   Which shapeless figures in each piece
>   Reveals without connection.[12]

In fact, at the death of James Hogg, known as the Ettrick Shepherd,
who had been a regular correspondent to *Blackwood's Magazine*,
Branwell, at eighteen years of age, fancied he might admirably fill the
vacant post and wrote to the editor accordingly. When writing such
letters of introduction or application, he usually employed a singularly
unfortunate style, mixing flattery, browbeating, over-confidence and

self-abnegation. His letters remained on *Blackwood's* files as oddities, probably from a madman, and it was only much later that anyone gave a further thought to them.

I *know* that I possess strength to assist you beyond some of your own contributors; but I wish to make you the judge in this case and give you the benefit of its decision [he declared when asking permission to send some of his work]. Now, sir, do not act like a man willing to examine for himself. Do not turn from the naked truth of my letters, but *prove me* – and if I do not stand the proof, I will not further press myself on you. If I do stand it – why – you have lost an able writer in James Hogg, and God grant you may gain one in

Patrick Branwell Brontë.

Not surprisingly, this letter received no reply, but when Branwell had completed his poem 'Misery Part I' with 'Misery Part II', he wrote again, saying rather endearingly, 'But don't think, sir, that I write nothing but Miseries. My day is far too much in the morning for such continual shadow. Nor think either (and this I entreat) that I wish to deluge you with poetry. I sent it because it is soonest read and comes from the heart.'[13]

This and a still further letter requesting a personal interview were never answered. But Branwell's biggest disappointment must have been the calculated silence that followed the letter and poem he sent to William Wordsworth some time later. Unfortunately, perhaps, he sent the by then somewhat crusty old poet a poem which, although it has undoubted merits, in part echoes all too clearly Wordsworth's own great 'Intimations of Immortality' Ode.

Yet did Man's soul descend from heaven
With feelings by its Maker given
All high, all glorious, all divine,
   And from his hand perfected gone
With such a bright reflected shine
   As the full moon bears from the sun.
But then – the soul was clothed in clay,
So straight its beauty passed away,
And through a whirl of misery driven

Earth's shadow came 'tween it and heaven.
A darkened orb the moon became,
Lost all its lustre, quenched its flame![14]

In much of his poetry, Branwell — like so many influenced by Byron
was to exhibit all the worst faults of that poet's poorer writing. But
passages here and there rise above this mundane level. What might he
have achieved with a more disciplined routine; someone to encourage
and constructively criticize him; and, above all, a little early success to
strengthen his always precarious resolve?

I thought just now that Life or Death
    Could never trouble me,
That I should draw my future breath
    In silent apathy,
That o'er the pathway of my fate
Though steady beat the storm,
As I walked alone and desolate
I'd to that path conform.
Affection should not cherish me,
Or Sorrow hold me down,
But despair itself sustain me,
Whom itself had overthrown.[15]

4. Tension and Change, 1835–8

Whatever they had to look back on and regret, there can be no doubt that in the months between January and December 1836 Branwell and Emily were much happier than Charlotte and Anne.

Charlotte found her position in the school as a paid employee somewhat different from when she had been a paying pupil. To a certain extent she was the victim of her own conscientiousness, forcing herself in marking and lesson preparation beyond the bounds of duty. Although she knew that Anne was unhappy, in her official position she was over-careful not to show her sister any favours. Anne, always so sensitive to other people's responses, kept to what she saw Charlotte regarded as her place. This was a pity. The sisters were congenial companions and very fond of each other. More than anyone else there, each could have allayed the other's sufferings, which, whether they recognized it at the time or not, had a great deal in common.

To fit into this narrow, regimented atmosphere, Charlotte was having to deny her own emotional and highly romantic nature. She had to suppress the continual upsurge and spring of her literary creativity. By comparison with the religious and social principles instilled in their pupils by the Misses Wooler, Charlotte knew very well that she had been living in her imagination what would appear to them a life of sin. Wronged wives, adulterous husbands, passionate and patient mistresses, 'love-children' – were all features of her Angrian scene, without the redeeming moral limitations she was to impose on the narrative of *Jane Eyre*. The Angrian Chronicles had not been written for publication, so there was no need for such discretion. But although she was to continue them for a while yet, Charlotte, in the atmosphere of the school and in her now somewhat intense friendship with the conventional and religious Ellen Nussey, was beginning to feel increasingly guilty. And yet, penned and confined, mentally and emotionally starved as she was, her only escape from this misery was into the world of her imagination. Her feelings are poignantly expressed in the journal she kept during these months at Roe Head.

> I am just going to write because I cannot help it ... A Cook on one side of me, E Lister on the other and Miss Wooler in the background, stupidity the atmosphere, schoolbooks the employment, asses the society. What in all this is there to remind me of the divine, silent, unseen land of thought, dim now and indefinite as the dream of a dream, the shadow of a shade. There is a voice, there is an impulse that wakens up that dormant power which in its torpidity I sometimes think dead. That wind pouring its impetuous current through the air, sounding wildly unremittingly from hour to hour, deepening its tone as the night advances, coming not in gusts, but with a rapid gathering stormy swell, that wind I know is heard at this moment far away on the moors at Haworth. Branwell and Emily hear it and as it sweeps over our house down the church-yard and round the old church, they think perhaps of me and Anne – Glorious! that blast was mighty it reminded me of Northangerland, there was something so merciless in the heavier rush, that made the very house groan as if it could scarce bear this acceleration of impetus. O it has awakened a feeling that I cannot satisfy – a thousand wishes rose at its call which must die with me for they will never be fulfilled ...[1]

At the same time as Charlotte was so miserable, Anne was undergoing a most distressful crisis in her Christian faith. Of all the family, undoubtedly she was the most religious in the Christian sense. Yet, surprisingly, at no time did she share in any way Charlotte's sense of guilt when she entered into the delights of her Gondal creation. Perhaps this was because, in the world of Gondal, Emily was her leader and her inspiration, and in Emily's cosmic and objective view there was no place for such intensely subjective personal guilt.

Anne's crisis was of quite a different kind from Charlotte's but it seems a sad waste that these two loving sisters could not have shared and eased for each other the miserable months they spent together at Roe Head. Undoubtedly, each could have profited from this long period of companionship.

One of the reasons for this, which was unfair to both Anne and Miss Wooler, was that prompted by the forthright views of her friend Mary

Taylor. Charlotte may have been smarting under the feeling that she was suffering unnecessarily for the price of her sister's education: 'I went to see her, and asked how she could give so much for so little money, when she could live without it. She owned,' Mary Taylor was to remember, 'that, after clothing herself and Anne, there was nothing left, though she had hoped to be able to save something. She confessed it was not brilliant, but what could she do?'[2]

In fact, in several of her situations, Charlotte seems to have felt that she herself was being personally exploited, without fully realizing that such exploitation of genteel female staff was merely the generally accepted condition of employment of the day and in no way reflected on her or her sisters in particular.

Characteristically, to all outward appearances, Anne had soon settled down at the school; she worked hard and became a model pupil. She did not enjoy it, but the routine was not the torture to her that it had been to Emily. At the end of her first year, she received 'A Prize for good conduct presented to Miss A Brontë with Miss Wooler's kind love, Roe Head, Dec. 14th 1836.'[3] She does not appear to have made any close friends, as Charlotte had done with Mary and Ellen. This may, in fact, have been due to the other pupils' reaction to her own rather anomalous position in the school – a point which Charlotte does not seem to have considered. Affectionate as she was, there can be little doubt that Anne must have been hurt, puzzled and concerned by Charlotte's obvious tenseness and irritability at this time, especially as she had always been accustomed to the daily loving companionship of Emily, whom she missed desperately.

Moreover, it must be remembered that Anne was only sixteen, she had never been away from home before and, a lifelong asthma sufferer, she was in far from robust health. Not surprisingly, it was now that all her long repressed religious doubts came to the surface. All her life, Anne had been subjected to the rigorous teachings of her Aunt Branwell. She had appeared to subscribe to them, but some of the tenets her aunt upheld most zealously were utterly repugnant to the instinctive beliefs of this outwardly bending and gentle but inwardly courageous and stoical girl.

Some eighteen months after she joined the school, Anne became quite seriously ill. Whether because she suspected her illness was due to her religious conflict or because she felt she might be about to die is not clear but she felt in need of spiritual guidance which was not available to her from the usual clerical circle by which she was surrounded.

The doctrine that so oppressed the fair-minded Anne was that eternal punishment awaited the sinner, that for some of God's weak and unfortunate creatures there could be no salvation. Fortunately, she had heard that in the area there was a settlement of Moravian brothers, believers in 'salvation by faith', pardon and peace – perhaps one might say essentially true followers of the teachings of Jesus Christ. Miss Wooler had spoken of the settlement to her pupils, and in her hour of need Anne sent to them for help, She was lucky in that it was the sincere and sensitive Bishop James la Trobe who came to see her. Immediately he recognized that the sick girl was oppressed not by the fear of death but by the fear of judgement and eternal punishment, not so much for herself but for others – a creed in which she could not truly believe. Without hesitation, he was able to reassure her, 'The words of love, from Jesus, opened her ear to my words, and she was very grateful for my visits. I found her well acquainted with the main truths of the Bible respecting our salvation, but seeing them more through the law than the Gospel, more as a requirement from God than His Gift in His Son, but her heart opened to the sweet views of salvation, pardon and peace in the blood of Christ, and she accepted his welcome to the weary and heavy-laden sinner, conscious more of her not loving the Lord her God than of acts of enmity to Him, and, had she died then, I should have counted her His redeemed and ransomed Child.'[4]

Fortunately, Anne did not die then and although, as was to be expected after so many troubled years, from time to time her old doubts reawakened, she was never again to feel such intensity of spiritual despair. From then onwards, Anne's Christian faith was always to be a comfort and support rather than a torment to her.

Poems that she wrote at this time for the Gondal saga are so deeply felt because they are so applicable to her own plight – her feelings of imprisonment and loss of liberty, and her spiritual quandary.

> Long have I dwelt forgotten here
> In pining woe and dull despair,
> This place of solitude and gloom
> Must be my dungeon and my tomb,
>
> No hope, no pleasure can I find;
> I am grown weary of my mind;

Often in balmy sleep I try
To gain a rest from misery,

And in one hour of calm repose
To find a respite for my woes;
But dreamless sleep is not for me
And I am still in misery.[5]

That wind is from the North: I know it well;
No other breeze could have so wild a swell.
Now deep and loud it thunders round my cell,
    Then faintly dies, and softly sighs,
And moans and murmurs mournfully ...

Confined and hopeless as I am,
    Oh, speak of liberty!
Oh, tell me of my mountain home,
    And I will welcome thee![6]

After this crisis, Anne recovered her health and went on benefiting from all she was learning at the school. In a way more consciously and realistically than either of her sisters, she was preparing herself for the life of a governess.

In those days, the school year was divided in two terms at Christmas and in the summer so that pupils in rural areas could return home to help with the harvest. In one of these summer breaks, Charlotte and Anne spent some time, not altogether happily, shy as they were, with Anne's godmother, Mrs Franks, and her family. Both gained, however reluctantly, insights into a more extended society which were to be reflected later in their published works. Unfortunately, Mrs Franks died the next year at the early age of forty, and was never to know the true quality of her god-daughter.

During Anne's first Christmas visit home in December 1836, their faithful old servant fell on the ice and broke her leg. In this state, Tabby could no longer be of any help in the parsonage, and Aunt Branwell decided she must be sent to her sister's until she was well enough to resume her duties. The girls were shocked to think of Tabby, who had looked after them so well, being thus deserted in her own hour of need.

Mrs Gaskell described how they went on strike until this harsh decree
was rescinded:

> 'They made one unanimous and stiff remonstrance. Tabby had tended
> them in their childhood; they, and none other, should tender her in her
> infirmity and age. At tea-time, they were sad and silent and the meal went
> away untouched by any of the three. So it was at breakfast; they did not
> waste many words on the subject, but each word they did utter was
> weighty ... and Tabby was allowed to remain a helpless invalid entirely
> dependent on them.'[7]

Since Charlotte and Anne were soon due back at school, the major part of
this new domestic burden fell, as so often, on the willing Emily.

It was during this holiday, around the same time as Branwell was
busily writing to *Blackwood's* and to Wordsworth, that Charlotte wrote to
the Poet Laureate, Robert Southey. Clearly her letter, which was not
preserved, would have been couched in very different terms from her
brother's, and Southey was kindlier and more courteous than
Wordsworth in that he wrote a careful and considered, if basically
discouraging, reply. Charlotte answered his letter, and he wrote again,
requesting that should she ever be in his neighbourhood in the Lake
District, she should visit him. As Charlotte must have realized, his
discernment had been penetrating:

> There is a danger of which I would, with all kindness and all earnestness,
> warn you. The day dreams in which you habitually indulge are likely to
> induce a distempered state of mind and, in proportion as all the ordinary
> uses of the world seem to you flat and unprofitable, you will be unfitted for
> them without becoming fitted for anything else ...
>
>   But do not suppose that I disparage the gift which you possess, nor that
> I would discourage you from exercising it. I only exhort you so to think of
> it, and so to use it, as to render it conducive to your own permanent good.
> Write poetry for its own sake; not in a spirit of emulation, and not with a
> view to celebrity; the less you aim at that the more likely you will be to
> deserve and finally to obtain it ...
>
>   Take care of over-excitement, and endeavour to keep a quiet mind ...

By the time she received Southey's replies, Charlotte was back in her
frustrating life at school. She read his letters over and over again,

endorsing them, 'Southey's advice to be kept for ever. My twenty-first birthday. Roe Head. April 21 1837.' [8] One wonders what her feelings would have been at that time had she been able to look into the future and learn that one day Southey's son would be requesting her permission to include this correspondence in his father's biography.

At home that summer of 1837, the family was thrilled to learn of the accession of the young Queen Victoria to the throne. After the long period of Hanoverian gloom, a bright and hopeful new reign had begun – a mood that was soon to be reflected in the annals of Gondal.

On Branwell's birthday, 26 June, Emily and Anne wrote one of their characteristic diary papers:

> A bit past 4 o'clock Charlotte working in Aunt's room, Branwell reading Eugene Aram to her – Anne and I writing in the drawing-room – Anne a poem beginning 'Fair was the evening and brightly the sun' – I Augustus Almeda's life 1st V – 4th page from the last. Fine rather coolish then grey cloudy but sunny day. Aunt working in the little room Papa gone out Tabby in the kitchen The Emperors and Empresses of Gondal and Gaaldine preparing to depart from Gaaldine to Gondal to prepare for the coronation which will be on the 12th of July Queen Vittoria ascended the throne this month. Northangerland in Monkeys Isle – Zamorna at Eversham. All tight and right in which condition it is to be hoped we shall all be on this day 4 years at which time Charlotte will be 25 and 2 months – Branwell just 24 it being his birthday – myself 22 and 10 months and a peice Anne 21 and nearly a half. I wonder where we shall be and how we shall be and what kind of a day it will be then let us hope for the best
>
> Emily Jane Brontë – Anne Brontë

> I guess that this day 4 years we shall all be in this drawing-room comfortable I hope it may be so. Anne guesses we shall all be gone somewhere together comfortable. We hope it may be so indeed.'

Perhaps Aunt Branwell had grown tired of listening to *Eugene Aram* or, on his twentieth birthday, Branwell had grown tired of reading, but in either event, at this moment, she came into the drawing-room:

> Aunt: 'Come, Emily, it's past four o'clock.'
> Emily: 'Yes, Aunt.'
> Evidently some regular duty was required to be performed at this time by Emily, but her sister enquires:

Anne: 'Well, do you intend to write in the evening?'
Emily: 'Well, what think you?'
('We agreed to go out 1st to make sure if we got into the humour. We
may stay in …')[9]

Whether they went out or stayed in, it seems likely that some pages
were added to the Gondal chronicles that evening, and it is interesting to
note that, in spite of their own preoccupation, at this time Emily and
Anne were still interested in following Branwell and Charlotte's
Northangerland adventures.

Anne's poem beginning 'Fair was the evening and brightly the sun',
later entitled 'Alexander and Zenobia', sixty-seven four-line and one
six-line stanza, written at the age of seventeen, can be accurately dated by
this diary paper:

Zenobia, do you remember
    A little lonely spring
Among Exina's woody hills
    Where blackbirds used to sing?

And when they ceased as daylight faded
    From the dusky sky,
The pensive nightingale began
    Her matchless melody.

Sweet bluebells used to flourish there
    And tall trees waved on high,
And through their ever sounding leaves
    The soft wind used to sigh.[10]

Already, so early, Anne had found her own particular poetic voice:
clarity, simple beauty and regret.

When the girls returned after the summer break of 1837, Miss Wooler's
school had been moved from the gracious and beautiful house of Roe
Head, Mirfield, to an altogether less pleasing establishment two or three
miles away at Heald's House, Dewsbury.

Heald's House had at that time a commanding position on Dewsbury
Moor. It was a rambling old house which had been much added to and

altered during its long history, and it can still be seen today. But it had a much smaller garden than Roe Head, and since its original Heald owner had been a maltster, the kilns used in his trade were then still in existence, and there was a fresh-water well running under the house, which no doubt, without adequate heating, made it chilly and damp. Miss Wooler, forced to reduce her establishment by family circumstances, had purchased the house from the Reverend Mr Heald, the Rector of Birstall, well known to Charlotte, who later introduced him in her novel *Shirley* as the Reverend Cyril Hall.

From the start of that second half of 1837, both Charlotte and Anne were even unhappier than they had been before. Both girls had been saddened by the untimely death of their loyal friend, Anne's godmother, Elizabeth Franks. Miss Wooler was often away and pre-occupied, and Charlotte found she was not only doing much more than her share of the teaching but supervising the domestic arrangements, even caring for Miss Wooler's little nephew and baby niece. Perhaps because the situation of the house did not suit her, Anne's health began noticeably to decline.

Apart from their own plight, both girls had another cause for worry at this time. Unexpectedly, perhaps feeling it was time for her to help ease the family's financial situation, Emily had found employment. Possibly through an introduction of Charlotte's, she had accepted a teaching post in the school known as Law Hill run by Miss Elizabeth Patchett, whose sister Maria who had helped her in the school had recently left to get married. Emily was to replace her.[11]

Law Hill, in an elevated position on Southowram Bank overlooking Halifax, commanded splendid views and enjoyed fresh, breezy air, similar to that of Haworth moor. The house was large and had the advantage of various outbuildings, and the Miss Patchetts, sisters of a Halifax banker, had many useful contacts when it came to finding pupils. During Emily's stay, there was an attendance of nearly forty girls.

Soon after Emily's arrival there, Charlotte wrote to Ellen Nussey: 'I have had one letter from her since her departure … it gives an appalling account of her duties – hard labour from six in the morning until near eleven at night, with only one half-hour of exercise between. This is slavery. I fear she will never stand it.'[12]

Charlotte and maybe Emily too were sometimes prone to exaggeration, and when Mrs Gaskell published this letter, Miss Patchett, by that time Mrs Hope, a vigorous old lady who lived to be well over eighty, took the greatest exception to it – to the extent that she could never be persuaded to give her own version of Emily's stay with her, which must be accounted a great loss. Clearly a cultivated and intelligent lady, her impressions of Emily at this time would have been of the greatest interest.

But whatever her stay at Law Hill was truly like, it did Emily one inestimable service. The story of the Walker family, who had previously owned both it and the nearby Walterclough Hall, and their adopted nephew, Jack Sharp, provided her with the bare bones of the plot she was later to expand with such consummate skill in *Wuthering Heights*. A mile and a half away was the old house of High Sunderland Hall, which may well have a greater claim than Top Withens nearer to Haworth to be the model for the house Emily was to call Wuthering Heights. One of the Latin inscriptions carved in its time-weathered stone reads:

Hic Locus odit, amat, punit, conservat, honorat nequitiam, pacem, crimina, jura, probos.

This place hates, loves, punishes, observes, honours wickedness, peace, crimes, laws, virtuous persons.

This extraordinary claim might, as Winifred Gérin points out 'be thought to have prompted the *leitmotif* of Emily's novel'.[13]

It is not certain for how long Emily did force herself to 'stand' life at Law Hill. But however well or ill she was treated, for her it was clearly a prison sentence, and it seems most likely she endured it only for some six months. Both Anne and Charlotte worried about her, perhaps Charlotte in particular, if she had been instrumental in recommending Emily for the post. She herself was feeling more and more put upon at Heald's House, and Anne was becoming increasingly delicate.

For just a few months, with all three sisters away, Branwell was at home alone with his father and aunt. From some of his prose writings of about this time, fictionalized autobiographical sketches set in Northangerland as many of them are, it appears that excessive drinking and probably gambling were already becoming personal problems. In the character of Henry Hastings, he writes with convincing authenticity: 'Now, with respect to the reports about my conduct, I must say one word further. It has been stated that within the last year past I have done nothing but drink and gamble and do everything that is Bad ... I like my glass of a night, the same as another. Well, "I am in a continual and beastly state of intoxication." I bet a nominal guinea on the issue of our topics of daily curiosity, I am "an abandoned gambler", and if successful, "an arrant swindler" ... Altogether, Henry Hastings is pronounced to be a "debauched and reckless desperado".'[14] It need hardly be stressed that in the financial context of the Brontë family, a guinea was far from a 'nominal' figure.

With no replies from *Blackwood's*, no success so far at getting into print with his serious attempts at poetry, typically Branwell, and no doubt his anxious father, was beginning to turn back to the prospect of an artistic career.

But the next important event in the life of the family was taking place at Heald's House school, where Charlotte's morbidity and self-preoccupation had increased to such an extent that she wrote later to Miss Wooler, 'I can never forget the concentrated anguish of certain insufferable moments, and the heavy gloom of many long hours, besides the preternatural horrors which seemed to clothe existence and nature, and which made life a continual walking nightmare.'[15]

Suddenly Charlotte was awakened from her gloomy self-absorption by the terrifying realization that Anne was not just ailing but seriously ill. Several of the girls had been suffering from influenza-type colds, but the always uncomplaining Anne's condition had rapidly worsened until Charlotte was thoroughly alarmed by her feverish appearance, weakness, difficulty in breathing and painful cough. She began to fear the dreaded spectre of the consumption which had killed her two older sisters. Evidently Miss Wooler thought she was exaggerating Anne's case, and as Charlotte was to describe to Ellen, an angry scene took place:

I told her one or two rather plain truths, which set her a-crying, and the next day, unknown to me, she wrote to papa telling him that I had reproached her bitterly – taken her severely to task, etc. etc. Papa sent for us the day after he received her letter. Meantime, I had formed a firm resolution – to quit Miss Wooler and her concerns for ever – but just before I went away she took me into her room, and giving way to her feelings, which in general she restrains far too rigidly, gave me to understand that in spite of her cold repulsive manners she had a considerable regard for me and would be very sorry to part with me. If anybody likes me I can't help liking them, and remembering that she had in general been very kind to me, I gave in and said I would come back if she wished me − so we're settled again for the present; but I am not satisfied.[16]

The girls were home for Christmas, and the ordeal of 2 unhappy years away at school was over for Anne, who was not to leave home again until the spring of 1839. Charlotte returned, as promised, to Heald's House, but soon she was in even lower spirits than before. After just a few months, it became clear that she was heading for a nervous breakdown. Some of her suffering at this time was later described vividly in *Villette*. When she at last sought medical advice, the doctor urged her immediately to go home. This was advice that Charlotte accepted with joy and with which, this time, Miss Wooler made no attempt to quarrel. She parted with Charlotte on cordial terms, presenting her with an illustrated edition of Scott's *The Vision of Don Roderick*, inscribed '… with the love and best wishes of a Sincere Friend.'[17] It is good to be able to say that Miss Wooler remained Charlotte's sincere friend until the end.

Charlotte arrived home towards the end of May, Emily may have been there before her or was to arrive soon afterwards, and for some happy months the three young women were reunited at Haworth, while it was Branwell's turn to go away.

With his ambitious sights more realistically lowered, Branwell had been offered a second chance to make a success as a portrait painter. This time he was not to go far away to London but was to be sensibly set up in Bradford, where friends could keep an eye on him, and he would regularly be able to get home. His father's great friend, the Reverend William Morgan, was vicar of Christchurch and living in Fountain Street, where Branwell found lodgings with the family of Mr Isaac Kirkby, appropriately enough a 'Porter and Ale Merchant', at number 3, where he set up his studio. Fanny Cuthwaite, Anne's surviving godmother, and her father lived nearby and the Brontës had never lost touch with their affectionate old servant Nancy Garrs, who had settled in Bradford after her marriage.

Preparatory to this venture, Branwell had resumed his lessons with William Robinson in Leeds, and there is no reason to doubt that he had every intention of settling down and working hard.

Two requisites are essential for success as a portrait painter: the ability to strike a good likeness, which was perhaps more important then than it is now, and a regular supply of sitters. Some portraitists invariably succeed in getting a likeness; others sometimes hit it but not always, and it seems likely that Branwell was in the latter category. Moreover, technically, he was perhaps not ready to launch out on his own. His friends introduced a few clients to him, but gaining a living in Bradford in this fashion was not easy, and the local artists who had succeeded were those who had left home.

One of the few favourable accounts of Branwell at this time was given by Margaret Hartley, a niece of the Kirkby family, who was then living with them:

> ... he came to lodge with us and had one room as his studio, and there painted many portraits. He was low in stature, about 5ft 3 inches high, and slight in build, though well proportioned. Very few people, except sitters, came to visit him; but I remember one, a Mr Thompson, a painter also. I recollect his sister Charlotte coming and I remember her sisterly ways ... It was young Mr Brontë's practice to go home at each weekend, and I remember that while sometimes he took the coach for Keighley, he on other occasions walked to Haworth across the moors. He was a very steady young gentleman, his conduct was exemplary, and we liked him very much. He stayed with us about two years ... Whilst lodging with us he painted my portrait and those of my uncle and aunt, and all three were accounted good likenesses.[18]

The Mr Thompson Margaret recollects was already an accomplished artist, though starting from humble beginnings, some nine years Branwell's senior. The two soon became friends, and John Hunter Thompson was responsible for introducing Branwell to the more lively and artistic side of Bradford society. Unfortunately, the various elements of this society tended to make their headquarters in some of Bradford's many inns. Literary men met at the George Hotel, musicians at the Bull's Head and artists at the Queen's. Branwell was soon at home in all these establishments, plus the New Inn, where the Bradford Philosophical Society met, and the Tory Talbot, where he could pursue his interest in politics. Here, as all too often in his life, Branwell's social activities began to revolve around a series of pubs, and maybe he did not always return home to his lodgings quite the 'steady' young man Margaret Hartley described. On the other hand, it is clear that this period represented one of the most hopeful in Branwell's chequered life.

But, however able he was as a portraitist (and certainly, apart from those of his sisters, he left a vivid portrait of John Brown), the sitters simply failed to come Branwell's way. Instead, his spare time was devoted to idleness and at various hostelries as a drinker, using perhaps the greatest of his talents, as a talker.

Apart from this, his stay in Bradford was made pleasant by his circle of friends, visits from his family and trips home. On one of these, he found that Charlotte's great friend from Roe Head, Mary Taylor, and her vivacious younger sister, Martha, were paying a visit to Haworth. Charlotte recorded the occasion in a letter to Ellen Nussey: 'They are making such a noise about me I cannot write any more. Mary is playing on the piano; Martha is chattering as fast as her little tongue can run; and Branwell is standing before her, laughing at her vivacity.'[19]

Perhaps it was on this occasion that sensible Mary became affectionately interested in Branwell. It sounds an incongruous attraction, but not entirely unlikely that the capable, managing Mary might have seen in Branwell the raw material from which she might have fashioned a worthy mate. Only vague hints remain of this elusive affair, but it seems that, as soon as Branwell became aware that Mary might be involving herself emotionally with him, he backed away, and she was far too proud and independent to pursue him. If anyone might have rescued Branwell from his self-destructive course, then or even much later, it must have been Mary Taylor. But Branwell denied her the opportunity. At this stage, it must be remembered, Mary was not the somewhat masterful Victorian lady she became later but an exceedingly pretty girl. Charlotte concluded that this was because Mary had made her feelings too plain, but it may equally well have been that Branwell knew he was unable to respond to them.

Early in the spring of 1838, when any return from his and his family's outgoings on his behalf had dwindled to nothing, Branwell recognized there was no point in staying any longer in Bradford to pursue his career as a portrait painter. He gave up his lodgings and returned to the parsonage – home again after another failure.

Two sisters were there to comfort him: Charlotte, still his great ally and collaborator, and the enigmatic Emily. Their little sister, Anne, against the advice of all the family, had determined to make her own way in the world. She had left home and gone as a governess to the Ingham family at Mirfield.

5. Three Lost Posts, 1839–40

Anne Brontë was the youngest and, in physical terms, the weakest of the family. Always delicate, she was prone to bronchitis and suffered from asthma. Her aunt had early implanted in her an almost ineradicable vein of pessimism. But frail though she might appear, Anne was stoical, tenacious, enduring, patient and humorous. In the end, only her ill health defeated her, and even when facing her early death, she was to prove indomitable.

When she determined to go out into the world to earn her own living and help the family, the rest of them were united against her decision. It might be possible for the other three, but not for their little Anne. Yet she was resolved and, against all advice and opposition, persevered in finding a post. Although she was to be dismissed from her first post, as an employee she must be considered the most successful of the family, staying doggedly in her second position for an uninterrupted four years.

It was perhaps an unlucky omen that Anne's first situation was to take her back to Mirfield, where she had been so unhappy at school. This was probably because Miss Wooler had heard of the vacancy and recommended her. The Inghams were a well-known local family who had lived at Blake Hall since the time of Charles I. They attended Mirfield church, where Miss Wooler's brother-in-law, the Reverend Edward Carter, officiated and where Anne had worshipped on Sundays when she was at school. In the eighteenth century Benjamin Ingham had had close associations with Wesley and the Evangelical Revival, and he had enabled the establishment of the Mirfield Settlement of the Moravian Brotherhood of which the current Bishop – the Reverend James la Trobe – had done so much to restore Anne's peace of mind during her crisis two years before. All these connections, plus the fact that Miss Wooler had described Mrs Ingham as 'a very nice woman', must have helped to allay

Anne's fears and her family's objections. The Ingham family consisted already of five children (there were ultimately to be thirteen), but Anne was to have charge only of the two eldest, Joshua, aged six, and Mary, who was five. She was to receive a salary of £25 per year.

In her first novel, *Agnes Grey*, which Anne was to write six years later, her career at Blake Hall is simply and honestly described: her high hopes on setting forth, her dismay at realizing the conditions of her job, the almost incredible bad behaviour of the young children she was to care for, and the totally uncooperative attitude of their parents, who appear to have had some 'modern ideas' about bringing up children.

To we who are accustomed to thinking of Victorian children as being extremely strictly controlled and trained to be seen but not heard, the children Anne depicts in her book come as a great shock. To Anne, who had been very strictly brought up both at home and at school, the shock must have been even greater.

As her novel makes plain, she had anticipated that she would be able to manage them 'delightfully': 'I do not pretend to be able to instruct great girls; but surely I could teach little ones; and I should like it *so* much: I am so fond of children.'[1]

In her book, Anne transformed the Inghams into the Bloomfield family; Joshua became Tom, and Mary was given an additional name as Mary Anne. She changed certain of the family details for obvious reasons, but there can be no reason to doubt that the harsh facts she related in *Agnes Grey* were substantially true. It has been suggested that she greatly exaggerated details of her stay with the Inghams when she came to write her autobiographical fiction, but an article by Susan Brooke, a descendant of the family, in the *Transactions of the Brontë Society*,[2] firmly refutes this and reinforces the view that to a considerable extent Anne was reporting fairly and accurately her life there:

> The lack of parental discipline which Anne found such a disturbing feature of the children's upbringing was characteristic of many Yorkshire families at this period, for among the newly enriched folk of the West Riding there had been a certain reaction against the stricter code of an earlier generation, and those who aspired to any position in the countryside were particularly anxious to avoid the stigma of middle class manners. Boys were frequently over-indulged by their parents and if they teased or bullied their sisters it was merely considered a sign of manliness.

For anyone who knew the famly at Blake Hall it must have been obvious that there was a close resemblance between the young Inghams and the Bloomfields in *Agnes Grey*. Their ages more or less corresponded and their psychological tendencies seem to have been precisely similar. In fact there can be little doubt that *Agnes Grey* contains an accurate description of Anne's first experience as a governess.

Susan Brooke goes on to recount that once Frances, one of the daughters, 'was so frightened to see her father standing motionless at the top of a dark flight of stairs, that she fell and injured her back'.

It was not until later that Anne's family realized the full extent of the ordeal she had undergone. She was so determined to make a success of her first post, which she had fought so hard to be allowed to accept, that she put on a cheerful face for the sake of her family when writing home. Unfortunately her letters were not preserved, but Charlotte's to Ellen Nussey make this clear.

> We have had one letter from her since she went. She expresses herself very well satisfied, and says that Mrs Ingham is extremely kind; the two eldest children alone are under her care, the rest are confined to the nursery, with which and its occupants she has nothing to do. Both her pupils are desperate little dunces; neither of them can read, and sometimes they profess a profound ignorance of their alphabet. The worst of it is they are excessively indulged, and she is not empowered to inflict any punishment. She is requested, when they misbehave themselves, to inform their mamma, which she says is utterly out of the question, as in that case she might be making complaints from morning till night. So she alternately scolds, coaxes, and threatens, sticks always to her first word, and gets on as well as she can.[3]

Anne left home for this uncongenial post on 8 April 1839, and although she was looking forward to going out into the world, quite naturally leaving her home and, above all, leaving Emily was a bitter wrench. Her painful feelings were described in *Agnes Grey*.

> ... when all was ready for my departure on the morrow, and the last night at home approached – a sudden anguish seemed to swell my heart. My dear friends looked so sad, and spoke so very kindly, that I could scarcely keep my eyes from overflowing: but I still affected to be gay ... I had

played my last tune on the old familiar piano, and sung my last song to papa: not the last, I hoped, but the last for what appeared to me, a very long time. And perhaps when I did see these things again, it would be with different feelings: circumstances might be changed, and this house might never be my settled home again. My dear little friend, the kitten, would certainly be changed: she was already growing a fine cat; and when I returned, even for a hasty visit at Christmas, would, most likely, have forgotten both her playmate and her merry pranks. I had romped with her for the last time; and when I stroked her soft bright fur, while she lay purring herself to sleep in my lap, it was with a feeling of sadness I could not easily disguise. Then, at bedtime, when I retired with Mary [Agnes's sister] to our quiet little chamber, where already my drawers were cleared out and my share of the bookcase empty – and where, hereafter, she would have to sleep alone, in dreary solitude, as she expressed it – my heart sank more than ever.[4]

Anne was always to remember with pain such details, but without sentimentality. Most people will understand and appreciate how this shy girl of not quite nineteen was feeling as she approached the end of her journey and the beginning of her first experience of paid employment: '... when we entered the lofty iron gateway, when we drove softly up the smooth, well-rolled carriage road, with the green lawn on each side, studded with young trees, and approached the new but stately mansion of Wellwood, rising above its mushroom poplar groves, my heart failed me, and I wished it were a mile or two farther off. For the first time in my life, I must stand alone: there was no retreating now. I must enter that house, and introduce myself among its strange inhabitants.'[5]

An affliction Anne suffered, but with which she did not burden Agnes, was her tendency to stutter when nervous, which is likely to make any form of introduction an ordeal. Charlotte had been worried about this and feared that Mrs Ingham 'will sometimes conclude that she has a natural impediment in her speech'.[6] No doubt her small charges and their parents took advantage of this occasional disability.

If Mrs Ingham resembled the fictitious Mrs Bloomfield, Anne's last-minute cold feet were well justified. Most likely, too, after her seventeen-mile journey, Anne was as cold as her heroine had been when she arrived: 'The cold wind had swelled and reddened my hands, uncurled and entangled my hair, and dyed my face of a pale purple; add to this my collar was horribly crumpled, my frock splashed with mud, my feet clad in stout new boots, and as the trunks were not brought up, there was no remedy; so having smoothed my hair as well as I could, and repeatedly twitched my obdurate collar, I proceeded to clomp down the two flights of stairs, philosophising as I went; and with some difficulty found my way into the room where Mrs Bloomfield awaited me.'[7]

Anne's mistress was evidently very far from the 'very nice woman' Miss Wooler had described and was more probably like her counterpart in Anne's novel, 'a tall, spare, stately woman, with thick black hair, cold grey eyes, and extremely sallow complexion'. She conversed with the shy young governess with 'frigid formality', roused to enthusiasm only when describing the virtues and abilities of her offspring.[8]

Used to simple, well-cooked, wholesome food at home, one of Anne's trials (and, if Mr Ingham resembled Mr Bloomfield, one shared by the master of Blake Hall) seems to have been the poverty of the table. This aspect of her new life is described by her heroine with spirit and humour, from her first painful meal of tough beef and half-cold potatoes to Mr Bloomfield's later embarrassing attack on his wife's household management:

There was a roast leg of mutton before him: he helped Mrs Bloomfield, the children, and me, desiring me to cut up the children's meat; then, after twisting about the mutton in various directions, and eyeing it from different viewpoints, he pronounced it not fit to be eaten, and called for the cold beef.

'What is the matter with the mutton, my dear?' asked his mate.

'It is quite overdone. Don't you taste, Mrs Bloomfield, that all the goodness is roasted out of it? And can't you see that all that nice, red gravy is completely dried away?'

'Well, I think the *beef* will suit you.'

The beef was set before him, and he began to carve, but with the most rueful expressions of discontent.

'What is the matter with the *beef*, Mr Bloomfield? I'm sure I thought it was very nice.'

'And so it *was*, very nice. A nicer joint could not be; but it is *quite* spoiled,' replied he dolefully ...

Notwithstanding the ruinous state of the beef, the gentleman managed to cut himself some delicate slices, part of which he ate in silence. When he next spoke, it was, in a less querulous tone, to ask what there was for dinner.

'Turkey and grouse,' was the concise reply.

'And what besides?'

'Fish.'

'What kind of fish?'

'I don't know.'

'*You don't know?*' cried he, looking solemnly up from his plate, and suspending his knife and fork in astonishment.

'No. I told the cook to get some fish – I did not particularise what.'

'Well, that beats everything! A lady professes to keep house, and doesn't even know what fish is for dinner! professes to order fish, and doesn't specify what!'

'Perhaps, Mr Bloomfield, you will order dinner yourself in future.'[9]

This conversation has the ring of a straightforward piece of verbatim reporting. It would certainly never have taken place in the Brontë family.

But none of this, nor Anne's other problems, the loneliness, the long hours, the undermining of her authority over the children by the parents, compared with the horrifying major difficulty, the children themselves.

Very soon after she met them, Anne must have realized how vain had been that prospect of managing them 'delightfully'. Having been imagined as small, charming, malleable creatures, both her young charges turned out to be spoilt, ill-trained, unruly children, with exceptionally strong characters and unpleasant dispositions. From the moment she met the young Inghams, Anne Brontë had no doubts about the importance of early training – a theme she was later to expand with great power and force in *The Tenant of Wildfell Hall*.

Even at this early age, aware that for social reasons their parents would never place the views of their governess, however just, above their own wishes, Joshua and Mary enjoyed their game of thwarting, tormenting and humiliating their young governess, making her task of teaching and disciplining them thoroughly impossible, and her life a misery. Drawn as they were from living characters, Tom and Mary Anne are very far from any idealized view of children and are in the same tradition of, for example, the boys in *The Lord of the Flies* and the girls and boys in *High Wind in Jamaica*.

Agnes Grey, in the section devoted to the Bloomfield family, tells the story with painful exactitude and if, as Mrs Ingham claimed much later, Anne occasionally tied Joshua and Mary to the legs of the table, who could blame her?

The following well-known passage from *Agnes Grey* throws much light on Anne's character. Tom's maternal Uncle Robson, a justifiable thorn in the governess's side, has given his nephew a nest full of fledglings. His sisters run out 'to admire his spoils, and to beg each a bird for themselves'.

'No, not one!' cried Tom. 'They're all mine: Uncle Robson gave them to me – one, two, three, four, five – you shan't touch one of them! no, not one, for your lives!' continued he exultingly; laying the nest on the ground, and standing over it with his legs wide apart, his hands thrust into his breeches-pockets, his body bent forward, and his face twisted into all manner of contortions in the ecstacy of his delight.

'But you shall see me fettle 'em off. My word, but I *will* wallop 'em! See if I don't now. By gum! but there's rare sport for me in that nest.'

'But, Tom,' said I, 'I shall not allow you to torture these birds. They must either be killed at once or carried back to the place you took them from, that the old birds may continue to feed them.'

'But you don't know where that is, madam: it's only me and Uncle Robson that knows that.'

'But if you don't tell me, I shall kill them myself – much as I hate it.'

'You daren't. You daren't touch them for your life! because you know papa and mamma and Uncle Robson would be angry. Ha, ha, I've caught you there, miss!'

But the boy had underestimated the moral force of his governess who, rather than allow the helpless small creatures to suffer the various refinements of torture he had in mind, killed them quickly and mercifully by dropping upon them a heavy stone.

This action swiftly brought upon her her mistress's disapproval.

'I'm sorry, Miss Grey, you should think it necessary to interfere with Master Bloomfield's amusements; he was *very* much distressed about your destroying the birds.'

'When Master Bloomfield's amusements consist in injuring sentient creatures,' I answered, 'I think it my duty to interfere.'

'You seem to have forgotten,' she said calmly, 'that the creatures were all created for our convenience.'

I thought that doctrine admitted some doubt, but merely replied –

'If they were, we have no right to torment them for our amusement.'

'I think,' she said, 'a child's amusement is scarcely to be weighed against the welfare of a soulless brute.'

'But for the child's own sake, it ought not to be encouraged to have such amusements,' answered I, as meekly as I could to make up for such unusual pertinacity. 'Blessed are the merciful, for they shall obtain mercy.'

'Oh! of course, but that refers to our conduct towards each other.'

'The merciful man shows mercy to his beast,' I ventured to add.

'I think you have not shown much mercy,' replied she, with a short bitter laugh, 'killing the poor birds by wholesale in that shocking manner, and putting the dear boy to such misery for a mere whim.'

I judged it prudent to say no more. This was the nearest approach to quarrel I ever had with Mrs Bloomfield; as well as the greatest number of words I ever exchanged with her at one time, since the day of my first arrival.[10]

Shown here are Anne's love of helpless creatures, her compassion for their suffering, her necessary ruthlessness in destroying them (in the same way as her sister Emily was ruthless in training her dog Keeper) and her characteristic courage and unusual verbal aggression in justifying her action to her employer.

Another of Anne's characteristics was her fair-mindedness. To a certain extent, she understood just why the children were as they were, and she sympathized. Accordingly, she did her patient best to bring them into line and to teach them something. She tried discipline, kindness and above all perseverance. Slowly but surely, she felt she was making some headway.

But [in the words of Agnes Grey] soon my trials in this quarter came to a close — sooner than I either expected or desired; for one sweet evening towards the close of May, as I was rejoicing in the near approach of the holidays, and congratulating myself upon having made some progress with my pupils (as far as their learning went at least, for I *had* instilled *something* into their heads, and I had at length brought them to be a little — a very little — more rational about getting their lessons done in time to leave some space for recreation, instead of tormenting themselves and me all day long to no purpose) Mrs Bloomfield sent for me, and calmly told me that after Midsummer my services would no longer be required.[11]

Just as for Agnes Grey, this unkind and evidently unjust dismissal was a very hard blow to Anne Brontë. She had tried so hard and in such adverse circumstances, then, just as she began to see a little progress, she had been summarily dismissed. 'I wished to say something in my own justification: but in attempting to speak, I felt my voice falter; and rather than testify any emotion, or suffer the tears to overflow that were already gathering in my eyes, I chose to keep silence, and bear all like a self-convicted culprit.'[12]

Naturally enough, Anne disliked the thoughts of returning home, apparently having failed in her first situation. But she was determined, come what may, to try again. 'I knew all parents were not like Mr and Mrs Bloomfield, and any change must be for the better. I had been seasoned by adversity, and tutored by experience, and I longed to redeem my lost honour in the eyes of those whose opinion was more than that of all the world to me.'[13]

Anne returned to Haworth for the Christmas of 1839. Her disappointment must surely have been offset by her happy reunion with her family, the immediate renewal of her partnership with Emily, and the cheerful addition to their circle of her father's new curate, Mr William Weightman.

The year 1839 had brought to Charlotte Brontë two proposals of marriage and an even less successful spell as a governess than Anne's.

Charlotte had spent three months with the Sidgwick family at Stonegappe, near Skipton. Once more, Miss Wooler's brother-in-law, the Reverend Edward Carter, now appointed curate-in-charge of the church at Lothersdale, had made the recommendation. The post he found for Charlotte was no more congenial than that with the Inghams at Blake Hall had been for Anne.

When Charlotte arrived, Mrs Sidgwick was five months pregnant, and the new nursery governess was put in charge of the two youngest children in the family of four, Mathilda and John Benson, aged six and four respectively. Writing home to Emily, she complained, 'The children are constantly with me, and more riotous, perverse, unmanageable cubs never grew. As for correcting them, I soon found that was entirely out of the question: they are to do as they like. A complaint to Mrs Sidgwick brings only black looks upon oneself, and unjust, partial excuses to screen the children.'

Mrs Sidgwick was no improvement on Mrs Ingham although, Charlotte says, '... she is universally considered an amiable woman. Her manners are fussily affable. She talks a great deal, but as it seems to me not much to the purpose … Mr Sidgwick is in my opinion a hundred times better – less profession, less bustling condescension, but a far kinder heart. It is very seldom that he speaks to me, but when he does I always feel happier and more settled for some minutes after.' (Charlotte was always to prefer the masters to the mistresses in her posts.)

She had the added imposition of a huge volume of needlework in addition to her other duties: 'I now begin to find that she does not intend to know me, that she cares nothing in the world about me except to contrive how the greatest possible quantity of labour may be squeezed out of me, and to that end she overwhelms me with oceans of needlework, yards of cambric to hem, muslin nightcaps to make, and, above all other things, dolls to dress.[14]

Charlotte endured unhappily through to 19 July and then returned home about a month before Mrs Sidgwick's baby was born, which no doubt put the family to some inconvenience. Charlotte wrote to her friend Ellen, 'I was never so glad to get out of a house in all my life.'[15]

Later she and Anne must have had many points of similarity to discuss about their situations in the Sidgwick and Ingham establishments, but apparently Charlotte did not face her next venture into employment with the same stoic courage as her youngest sister.

Her two proposals came from clergymen. One was from Ellen Nussey's brother, Henry, who was busily looking for a wife without the same need but in rather the same spirit as Mr Brontë had once done. Charlotte's romantic soul could only reject him and, from his subsequent rather miserable history (six years later he married a Miss Emily Prestcott, their marriage ended in a separation, Henry left the Church and spent the rest of his life in France), it seems her instinct also guided her correctly in a practical sense.

Her other suitor, David Bryce, a young Irish curate fresh from Dublin University, who with a former curate of Mr Brontë's spent just one day with them, appears to have fallen in love with Charlotte at first sight, since a short while later his visit was followed by a letter proposing marriage expressed 'in the ardent language of the sapient young Irishman'.[16] Charlotte had enjoyed his company but had perceived some faults, evidently sufficient for her to refuse him. As it happened, pursuing this strange romance could only have led to heart-break, since the apparently strong, athletic-looking man died suddenly of 'the rupture of a blood vessel'[17] just a few months later, in January 1840.

Thinking herself, so she said, plain and doomed to be an old maid, Charlotte was waiting for love to dawn on her in the way it was to for her heroines. In fact, perhaps because she communicated in some way her capacity for sexual passion, she was the only one of the sisters to receive proposals and finally to marry.

There can be no doubt that the greatest event for Charlotte in 1839 was her first sight of the sea. She had read so much about the sea throughout her life in poetry and prose but even her vivid imagination failed to reproduce or to foresee the tremendous impact of the reality.

She had gone on holiday with her friend Ellen Nussey, and at first the two young women were constrained to stay with Henry Nussey's friends, Mr and Mrs Hudson at Easton House Farm, two miles from the sea. Disappointed, because she had wanted to take lodgings on the seafront, on their second day she and Ellen set off to walk to Bridlington on the coast.

Ellen has left her impression of the effect of the occasion on her friend: 'She was quite overpowered ... she could not speak till she had shed some tears ... her eyes were red and swollen, she was still trembling ... for the remainder of the day she was very quiet, subdued and exhausted.'[18] Later Charlotte was to write to Henry: 'I will not tell you what I thought of the sea, because I should fall into my besetting sin of enthusiasm. I may, however, say that its glories, changes, its ebbs and flow, the sound of its restless waves, formed a subject for contemplation that never wearied either the eye, the ear, or the mind.'[19] Less cautiously, she wrote to Ellen, his sister and her companion, 'Have you forgotten the sea by this time? Is it grown dim in your mind? Or still can you see it, – dark blue, and green, and foam-white; and hear it roaring roughly when the wind is high, or rushing softly when it is calm?'[20]

The sea was to have a similar effect on Anne, but it does not appear to have tempted Emily from her first allegiance to the rolling inland spaces of the moors.

January 1840 saw the three sisters reunited at home, and it was now time again for Branwell to attempt to earn a living. He had found, perhaps through the good offices of William Weightman, a position as a tutor. This was his first venture in the role, and he was to have charge of the two sons of Mr and Mrs Robert Postlethwaite of Broughton House, Broughton-in-Furness, Lancashire. The boys, John, aged twelve, and William, ten, were the only survivors of their family of six.

In order to get to Broughton, it was necessary for Branwell to break his journey at Kendal. The letter he wrote to his old friend and drinking companion John Brown about the evening he spent there sheds light on Branwell as he was and had behaved, or as he had imagined and would like to have acted – which now be only a matter for conjecture; perhaps it is a mixture of both.

> I took half-year's farewell of old friend whisky on the night after I left. There was a party of gentlemen at the Royal Hotel; I joined them and we ordered in supper and 'toddy' as "hot as hell!" ' They thought I was a physician, and put me in the chair. I gave them some toasts, of the stiffest sort ... washing them down at the same time, till the room spun round and the candles danced in their eyes ... a respectable old gentleman with powdered head, rosy cheeks, fat paunch, and ringed fingers ... led off with a speech, and in two minutes, in the very middle of a grand sentence, he stopped, wagged his head, looked wildly around, stammered, coughed, stopped again, and called for his slippers and so the waiter helped him to bed. Next a tall Irish squire and a native of the land of Israel began to quarrel about their countries; and, in the warmth of argument, discharged their glasses, each at his neighbours throat instead of his own. I recommended bleeding, purging, and blistering; but they administered each other a real 'Jem Warder', so I flung my tumbler on the floor too, and swore I'd join 'Old Ireland'! A regular rumpus ensured, but we were tamed at last, and I found myself in bed next morning, with a bottle of porter, a glass, and a corkscrew beside me. Since then I have not tasted anything stronger than milk and water, nor, I hope, shall, till I return at Midsummer; when we will see about it.[21]

Broughton is a beautifully situated, gracious little market town, and Broughton House stood in a corner on the market square opposite the King's Head. Mr Postlethwaite was, as Branwell said, 'of a right hearty and generous disposition', and his wife a quiet, amiable woman. Branwell seems to have been subjected to very few restrictions; he did not live with the family but lodged with the local doctor, a Dr Gibson, who evidently had a pretty daughter, 'fair-faced, blue-eyed, dark-haired, sweet eighteen'.[22]

Teaching the two 'fine, spirited boys' was well within his capabilities and did not tax him. Coming and going independently as he was able to do was not good for him, giving him a great deal of spare time. No doubt he was lonely, and all too soon he gravitated for some congenial company to the King's Head and further afield, to Ulverston, where he may have been in contact with fellow Masons. There were four attractive inns in the town and, for once in his life, Branwell had some money he had earned jingling in his pockets. He rode into Ulverston every week with Mr Postlethwaite, who visited his bank and shopped, and most probably he went there alone on other occasions.

But it is only fair and important to remember that Branwell did not waste all his precious leisure time, and during his stay in Broughton he turned again from art to literature. It was now that he completed his highly regarded translations of Horace's Odes, and there can be no doubt that the curb and discipline of translation were of great benefit to his own poetic style.

Privately printed in a limited edition in 1923, edited and with a preface by John Drinkwater, the Odes are not easily available, so it is good to know that Mr Everard Flintoff of Leeds University is preparing a new edition of this neglected aspect of Branwell's work.

In Drinkwater's opinion, 'Charlotte and Anne were not poets, Emily and Branwell were. These two had the wildness, the sense of loneliness, the ache for some indefinable thing called freedom that mark the poet from infancy.' He asserts, 'Branwell Brontë's translations of the First Book of odes need at their best fear comparison with none ... In a few instances I should say that they are decidedly the best of all ... in some whole poems, as in the lovely rendering of XXI, there is hardly a flaw from beginning to end. At his best he has melody, and phrase, and he builds his stanzas well. Further, he was happier in verse with Horace's subject matter than he generally was with the experience of his own confused and frustrated life.'

To Apollo and Diana (from Ode XXI)

Virgins, sing the Virgin Huntress;
   Youth, the youthful Phoebus, sing;
Sing Latona, she who bore them
   Dearest to the eternal King:
Sing the heavenly maid who roves
Joyous through the mountain groves;
She who winding waters loves;
   Let her haunts her praises ring![23]

Branwell was also much moved by the beauty of the countryside in which he now found himself, the great mass of Black Combe, which rises to a height of nearly two thousand feet, inspiring the following sonnet:

Far off, and half revealed, 'mid shade and light,
Black Combe half smiles, half frowns; his mighty form
Scarce bending into peace, more formed to fight
A thousand years of struggle with a storm
Than bask one hour subdued by sunshine warm
To bright and breezeless rest; yet even his height
Towers not o'er this world's sympathies; he smiles –
While many a human heart to pleasure's wiles
Can bear to bend, and still forget to rise –
As though he, huge and heath-clad on our sight,
Again rejoices in his stormy skies.
Man loses vigour in unstable joys.
Thus tempests find Black Combe invincible,
While we are lost, who should know life so well![24]

Once again he decided to send some of his poems to well-known literary figures, this time to Thomas De Quincey and Hartley Coleridge. De Quincey was to have a far from fortunate influence on Branwell's life, for it was most likely his *Confessions of an English Opium Eater* which inspired Branwell to try the effects of the drug. The correspondence has not been preserved, but after so much disappointment it is good to know that Hartley Coleridge responded not just with words but with an invitation for Branwell to visit him at his home, Nab Cottage, Rydal Water, where his neighbours and great friends were the Wordsworths.

Hartley Coleridge's early life bore considerable resemblance to Branwell's except that he was the son of a father of undoubted, if flawed, genius, and he grew up surrounded by helpful influential friends. Moreover, feckless and improvident though he was in many ways, the elder Coleridge had left provision enough for his son to pursue the life of literature he loved and which was the only life possible for him. At this time, he was about forty-five, small, strange and quaint. He was learned and talented but subject to unreasoning rages; as a boy, he had invented his own dream world, which in spirit was not too far away from Branwell's Angria; disappointed by his career at Oxford, he had taken to drink and lost his Fellowship; he had done some teaching and tutoring. But his great advantage over Branwell was that, when he wrote, literary doors were automatically opened to him. Finally, like Branwell and his own celebrated father, he was a brilliant talker.

The meeting of these kindred spirits took place on 1 May 1840. Undoubtedly, this was one of the high spots of Branwell's life, finding he was accepted on almost equal terms by a well-known literary figure he greatly admired.

On this occasion, Branwell had written a more modest letter of introduction and had said sensibly, 'I love writing too well to fling aside the practice of it without an effort to ascertain whether I could turn it to account, not in *wholly* maintaining myself, but in *aiding* my maintenance ... I do seek to know, and venture ... to ... ask ... whether by periodical or other writing, I could please myself with writing, and make it subservient to living.'[25]

To Branwell's credit, there can be no doubt that Hartley would not have welcomed him as he did had he not been impressed by his poetry. He himself had translated the XXXVIIIth Ode of Horace, and when Branwell reached it at the end of Book One, he wrote, 'This Ode I have no heart to attempt, after having heard Mr H. Coleridge's translation, on May Day, at Ambleside.' It is good to imagine Branwell, excited and elevated, for once, as he must have thought, in his proper element, listening to Hartley Coleridge declaiming, vicariously sharing at that sublime moment, in the life of the Lake Poets.

Nay, nay, my boy – 'tis not for me,
This studious pomp of eastern luxury:
Give me no various garlands – fine
    With linden twine,
Nor seek, where latest lingering blows
    The solitary rose.[26]

Hartley not only encouraged Branwell to continue with his translations but said he would be pleased to see and comment on the finished work. At last, he must have felt, here was a beginning. Unfortunately, it proved to mark an end.

From Nab Cottage, most probably the two small literary men repaired for a cheerful evening at the Low-Wood Inn, and Branwell returned to Broughton tardily and in a noticeably elevated mood.

Hartley's words of praise undoubtedly had a good effect on Branwell's translation of Horace, but an unsettling one on his teaching career.

Having heard a description of Branwell's stumbling return from Ambleside, Mr Postlethwaite began to pay closer attention to the day-to-day behaviour of his boys' tutor and soon realized that Branwell's duties were being honoured more in the breach than the observance. No doubt the two pupils had rather enjoyed their undemanding and infrequent lessons, and certainly Branwell had delighted in the long walks he had taken in the beautiful countryside in the late spring, and the pleasant times he had spent in the various hostelries he had discovered. Mr Postlethwaite was a generous and understanding man, but he knew very well when advantage was being taken of him. It appears that one final binge led to Branwell's dismissal, and in June 1840 he was back at Haworth with his sisters, no doubt, and in his case quite unfairly, comparing notes with Anne and Charlotte about the injustices of life as a tutor in a private family.

He had sent his translations of Horace's Odes to Hartley Coleridge, but, excellent though they were, they remained unpublished and can only have become to Branwell another source of disappointment. So far, he must have felt, all his efforts, in both art and literature, had gone unrewarded. What fields must he hope to conquer next?

For the three girls, all at home together, it had been a happy time, made even happier by the presence of their father's new curate.

William Weightman was clearly an exceptional young man. He was clever, handsome and kind and caused a good deal of local flutter on his coming to Haworth parsonage. When he first arrived, he claimed to be engaged to Miss Agnes Walton, a young lady of his home town of Appleby, but this soon fell away and left him free to be flirtatious in a perfectly harmless way in the new circle in which he now found himself. This included not only the three Brontë sisters but their friend Ellen Nussey and various other susceptible local young ladies. No doubt on account of his somewhat girlish good looks, Charlotte christened him 'Celia-Amelia'; he responded to the teasing with gallantry and humour and went out of his way to delight the girls with Valentines posted in far-away Bradford. It is not hard to feel that he was sorry for them and did his best to cheer them up and provide a little light relief in their all too serious lives.

When Branwell dejectedly arrived home, the curate set about cheering him up too, and there can be no doubt that Willie Weightman was the best and most suitable friend Branwell Brontë was ever to have.

Haworth Old Church in the 1860s, and below Haworth Parsonage at a similar date

HAWORTH OLD RECTORY.

Patrick, the father of the Brontës, still a handsome man in his old age

A portrait very likely to have been of Aunt Branwell, who played such an influential part in the life of the young

The Brontë Bridge, as it is now known, which provided a favourite moorland walk for the sisters. Inset: A badly damaged but beautiful profile study of Emily by her brother Branwell

Inset: Charlotte's drawing of her fourteen-year-old sister Anne

december 15 1836

One of Anne's typical pencil drawings

Anne, Emily, and Charlotte, portrayed by Branwell. The gap in the centre is
likely to have been a self-portrait painted out

A selection of Charlotte's juvenile manuscripts

The dining room at the Parsonage, showing the grim black sofa on which
Emily died, and portraits of Charlotte and Branwell

Two pages from Branwell's Luddenden Foot Notebook. The poem on the left
is reproduced below. The poem on the right appears on p. 97

The desolate earth, the wintry sky,
The ceaseless rain-showers driving by –
  The farewell of the year –
Though drear the sight, and sad the sound,
While bitter winds are wailing round,
Nor hopes depress, nor thoughts confound,
  Nor waken sigh or tear.

For, as it moans, December's wind
Brings many varied thoughts to mind
  Upon its storm-drenched wing,
Of words, not said 'mid sunshine gay,
Of deeds, not done in summer's day,
Yet which, when joy has passed away,
  Will strength to sorrow bring.

For, when the leaves are glittering bright,
And green hills lie in noonday night,
  The present only lives;
But, when within my chimnies roar
The chidings of the stormy shower,
The feeble present loses power,
  The mighty past survives.

I cannot think – as roses blow,
And streams sound gently in their flow,
  And clouds shine bright above –
Of aught but childhood's happiness,
Of joys unshadowed by distress
Or voices turned the ear to bless
  Or faces made to love.

15 December 1841

6. Wish for Wings, 1840–41

Art and literature having so far failed to earn him a living, dismissed from tutoring, after a two months' rest Branwell Brontë next turned to technology.

Today it might seem strange that such a being as Branwell even thought of a career on the railways, but at that time they represented science, the future and adventure. As far as transport was concerned, the harnessing of steam power was the first great advance since the invention of the wheel. Percy Bysshe Shelley, for example, might seem an unlikely figure to have been one of the first advocates of the steam-ship, but he was, while Turner was inspired to one of his greatest paintings by his vision of *Rain, Steam and Speed.* In the new steam-age, the lives of ordinary people were transformed and enlarged by the network of railways which began tracing the land, and by the steam trains chugging them up and down the countryside in comparatively inexpensive comfort. It was an extension of movement similar to that provided by cheap air travel in the mid twentieth century.

At this time in his life, Branwell Brontë was an optimistic character, and each new venture he started, however dismally it was to end, he embraced with enthusiasm. So it was in no glum spirits that he set off to his first post in the Manchester-Leeds Railway Company as assistant clerk at Sowerby Bridge Station. He was to be paid £75 annually, with an increase of £10 each year until he reached the maximum for that particular job of £105, and there was no reason to doubt that this humble beginning might lead to greater prospects before long.

Branwell arrived at Sowerby Bridge, just two miles south-west of Halifax, in early October 1840. The stretch of line had only recently been opened, and Sowerby Bridge was to remain the nearest important stop to Halifax for the next four years. Taking lodgings in an old house in

Sowerby Street, he soon acquainted himself with the nearby inns, the Royal Oak, the Bull's Head, the Wharf and Navigation Inn, where rough customers from the canal barges were also entertained. Best of all, he was within easy reach of Halifax, which enabled him to seek out his friends among the talented Leyland family. Robert Leyland was a publisher and printer and one-time editor of the *Halifax Guardian*; his eldest son, Joseph, Branwell's particular friend, was a talented but mercurial sculptor, while Francis, the youngest, was a steadier character more resembling their father. Forty years later Francis described Branwell as he remembered him at the time of their first meeting:

> The young railway clerk was of a gentleman-like appearance, and seemed to be qualified for a much better position than the one he had chosen. In stature he was a little below the middle height ... He was slim and agile in figure yet of well formed outline. His complexion was clear and ruddy, and the expression of his face, lightsome and cheerful. His voice had a ringing sweetness, and the utterance and use of his English was perfect: Branwell appeared to be in excellent spirits, and showed none of those traces of intemperance with which some writers have unjustly credited him about this period of his life. My brother had often spoken to me of Branwell's poetical abilities, his conversational powers, and the polish of his education; and, on a personal acquaintance I found nothing to question in this estimate of his mental gifts, and of his literary attainments.[1]

During his first six months with the railway company, Branwell must have attended to his duties and given satisfaction, for on 1 April 1841 he was promoted to the position of clerk in charge, at a starting salary of £130 per annum, at Luddenden Foot station, about a mile up the line nearer Hebden Bridge.

For Branwell, this station in the valley proved a dreary and depressing place, from which, all too soon, he strove to escape to the more congenial atmosphere of the Lord Nelson, the principal tavern of the attractive Luddenden village, half a mile or so away up the hill. Built in 1634, the cosy, low-ceilinged, beamed inn remains an attractive refuge today. Unfortunately, he was aided and abetted all too often in his dereliction of duty which became increasing and longer as time wore on, by the obliging and helpful porter, who was always ready to volunteer to take charge of the ticket office in his absence.

Early in 1841 life also took a different turn for Anne and Charlotte.
While, as he described, Branwell sat amid

> The bustle of a Town-like room
> 'Neath skies, with smoke-stain'd vapours hid –
> By windows made to show their gloom.
> The desk that held my Ledger book
> Beneath the thundering rattle shook
>   Of engines passing by:
> The bustle of the approaching train
> Was all I hoped to rouse the brain
>   Or startle apathy ... [alt. reading: of stealthy apathy][2]

two of his sisters had steeled themselves to bring to an end what must
have been one of the pleasantest periods they were ever to enjoy. For a
little over a whole year the three girls had been at home together, and in
addition they had the bright company of their father's much valued and
invaluable curate.

Her subsequent poems seem to show that Anne was strongly attracted
to him at first sight and that she alone of the girls saw through Willie's
gay social exterior to the essential integrity of the man, which was
appreciated by her father as much as herself. But at first he paid her no
particular attention.

As soon as Anne arrived home, she and Emily resumed their natural
partnership in the recording of the affairs of Gondal, and it seems likely
that the poem she wrote for Olivia Vernon on 1 January 1840 was
inspired by the powerful and unsettling feelings she was experiencing
within herself as she began to fall in love with William Weightman.

> Last night as we sat round the fire
>   Conversing merrily,
> We heard, without, approaching steps
>   Of one well known to me!
>
> There was no trembling in my voice,
>   No blush upon my cheek,
> No lustrous sparkle in my eyes,
>   Of hope, or joy, to speak;

But, oh! my spirit burned within,
   My heart beat full and fast!
He came not nigh – he went away –
And then my joy was past.

And yet my comrades marked it not!
   My voice was still the same;
They saw me smile, and o'er my face
   No signs of sadness came.
They little knew my hidden thoughts;
   And they will *never* know
The aching anguish of my heart,
   The bitter burning woe![3]

Like Jane Austen's Anne Eliot, Anne Brontë was to know the pain of 'loving longest, when existence or when hope is gone'. It was to be some while before Willie Weightman recognized, among all these young women, how important to him was quiet, gentle, lion-hearted Anne.

As well as the flattering Valentines, another example of Weightman's kindness to all three sisters and to Ellen Nussey occurred in February 1840. He was keenly aware of how circumscribed were their lives and how few treats ever came their way. Without vanity, he knew how much pleasure it would give them to hear the lecture he was due to deliver at the Mechanics Institute in Keighley on the Classics. Weightman anticipated and overcame the objections to their going raised by Mr Brontë and Miss Branwell; he arranged for the sisters and their friend to have tea with the Reverend Theodore Dury, Vicar of Keighley, and his kind wife, and luckily the weather co-operated with him too. After an exhilarating evening, the girls cheerfully walked the four chilly but dry and moonlit miles home, arriving in high spirits to a somewhat frosty reception at midnight from their father and aunt – not frosty enough to spoil their pleasure. This episode was recorded by Ellen, who was there at the time, and no doubt similar stimulating departures from routine were organized by Mr Weightman during this happy year of 1840.

That he was the model for Mr Weston in Anne's novel *Agnes Grey* seems very clear. Charlotte, who, feeling somewhat piqued, was not always too kind about him by then, wrote to Ellen Nussey in late September 1840, telling her that their father had been visiting one of his best Sunday School scholars, Susan Bland, who was dying. 'After sitting with her some time,' Mr Brontë said, 'I happened to ask her mother if she thought a little port wine would do her good. She replied that the doctor had recommended it, and that when Mr Weightman was last there he had sent them a bottle of wine and a jar of preserves. She added that he was always good to poor folks, and seemed to have a deal of feeling and kindness about him.'[4] A scene echoed in Mr Weston's visits to Nancy Brown in *Agnes Grey*.

Perhaps because of the watchful eye Emily was keeping on her sisters at this time, Weightman began calling her 'the Major', a nickname that was to stick through the years, and one she rather appreciated.

Happy in this present companionship, yet always aware of its ephemeral quality, Anne was now to write two of her most characteristic poems. In 'The Bluebell', she describes how the sight of this familiar flower filled her with delight and nostalgia when she saw it growing far from home:

> Oh, that lone flower recalled to me
>   My happy childhood's hours,
> When bluebells seemed like fairy gifts,
>   A prize among the flowers.
>
> Those sunny days of merriment
>   When heart and soul were free
> And when I dwelt with kindred hearts
>   That loved and cared for me.
>
> I had not then mid heartless crowds
>   To spend a thankless life,
> In seeking after other's weal
>   With anxious toil and strife.
>
> 'Sad wanderer, weep those blissful times
>   That never may return!'
> That lovely floweret seemed to say,
>   And thus it made me mourn.[5]

A short poem written in December 1840, though without such powerful intensity, is akin in spirit to Emily Brontë's poetic record of her mystical experiences: 'Then dawns the Invisible, the Unseen its truth reveals; My outward sense is gone, my inward essence feels ...':

Retirement

O let me be alone awhile:
No human form is nigh;
And I may sing and muse aloud,
    No mortal ear is by.

Away! ye dreams of earthly bliss,
    Ye earthly cares be gone:
Depart! ye restless wandering thoughts,
    And let me be alone!
One hour, my spirit, stretch thy wings
    And quit this joyless sod:
Bask in the sunshine of the sky,
    And be alone with God![6]

It can easily be appreciated how much the three sisters enjoyed these precious months spent together, if only because they knew it must soon come to an end, perhaps already wondering if they could secure independence, not just by becoming employees but after gaining experience, by one day opening a modest school of their own.

Mrs Gaskell describes the even tenor of their routine, which, for Emily and Anne especially, was punctuated by the freedom and inspiration of their long rambles together over their dearly loved, familiar moors.

People in Haworth have assured me [says Mrs Gaskell] that according to the hour of day – nay, the very minute – could they have told what the inhabitants of the parsonage were about. At certain times the girls would be sewing in their aunt's bedroom – the chamber which, in former days, before they had outstripped her in their learning, had served them as a schoolroom; at certain (early) hours they had their meals; from six to eight, Miss Branwell read aloud to Mr Brontë; at punctual eight, the household assembled to evening prayers in his study; and by nine he, Miss Branwell, and Tabby, were all in bed, – the girls free to pace up and down (like restless wild animals) in the parlour, talking over plans and projects, and thoughts of what was to be their future life.[7]

The first to leave this period of happiness to answer the call of duty was

Charlotte, who had finally found a suitable post with Mr and Mrs White at Upperwood House, Rawdon, a few miles from Bradford and only some twelve miles from Haworth. While not ideal, it was a happier post for Charlotte than that with the Sidgwicks had been. Her pupils were a little girl of eight and a boy of six, and there was also a 'fat baby' of whom she was to grow rather fond.

She was homesick at first and, as usual, preferred Mr White to his wife: 'I like Mr White extremely. Respecting Mrs White I am for the present silent. I am trying hard to like her. The children are not such little devils incarnate as the Sidgwicks, but they are over-indulged, and at times hard to manage.'[8] However, after her summer holiday, Charlotte appears to have settled down more happily, and it is no doubt to the credit of both parties that when she left the Whites at Christmas they parted on good terms and with regret.

The post Anne found was further afield, some fifty miles away from home, with the family of the Reverend Edmund and Mrs Lydia Robinson at Thorp Green Hall. She was excited by her prospects as her pupils were to be young ladies, not children, so she would be teaching more rewarding and interesting subjects, and, best of all, she was to receive double her previous salary, the handsome sum of £50 a year.

When Agnes Grey rejoices in her good fortune at obtaining her new post at Horton Lodge, she is surely echoing the sentiments of her author:

> My pupils, being older, would be more rational, more teachable, and less troublesome than the last ... and fifty pounds appeared to me no ordinary sum. I must have decent clothes becoming my station. I must, it seemed, put out my washing, and also pay for my four annual journeys between Horton Lodge and home; but with strict attention to economy, surely twenty pounds, or little more, would cover those expenses, and then there would be thirty for the bank, or little less; what a valuable addition to our stock! Oh, I *must* struggle to keep this situation, whatever it might be! both for my honour among my friends and for the solid services I might render them by my continuance there.[9]

There can be little doubt that Anne's dismissal from her first post continued to rankle and had a great deal to do with her dogged determination to prove herself in her second. But when she set off with such high hopes, mercifully she could have had no idea of the tragic role Thorp Green was to play in the Brontë drama.

Anne arrived at her new post towards the end of March. It was a long, cold journey, during which, no doubt, some of her shaky confidence ebbed away. From *Agnes Grey*, the impression is given of a welcome that was only minimally more cordial and considerate than the one she had received from the Inghams.

Thorp Green Hall, now the home of the Martin family of Yorkshire and known as Thorp Underwood Hall, is situated in pleasant agricultural countryside near the village of Little Ouseburn on the road between York and Boroughbridge. Of the original building, most of which was destroyed by fire, only the kitchen area and stables now remain. It was a Georgian house, and the third to be built on the same spot. The nearby fourteenth-century Monk's House indicates there had once been a monastery on the site. When the Reverend Edmund Robinson's father bought the property, the same family had been occupying it from the time of the Tudors. Even with the changes it has undergone, a glance through the wrought-iron gates, up the long wide drive between the avenue of trees leading to the mellow red brick mansion must still give an impression similar to that received by Anne when she first saw it.

Some years later, when it was advertised for letting, Thorp Green Hall was described as a mansion containing:

Entrance Hall, Dining Room (32 ft 4 in. by 18 ft.,) Drawing Room (30ft. by 19ft.) Library (19 ft. 7 in. by 18 ft. 4 in.,) Spacious breakfast, Ante and other Rooms, large and convenient Kitchens. Servants' Hall, Cellars, and other Offices; Eight Lodging Rooms on the first floor and nine Lodging Rooms on the second floor.

The Outbuildings comprise Brewhouse, Wash-house, Laundry, Dairy, Stabling for 14 horses, Loose Box, Coach-house, Hay Chambers, Saddle Rooms & c.[10]

Splendid though their dwelling was, Anne's illusions about her employers were soon to be dashed. It is evident she had been expecting the Robinsons, from their station in life, to be altogether more courteous and cultivated than the Inghams.

When she entered their home, the Reverend Edmund Robinson was forty-one years of age and his wife a few months younger. Although ordained, he had never taken a living. Again, it is not possible to say just how far Agnes Grey's Mr and Mrs Murray resemble her author's employers, but the following character sketches might well have contained aspects of them. By all accounts, Mr Murray was 'a blustering, roystering country squire: a devoted fox-hunter, a skilful horse-jockey and farrier, an active practical farmer, and a hearty bon vivant. By all accounts, I say, for, except on Sundays, when he went to church, I never saw him from month to month; unless, in crossing the hall or walking in the grounds, the figure of a tall, stout gentleman, with scarlet cheeks and crimson nose, happened to come across to me; on which occasions, if he passed near enough to speak, an unceremonious nod, accompanied by a ''Morning, Miss Grey,'' or some brief salutation, was usually vouchsafed ...'[11] Although this does not accord with the later picture of the Reverend Edmund Robinson as a dyspeptic invalid, it must be remembered that Anne's first impressions of her employer were gained some while before he became so ill.

> Mrs Murray was a handsome, dashing lady of forty, who certainly required neither rouge nor padding to add to her charms; and whose chief enjoyments were, or seemed to be, in giving or frequenting parties, and in dressing at the very top of the fashion. I did not see her till eleven o'clock on the morning after my arrival; when she honoured me with a visit, just as my mother might step into the kitchen to see a new servant-girl; yet not so, either, for my mother would have seen her immediately after her arrival, and not waited till next day; moreover, she would have addressed her in a more kind and friendly manner, and given her some words of comfort as well as a plain exposition of her duties, but Mrs Murray did neither the one nor the other.[12]

Anne's pupils were Lydia (fifteen), Elizabeth, usually known as Bessy (fourteen), Mary (eleven) and, for the time being, the one son of the family, Edmund (nine). The Robinsons had recently lost a little daughter, Georgiana Jane, only two years of age.

Anne was soon to find that these older, untrained and morally neglected children presented as many, if different, problems as the unruly young Inghams. Lydia, appropriately named after her mother, already had her gaze fixed on acquiring all the graces and accomplishments necessary for social success, while Bessy was the horsy tomboy of the family. No doubt because she was the youngest Mary was the most congenial and to profit most from Anne's influence and integrity. As far as Edmund was concerned, Anne was to do all she could to prepare him, principally in Latin, for his hoped-for entry to a public school.

From the start she wrote bravely to Charlotte, reporting her safe arrival and that she was very well – a statement Charlotte regarded somewhat sceptically. Although Anne was eventually to succeed in building up an affectionate relationship with the girls, this took time, and with no contact with her employers or their friends and guests, and little with the lower employees, she was miserably lonely. From March until June she soldiered on, yearning for her return home for the holidays.

Only Emily was at home when she arrived, Charlotte's holidays not beginning until nearly a month later. Their reunion must have been a happy and fruitful time for the two younger sisters, bringing new inspiration to their sagas of Gondal. Emily wrote:

Aye, there it is! It wakes tonight
   Sweet thoughts that will not die;
And feeling's fire flash all as bright
   As in the years gone by!

And I can tell by thine altered cheek,
   And by thy kindled gaze,
And by the words thou scarste dost speak,
   How wildly fancy plays.[13]

As Emily confided in her birthday paper written at the end of the month, uppermost in their minds was the idea that the three girls should start a school. Perhaps realizing how unhappy Charlotte and Anne had been in their posts, both Mr Brontë and Miss Branwell had come to the conclusion that this was a plan with many merits, and Miss Branwell was prepared to assist with the provision of some much-needed capital.

'A scheme is at present in agitation for setting us up in a school of our own; as yet nothing is determined, but I hope and trust it may go on and prosper and answer our highest expectations. This day four years ... I guess that at the time appointed for the opening of this paper we, i.e. Charlotte, Anne, and I, shall be all merrily seated in our ow. sitting room in some pleasant and flourishing seminary ...'[14]

Anne went back to her work with the Robinsons much heartened by this prospect, while Charlotte, sorry though she was to have missed her youngest sister, set about pursuing the idea with her customary enthusiasm and energy. Various possibilities were considered, including finding a healthily suitable spot on the coast or taking over Miss Wooler's school at Dewsbury. But a letter from Mary Taylor from Brussels, where she was spending some time with her sister Martha and brother Joe, suddenly inspired Charlotte with a wider vision.

'Mary's letter spoke of some of the pictures and cathedrals she had seen – pictures the most exquisite – and cathedrals the most venerable – I hardly know what *swelled to my throat as* I read her letter – such a vehement impatience of restraint and steady work. Such a strong wish for wings ...'[15]

Charlotte went back to the White family full of excitement. The extent to which her relations with them had been improved can be judged by the fact that she talked her plan over with them, and before very long she was writing to her aunt to suggest that some of her proffered loan should be spent in financing a period of some six months further education in Brussels. A thorough familiarity with French, an improved knowledge of Italian and a dash of German, she suggested, would help overcome the competition of the many schools already in existence, similar to the one they were proposing. 'These are advantages which would turn to vast account, when we actually commence a school – and, if Emily could share them with me, only for a single half-year, we could take a footing in the world afterwards which we can never do now.'[16]

During the next weeks and months, Charlotte succeeded in overcoming every objection and difficulty and persuaded her father, her aunt and, hardest of all, Emily to agree to her plan.

Perhaps because Charlotte had always considered Anne frail and delicate or because, uncongenial though it was, she had a settled and apparently secure post, Charlotte did not include her youngest sister in any immediate plans, '... but', she explained, 'if all goes well I trust she will derive her full benefit from it in the end'.[17]

After her month at home, Anne had returned to the Robinsons to accompany them on their own travels to York and Scarborough. Here she was to find two wonderful compensations for the 'baneful influence'[18] of her daily life: the soaring beauty and spiritual peace of York Minster and her first sight of the sea, which affected her very much as it had Charlotte:

The sea was my delight; and I would often gladly pierce the town to obtain the pleasure of a walk beside it ... It was delightful to me at all times and seasons, but especially in the wild commotion of a rough sea-breeze, and in the brilliant freshness of a summer morning ... when my foot was on the sands and my face towards the broad, bright bay, no language can describe the effect of the deep, clear azure of the sky and ocean, the bright morning sunshine on the semi-circular barrier of craggy cliffs surmounted by green swelling hills ... And then, the unspeakable purity and freshness of the air! There was just enough heat to enhance the value of the breeze, and just enough wind to keep the whole sea in motion, to make the waves come bounding to the shore, foaming and sparkling, as if wild with glee.[19]

Yet on her return with the family to Thorp Green, Anne wrote some nostalgic lines which show how exiled in spirit she was always to feel away from home:

But if the sunny, summer time,
And woods and meadows in their prime,
   Are sweet to them that roam;
Far sweeter is the winter bare,
With long dark nights, and landscape drear,
   To them that are at Home![20]

When the three sisters were reunited at Haworth for the Christmas of 1841, all was decided. Mr Brontë and Aunt Branwell were to manage at the parsonage with Martha Brown and her young sister Hannah; Anne would return to the Robinsons, since her health would never permit her to undertake the burden of baking and housework so cheerfully and efficiently performed by Emily; and, in the charge of their father, Charlotte and Emily were to travel to Brussels to broaden and polish their education at the respectable and reasonably priced Pensionnat Heger.

There was just one person unconsulted, unconsidered and quite left out of all these plans. Whether he knew this at the time, whether or not he cared, for Branwell Brontë the end was in sight of his once promising career on the railway.

7. Sorrows, Hopes and Fears, 1842–4

No description can convey the special impact on visitors of seeing the precious documents preserved at the Brontë Parsonage Musem. More than any words, these strange little papers, so carefully and patiently printed, drawn and stitched, or sometimes, as in Emily's diary papers, so untidily scrawled and blotched, give a vivid and intimate view into the busy, self-occupied lives of the young Brontës 150 years ago. A similar insight can be gained by reading the notebook Branwell used while he was at Luddenden Foot.[1] It is a little red book, six inches by four, containing twenty-eight pages, two of them blank, written and drawn on in both pencil and ink, sometimes in his special printing, sometimes in his natural hand.

There are references to railway affairs, such as '3 waggons and 2 covers for Sowerby'; 'Wool 1^T 4^C – 10th Oct', a note about the sale of shares for twenty miles of the Great Yarmouth and Norwich Railway, and some diagrams that look rather like duty rosters. There are some extremely vigorous little sketches of heads, a pair of pugilists and a particularly fine drawing of a man wearing a top hat in a high-backed wooden chair, with a heading, in Greek characters, 'John Murgatroyd' and a caption 'George Richardson'. Whichever is the gentleman represented, he certainly appears to have been drawn from life. Most importantly, the book contains – among other neatly or not so neatly written lines – Branwell's poem on Lord Nelson, commencing 'Man thinks too often of the ills of life', 'Oh God while I in pleasure's wiles', 'The desolate earth, the wintry sky', 'When side by side at twilight sitting' and 'Give me Great God, give all beneath thy sway'.

Certainly the overall effect is of a talented young man whose mind was much more on his poetry than on his work. But, of course, Branwell may have kept other, more businesslike notebooks which, without the poetry they contained, there was no reason to preserve.

Another valuable source of information about his life at this time is his new friend, Francis Grundy, in a volume of recollections, *Pictures of the Past,* even though these should sometimes be taken with a grain of salt. Three years younger than Branwell, Grundy was employed on the railway, as an engineer on the new line between Leeds and Bradford. He had been acquainted in his boyhood with the Martineau family, of whom Harriet, the famous novelist, writer and critic is best known today. At the time he was introduced to Branwell by their mutual friends, the Leylands, he was sharing a 'chummery' with the nephew of the great George Stephenson, creator of that famous train *The Rocket,* who no doubt influenced young Francis in his choice of career.

The two new friends soon began seeing a lot of each other, rambling among the beauty spots of the area on Sundays and talking by the hour in their free time in taverns. Grundy, from the first, seems to have both admired Branwell and understood him. Above all, right to the end, he was always to recognize his continual battle between the weak and dissolute and the good and aspiring elements of his sadly divided nature. 'Patrick Branwell Brontë', he said, 'was just a man in a mist who had lost his way.'

From his book, Grundy, who went on later to lead an adventurous life in the outback of Australia, appears to have been a brash, aggressive, shrewd yet naïve and likeable fellow, an outstanding civil engineer, with a great fondness for animals. The two young men seem to have hit it off from the start.

Soon after I came to Halifax, I made the acquaintance of a genius of the highest order, Patrick Branwell Brontë, who was at least as talented as any member of that wonderful family. [Grundy, it must be said, writing from hindsight, erred on the generous in his estimation of his friend.] Brontë took an unusual fancy to me, and I continued, perhaps, his most confidential friend through good and ill until his death. Poor brilliant, gay, moody, moping, wildly excitable, miserable Brontë.

When I first met him, he was stationmaster at a small roadside place on the Manchester and Leeds Railway, Luddenfoot by name. The line was only just opened. This station was a rough wooden hut, and there was no village near at hand. Had a position been chosen for this strange creature for the express purpose of driving him several steps to the bad, this must have been it. Alone in the wilds of Yorkshire, with few books, little to do, no prospects, and wretched pay, with no society congenial to his better tastes, but plenty of wild, rollicking, hard-headed, half-educated manufacturers, who would welcome him to their houses, and drink with him as often as he chose to come – what was this morbid man, who couldn't bear to be alone, to do?[2]

There is a mixture of truth and exaggeration in this statement. When he escaped, as he did so often, to the Lord Nelson, Branwell found there not only a drink and convivial company but the nine hundred volumes of the Luddenden circulating library. Although he does not seem to have been among the twenty-two members, subject to rules and a monthly fee of 4 pence each, it seems unlikely that his friendly landlord did not allow him upstairs to browse and read. Wherever he went, Branwell was a welcome companion in the society in which he found himself. In fact, a point worth noting is that, of the four surviving Brontë children, only Charlotte and Branwell, the childhood partners, appear to have had the wish to make, and the gift of making, friends. Emily and Anne were sufficient unto each other and evidently never attempted to attract and retain friends as Branwell did without effort and Charlotte so assiduously.

If Branwell had attended sensibly to his remarkably light duties, his increasing railway salary, not so wretched for the time as Grundy suggests, would have provided him with a financial cushion for life while he went on writing and painting, in much the same way as the East India Company did for Charles Lamb and Thomas Love Peacock, and the Postal Service was to do for Anthony Trollope. Admittedly, he had been a failure in his post with the Postlethwaites and wasted much time in dissolute idling, but Branwell had also managed a respectable amount of literary work while he was there. With some surveillance, encouragement, just that little more self-discipline and luck, he might have been able to combine with his railway job, a certain amount of roistering and a worthwhile output of writing and painting – his note-book shows that he wrote some of his best poetry during this period.

Unhappily for him and his family, this was not to be, for while he was away from his office, his all too accommodating porter had been dipping into the money the passengers paid for their fares. Careless and unaware of this, Branwell was only too glad to leave the station in the porter's charge while he sought more congenial company.

As this poem written in the notebook in December 1841 shows all too

clearly, in his stern and sober moments, Branwell had no illusions about
the course of conduct he was allowing himself to pursue.

O God! while I in pleasure's wiles
   Count hours and years as one,
And deem that, rapt in pleasure's smiles,
   My joys can ne'er be done,

Give me the stern sustaining power
   To look into the past,
And see the darkly shadowed hour
   Which I must meet at last;

The hour when I must stretch this hand
   To give a last adieu
To those sad friends that round me stand
   Whom I no more must view.

For false though bright the hours that lead
   My present passage on,
And when I join the silent dead
   Their light will all be gone.

Then I must cease to seek the light
   Which fires the evening heaven
Since to direct through death's dark night
   Some other must be given.[3]

During the last few months, Branwell had been a infrequent visitor to
Haworth, and it can easily be guessed how nervous he was about the
impending annual audit. He would hardly have enjoyed interested family
enquiries about his progress at work.

The blow fell when Messrs. Robinson and Greenish disclosed to the
Railway Directors that there was a deficit of £11.1s.7d in the station's
accounts. The amount was deducted from Branwell's salary, and although
it was appreciated that this was due to inattention and incompetence and
not dishonesty, he was immediately dismissed. A little later, some of his
more influential acquaintances presented an appeal on his behalf, which

suggests he had been well liked in the neighbourhood, but the Board adhered to its decision.

This was now the third time Branwell had returned home in debt and disgrace and, much as they loved him, his father and aunt were beginning to despair that, far from enjoying the golden future they had once predicted, he would ever be able to make even a modest success of his life. The effect on Branwell of this kindly but disapproving welcome can well be imagined. Moreover, having been drowning his sorrows in those last few nerve-racking months even more intemperately than usual – and by this time his 'little squibs' of spirits were sometimes joined by draughts of laudanum – morally and physically he was in a state verging on breakdown. Perhaps it was as well that Charlotte was not at home, as she would have expressed her own disapproval, but Branwell must have missed the less demanding more impartial companionship of his younger sisters. Luckily, he had a good friend of his own age to turn to in William Weightman.

It seems to have taken some weeks for him to pull himself together, but by 22 May he was writing to Grundy to see whether another place might yet be found for him: 'I have something still left in me which may do me service. But I ought not to remain too long in solitude, for the world soon forgets those who have bidden it "Good-by". Quiet is an excellent cure, but no medicine should be continued after a patient's recovery.'[4] Recovered or not, as Grundy saw all too plainly, Branwell's blotted copybook would effectively block him from being accepted as a railway employee again, and he could only urge his friend to look elsewhere.

Apart from the congenial companionship of Weightman, during the summer months of 1842, Branwell was sustained by his interest in obtaining a commission for a memorial in Haworth church for his friend Joseph Leyland, and the publication of some of his own poems.

Accomplished sculptor though he was, Joseph Leyland had been suffering financial difficulties and was only too grateful to undertake the modest memorial for Thomas Andrew, the local surgeon, that Branwell was so pleased to put in his way. Like so many well-meant local efforts, the memorial occasioned some disputes among the committee set up to implement it, but eventually Branwell was able to tell his friend that, '... your work at Haworth has given to all who have seen it the most unqualified satisfaction even where they understood nothing of its real merit ...'[5]

Even more rewarding for Branwell must have been the publication of his poems. On 7 and 14 May the *Halifax Guardian* published two sonnets from the sequence of 'Caroline' poems he had begun several years before, and on 7 May the *Leeds Intelligencer* printed some lines on 'The Afghan War', written after the humiliating British retreat from Kabul in January 1842. This sentimental patriotic piece, clearly undertaken with a view to publication, shows that Branwell might well have been able to take his place with the many writers who made or augmented their livings with similar occasional verses on topical themes with a broad appeal to the general public:

> Breasts and banners, crushed and gory,
>   That seemed once invincible;
> England's children – England's glory,
>   Moslem sabres smite and quell! ...
>
> England rises! Thine ancient thunder
>   Humbled mightier foes than these;
> Broke a whole world's bonds asunder,
>   Gave thee empire o'er the seas.[6]

In June Anne came home for her summer holidays. Since her return to Thorp Green after Christmas, she had continued to feel unsettled. She wanted to change her post, but her salary with the Robinsons was too good to allow her to take the risk; she may have been envying her sisters in Brussels and suffering at her parting from William Weightman at a time when perhaps he, as well as she, was beginning to fall in love.

Although, for some reason, Charlotte had never been able to think of William Weightman as other than a flirt, she had noticed on Anne's last visit home that he had begun to pay her more than ordinary attention: 'He sits opposite to Anne at Church sighing softly and looking out of the corners of his eyes to win her attention – and Anne is so quiet, her look so downcast – they are a picture.[7]

William Weightman must have been much in Anne's thoughts during these lovely months, when she perhaps had already begun to turn her experiences into the autobiographical novel known now as *Agnes Grey* but first entitled *Passages in the Life of an Individual*. There seems no

reason to doubt that his character inspired Mr Weston's, any more
than that Agnes's admiration and love of the curate mirrored Anne's own.

> He had not breathed a word of love, or dropped one hint of tenderness or
> affection, and yet I had been supremely happy. To be near him, to hear
> him talk as he did talk; and to feel that he thought me worthy to be so
> spoken to – capable of understanding and duly appreciating such discourse
> – was enough.
>   'Yes, Edward Weston, I could indeed be happy in a house full of
> enemies, if I had but one friend, who truly, deeply, and faithfully loved
> me; and if that friend were you – though we might be far apart – seldom
> to hear from each other, still more seldom to meet – though toil, and
> trouble, and vexation might surround me, still – it would be too much
> happiness for me to dream of! Yet who can tell,' I said within myself, as I
> proceeded up the park – 'who can tell what this one month may bring
> forth? I have lived nearly three-and-twenty years, and I have suffered
> much and tasted little pleasure yet; is it likely my life all through will be so
> clouded? Is it not possible that God may hear my prayers, disperse these
> gloomy shadows, and grant me some beams of heaven's sunshine yet!'[8]

A month's summer holiday was all Anne might enjoy at home, as
once again she was required to attend on the Robinsons at Scarborough.
Happy and excited though she was to be seeing Mr Weightman again,
she must have been upset by Branwell's story of his most recent failure
and current lack of prospects. Once again, Aunt Branwell's two favourites
were at home alone together, and Anne now joined with Mr Weightman
in his sensible and vigorous efforts to keep Branwell active, busy, in good
spirits and off the primrose path. With her sisters in Brussels, Anne must
have had many more opportunities during these brief weeks of seeing Mr
Weightman on her own and to reveal the strength and beauty of her shy
nature. Perhaps there were moments when, like her heroine, she felt
supremely happy.

It must have been now that the idea came to her that a vacancy might
exist for Branwell in the Robinson family. Hard though she had worked
with Edmund, under her tuition, he had not succeeded in reaching the
standard for admittance to a public school as had been planned. Anne
knew she had taken the boy as far as she could and that sooner or later his
parents would be considering hiring a tutor for him. It seemed to Anne,
who no doubt discussed her plan with both her father and Mr

Weightman, as well as their devoted Aunt Branwell, that it would be an excellent idea to recommend her brother for the post. Apart from being fully qualified academically to bring Edmund up to scratch, Branwell would provide the congenial intimate companionship she so sadly lacked, and she could keep a sisterly eye on him. Probably she had not been told a true account of Branwell's dismissal from the Postlethwaites, nor recognized how far he had gone towards dependence on alcohol and drugs. Fond of him though she was, it hardly seems likely she would have considered taking such a risk had she known the full facts.

While Anne was at home, news arrived from Charlotte that an arrangement had been made for her and Emily to remain in Belgium for another half year. In exchange for some teaching services, they would have free board and continue their studies in French and German. 'I am inclined to accept it ... I don't deny I sometimes wish to be in England, or that I have brief attacks of home-sickness; but, on the whole, I have borne a very valiant heart so far; and I have been happy in Brussels, because I have always been fully occupied with the employments I like. Emily is making rapid progress in French, German, music and drawing.'[9]

Letters from and to Brussels had not been very frequent because of the expense of the postage, but it is a great loss that none of Emily's letters have survived – surely she must have written occasionally fully and frankly to Anne.

Probably Emily agreed to stay on too, if only because, for the first time in her life, she was being intellectually stretched by a first-class mind. Monsieur Constantin Heger, one of the principal tutors in his wife's school, was not only a very cultured and intelligent man but an exceptionally gifted teacher. From the first he realized the outstanding qualities of the two painfully shy, gauche, badly dressed provincial young Englishwomen whom fate had sent under his charge. Moreover, although Charlotte was apt to take the lead and, having spent longer at school, to regard herself as the better educated, he soon perceived that Emily had the greater potential. Later he was to tell Mrs Gaskell that she had a head for logic and a capability of argument unusual in a man and rare indeed in a woman. 'She should have been a man – a great navigator. Her powerful reason would have deduced new spheres of discovery from knowledge of the old; and her strong imperious will would never have been daunted by opposition or difficulty; never have given way but with life.'[10] Such an assessment raises the interesting question of how far Emily's mind might have probed had she lived in the twentieth century.

It was said of M. Heger that he had an intellectual magnetism, and it was soon plain that as far as Charlotte was concerned he had a physical magnetism too. As early as May 1842 she was giving Ellen Nussey a character sketch of her teacher that might have come straight out of the page of *Villette,* where she was later to immortalize him as M. Paul Emanuel: 'He is professor of rhetoric, a man of power as to mind, but very choleric and irritable in temperament; a little black being, with a face that varies in expression. Sometimes he borrows the lineaments of an insane tom-cat, sometimes those of a delirious hyena; occasionally, but very seldom, he discards these perilous attractions and assumes an air not above 100 degrees from mild and gentlemanlike ...'[11]

Certainly one of Charlotte's principal reasons for wishing to stay was the fascinating and unpredictable M. Heger, although she was clearly quite unconscious at that time of the misery into which her preoccupation was to lead her.

When Anne returned to her duties with the Robinsons in August 1842, everything seemed to be going well. The two elder girls preparing for their own school in Brussels, herself with a settled job which included a prospect for her brother, and Branwell, in the meanwhile, in the affectionate and capable care of William Weightman.

Then, as so often in the Brontë story, tragedy intervened to upset this promising state of affairs. Its first blow struck from the most unexpected quarter, when William Weightman, handsome, healthy and twenty-six years of age, just a few weeks after Anne's departure, fell sick of the disease that visited Haworth all too often, the dreaded cholera.

He fought his disease for two weeks – two weeks when Branwell Brontë was seen at his best, staying bravely and without fear for his own safety by his friend's bedside. Mr Brontë, who had grown to love and depend on his curate, also visited daily. But there was nothing to be done, and William Weightman died on 6 September 1842, mourned by all his friends and the parishioners whose welfare he had tended so faithfully. Had he lived, the story of Anne and Branwell might have ended more happily.

Mr Brontë had lost not only an invaluable curate but a young man whom he must have seen as a hope of salvation for his son. Indeed, in the sermon he preached at William Weightman's memorial service, he spoke of him as 'another son'. He had been present at the end of the young man's 'bright but short career'. He had seen him 'in tranquillity close his eyes on this bustling, vain, selfish world – his end was peace and his hope glory'. In his moving tribute, which serves as a reminder of Mr Brontë's own gift for language, he said, 'There are many who for a short time can please, but who soon retrograde and fall into disrepute. Mr Weightman's character wore well; the surest proof of worth. He had, it is true, some peculiar advantages. Agreeable in person and manners, and constitutionally cheerful, his first introduction was prepossessing. But what he gained at first he did not lose afterwards. He had those qualities which enabled him rather to gain ground.'[12]

Mr Brontë, his son and his youngest daughter had perceived that William Weightman's attractive exterior was a true reflection on the worth of his character.

Under the circumstances, continuing and bringing to its happy conclusion her novel, *Agnes Grey*, must have been an agonizing experience for Anne, and it took many months for her to write the beautiful poems, whether or not they fitted into the Gondal Saga, that described her one sad experience of love.

All too soon, she was recalled home and to visit the church where William Weightman had so recently been buried, but the simple lines that so perfectly express her feelings were dated nearly two years later, April 1844.

> Yes, thou art gone! and never more
>   Thy sunny smile shall gladden me;
> But I may pass the old church door,
>   And pace the floor that covers thee.
>
> May stand upon the cold, damp stone,
>   And think that frozen lies below
> The lightest heart that I have known,
>   The kindest I shall ever know.
>
> Yet, though I cannot see thee more,
>   'Tis still a comfort to have seen;
> And though thy transient life is o'er,
>   'Tis sweet to think that thou hast been;

To think a soul so near divine,
    Within a form so angel fair,
United to a heart like thine,
    Has gladdened once our humble sphere.[13]

Again, a year later, she is writing, with moving, unforced feeling:

I love the silent hour of night,
For blissful dreams may then arise,
Revealing to my charméd sight
What may not bless my waking eyes.

And then a voice may meet my ear
That death has silenced long ago
And hope and rapture may appear
Instead of solitude and woe.

Cold in the grave for years has lain
The form it was my bliss to see,
And only dreams can bring again
The darling of my heart to me.[14]

Although it had been noted that only the weeping Branwell was in the Brontë family pew for William Weightman's memorial service, it was not until a few days later that it was realized just how ill Miss Branwell was. Almost as soon as he finished presiding at one death bed, Branwell was needed to help nurse and to comfort his aunt in her last, excruciatingly painful illness. Once again, rousing himself in spite of his grief, he rose to the occasion.

Branwell and Anne had always been their aunt's favourites – perhaps, since he was the only boy of the family, Branwell more than Anne. He was probably the most fond of her, because his temperament had done battle with, not submitted to, her morbid and depressing influence. As he said, she had been for twenty years his mother. On the day she died, 29 October, pitifully of 'exhaustion from constipation', he wrote to Grundy, 'I am incoherent, I fear, but I have been waking two nights witnessing such agonising suffering as I would not wish my worst enemy to endure; and I have now lost the guide and director of all the happy days connected with my childhood.'[15] In these words, Branwell paid his aunt, who in many ways had sacrificed her life to the Brontë family, a moving and worthy tribute.

Anne sought permission to return home but arrived only in time for her aunt's funeral. Now she could mourn openly, grieving for the brilliant, optimistic young man and the staunch elderly lady at one and the same time. For who was to know for whom she really wept?

Immediately the seriousness of Miss Branwell's condition had been realized, a letter had been despatched to Brussels, where Charlotte and Emily were still stunned by the totally unexpected death there on 12 October of the sparkling Martha Taylor, aged only twenty-three. Of all their friends and companions, William Weightman and Martha had been the liveliest and most brilliant, the two of their circle apparently destined for the happiest of lives, which made the shock of their sudden and untimely deaths all the greater.

Charlotte wrote to Ellen Nussey that Martha had died 'of exactly the same illness as Mr Weightman', implying that she had succumbed to cholera.[16] But the phrasing of a letter from her sister Mary, also to Ellen, and the somewhat unorthodox and hasty burial (even though haste was clearly required with a disease so contagious) suggest that perhaps in a foreign land the attractive Martha had fallen to some other temptation: 'You will wish to hear the history of Martha's illness – I will give it to you in a few months; till then you must excuse me ... There is nothing to regret, nothing to recall – not even Martha. She is better where she is. But when I recall her sufferings that have purified her, my heart aches ...'[17] This is strange language for the practical Mary Taylor to use of a much-loved sister dying so young of such a terrible disease.

The news of their aunt's death reached Charlotte and Emily too late for them to be able to attend her funeral but, like Anne, they decided they must return home to face the crisis with the rest of the family.

Probably Emily had immediately decided that, as far as she was concerned, the departure was to be for good. In her heart, she must have known that, once she was home again, she could not bear to leave. For Charlotte, it was very different, and she carried with her a warmly persuasive letter from M. Heger to their father, urging that at least one of the girls should go back for another year's tuition, with the added inducement of a small salary.

The Brontë family was reunited at Haworth parsonage on 8 November 1842, and it was clear that some new arrangements would now have to be made. Although she had done no manual work, Miss Branwell had held the household reins for nearly twenty years, and someone had to be appointed to take her place. Emily, who had always provided stalwart help in the house, was the obvious candidate and, much though she had benefited from her time in Brussels, she was relieved to have this perfectly valid excuse for staying at home. Charlotte might have felt guilty in so readily accepting her offer, aware as she must have been of her mixed motives, but at the same time her conscience was clear in the knowledge that neither she nor Anne could possibly manage the household as expertly and smoothly as Emily.

It was a time of change and sadness and, in spite of a visit from Ellen Nussey, it could not have been a happy Christmas, but sensible decisions were made and life went on. Anne had been recalled to Thorp Green immediately after her aunt's funeral, and when she returned for the holiday it was with a definite offer of a post for Branwell as Edmund's tutor at £80 per annum. This apparently meant a consequent reduction of £10 in Anne's salary since she would no longer be teaching Edmund, and Lydia, her eldest charge, was beginning to leave the schoolroom and take her own part in the social round so much enjoyed by her mother.

Aunt Branwell's will had been a surprise. The girls knew she had a little nest egg tucked away but not that she had been thrifty and frugal enough to leave nearly £1,500 to be divided between them and another niece, Elizabeth Jane Kingston, in Cornwall. Her will had been made in 1833, and the fact that no sum was allotted to Branwell was almost certainly because at that time her expectations for his future were so high. A realistic spinster herself, her first thoughts had been for her nieces, who might never marry and be less fortunate than she had been. For the first time in their lives, the girls had a little money behind them, and once Charlotte returned home for good, there seemed no reason why the school they had dreamed of should not become a reality. Unexpectedly practical in such matters, Emily took charge of their investments, perhaps influenced by Branwell's brief career, buying shares in the York & North Midland Railway Company.

By the end of January Emily was at home alone with her father and her inseparable companion, Keeper, their fierce housedog whom she had beaten and dominated into loyal, loving obedience; she had the help of the young Brown sisters, and she had brought old Tabby back into the household, where she was now to stay until a few days before the end of her life. After a period in Brussels, for Emily this was a welcome fallow time, when she was able to reflect and feel and to fall back into her own rhythms of work and thought and life. Disciplined studies, although she had profited from them, were not suited to her particular genius, but she had promised to be responsible for teaching German in their school. At that time, 'Anyone passing by the kitchen-door, might have seen her studying German out of an open book, propped up before her, as she kneaded the dough; but no study, however interesting, interfered with the goodness of the bread, which was always light and excellent.'[18]

This was a time when Emily grew close to her father and, since his sight was beginning to fail, she began to read to him and discuss what they read. Best of all, she was free to resume her solitary and fruitful walks on the moors.

Charlotte soon found that life in Brussels, shy and reserved though Emily had been even with her, was very different now that she was there on her own. When M. Heger began increasingly to dominate her thoughts and emotions, Mme. Heger noticed and tried to curb the dangerous symptoms which – such was her husband's innocent appeal to young ladies – must have been through the years a constant and sensible, not a jealous preoccupation, certainly not confined to Charlotte.

Anne and Branwell were together again, no longer in the parsonage in the shadow of their father and their loving aunt, or with their sisters and childhood partners, but in the totally different, expansive and luxurious atmosphere of Thorp Green Hall. Anne recognized by now the heights and depths, the social and moral texture of the household, but Branwell had to feel his way and learn. From the moment their carriage passed into the grounds, he felt that this was the ambience he had always dreamed of inhabiting. As he took stock of the park, the Hall and his own uniquely romantic lodgings in the Old Monk's House, after all his vicissitudes, still always hopeful at the beginning of a new experience, Branwell Brontë felt he had come into his own.

From the wreck of her own dearest hopes, Anne must have regarded her launching of Branwell into a new and suitable career at Thorp Green as a worthy salvage. William Weightman was no longer there to care for either of them, but at least she herself could try to guide her mercurial brother.

It appears that for the first few months all proceeded according to plan. Branwell worked away as best he could with what must have been Edmund's unpromising academic abilities; Anne's workload was lightened and her prestige had been increased by her introduction of her

cultured, charming, talkative and musical brother into the household –
though it must be remembered that, unless Anne herself had been highly
regarded, her recommendation would never have been accepted.

No doubt, in leisure moments, Mrs Robinson was pleased to sing to
Branwell's dashing piano accompaniments or listen to his reading of her
own and others' verses, and when there were no visitors or visits she was
sometimes glad of his conversation and company. Her treatment of him
from the first appears to have been very different from her manner to
Anne. Branwell was clearly charmed and flattered that so important and
grand a lady was taking such an interst in him. Quite probably, too, the
Reverend Mr Robinson was pleased that his son's tutor was also capable
of providing some innocent amusement for his wife, to whom he appears
to have been devotedly attached. But, like Anne, Branwell was to discover
that his employer had the caustic tongue and the short temper often
displayed by those suffering from his increasing martyrdom to dyspepsia,
which, whatever its cause, was to lead to his death at the age of forty-six
three years later. A modern diagnosis might have been that he had a
duodenal ulcer.

While Branwell apparently was accorded greater social status, *Agnes
Grey* makes it all too plain that, although in private together Anne's
young ladies might sometimes enjoy chatting to her and making her their
confidante, when they were with their own friends she virtually ceased to
exist.

> As none of the ... ladies and gentlemen ever noticed me, it was
> disagreeable to walk beside them, as if listening to what they said, or
> wishing to be thought one of them, while they talked over me, or across;
> and if their eyes, in speaking, chanced to fall on me, it seemed as if they
> looked on vacancy – as if they either did not see me, or were very desirous
> to make it appear so. It was disagreeable, too, to walk behind, and thus
> appear to acknowledge my own inferiority; for in truth I considered
> myself pretty nearly as good as the best of them, and wished them to know
> that I did so ...[19]

It is good to hear Anne, usually described as gentle, sounding so robust.
At this time she was to write one of her strongest poems. Not
surprisingly, all her life she was burdened by the legacy of melancholy
principles Aunt Branwell had done her best to instil in her and against
which she had at last triumphantly rebelled, but from time to time, and

especially in the period of deep sadness that followed William Weightman's death, she had to do battle anew with her doubts and fears, which centred mainly on the survival after death of all or – as her Aunt Branwell, in common with many others, believed – only the elect.

Like Jane Austen, Anne was very much drawn to the poetry of William Cowper, who had also struggled with his doubts:

Sweet are thy strains, celestial Bard;
   And oft, in childhood's years,
I've read them o'er and o'er again,
   With floods of silent tears.

The language of my inmost heart
   I traced in every line;
My sins, *my* sorrows, hopes, and fears,
   Were there – and only mine ...

Yet should thy darkest fears be true,
   If Heaven be so severe,
That such a soul as thine is lost, –
   Oh! how shall *I* appear?[20]

This poem to Cowper was dated November 1842, but six months later Anne was writing with firm confidence and courage 'A Word to the "Elect" ', which simply and clearly describes her own views and hopes and was to be echoed in the prose argument she conducted between her heroine, Helen Huntingdon, and her aunt when she came to write *The Tenant of Wildfell Hall*.

You may rejoice to think *yourselves* secure;
   You may be grateful for the gift divine –
That grace unsought, which made your black hearts pure,
   And fits your earth-borne souls in Heaven to shine,

But, is it sweet to look around, and view
   Thousands excluded from that happiness
Which they deserve at least as much as you –
   Their faults not greater, nor their virtues less?

And oh! there lives within my heart
　　A hope, long nursed by me;
(And should its cheering ray depart,
　　How dark my soul would be!)

That as in Adam all have died,
　　In Christ shall all men live;
And ever round his throne abide,
　　Eternal praise to give.[21]

Always Anne was striving to convince herself that there was eternal salvation, and that salvation was for all.

Here is Helen's aunt trying to persuade her, quite rightly as it turns out, not to unite her destiny to that of Arthur Huntingdon.

> 'And, remember, Helen,' continued she solemnly, 'The wicked shall be turned into hell and they that forget God!' And suppose, even, that he should continue to love you, and you him, and that you should pass through life together with tolerable comfort, – how will it be in the end, when you see yourselves parted for ever; you, perhaps, taken into eternal bliss, and he cast into the lake that burneth with unquenchable fire – there forever to –'
> 'Not for ever,' I exclaimed … 'He that "is able to subdue all things to Himself will have all men to be saved".'[22]

And for Helen at the end 'all men' included even her lost Arthur Huntingdon and his terrible companions.

During the rest of their stay at Thorp Green, while Anne went on writing (religious poems, additions to the Gondal Saga and *Agnes Grey*), it appears to have been a non-productive time for Branwell. He might have destroyed what he wrote then, or Charlotte may have done so, but he tended to preserve rather than discard, so, as far as can be known, during this period, his painting and writing virtually ceased.

Proof of the satisfaction that Branwell gave to his employers in these early days was that Mr Brontë was invited to spend a few days with his son and youngest daughter, a privilege that had never been extended to Anne. It was a happy visit, with Branwell delighting to show his father his impressive new surroundings, Anne happy at her own part in helping him to settle down, and Mr Brontë, no doubt, mightily relieved. Immediately on his return home, he wrote to Charlotte to assure her that Branwell was doing well and 'in good odour'.[23]

Her father's letter prompted Charlotte to write to her brother, requesting more news both from him and from Anne. By now she was homesick and lonely, and her thoughts, almost for the first time, returned to Angria and the close companionship they had shared in the parsonage while they 'wove a web in childhood',[24] evolving their wondrous, romantic and, as far as she was concerned, now forbidden world: 'Always in the evenings when I am in the great dormitory alone, having no other company than a number of beds with white curtains, I always recur as fanatically as ever to the old ideas, the old faces, and the old scenes in the world below.'[25]

Soon after their father's visit, it was time for Anne and Branwell to return to Haworth for the break allowed them before they accompanied the Robinsons on their annual Scarborough holiday. This time Anne was bringing home a delightful spaniel puppy, described by Ellen Nussey as 'long, silky-haired, black and white Flossy'.[26] She was to become Anne's devoted companion, evidently establishing a friendly relationship with the daunting Keeper, and lived for eleven contented and well-favoured years.

It was a glorious summer, and from her lonely exile in the suffocating heat in Brussels, Charlotte envied her sisters and brother their companionship and walks together on the moors. In her loneliness, she must have realized how much Emily appreciated having them home with her again, if for so brief a while. Even when they departed, Emily would still have her animals, her beloved moors and her free-ranging thoughts, while Anne and Branwell were to see York again and the sea.

Charlotte could have returned home herself; after Aunt Branwell's legacy, lack of funds did not prevent it. The Pensionnat Heger closed for the long summer vacation, the girls dispersed, and the Heger family departed for their annual holiday at Blankenberg. But perhaps because she knew that, if she were to return to Haworth at this juncture, she would never get back to Brussels and, much more important, to M. Heger, obstinately Charlotte stayed on, with only the cook-caretaker for company. The terrifying mental and emotional strains she endured during this period were to be translated imaginatively in some of the most highly charged and brilliant passages of *Villette*.[27] Writing to Emily on, 2 September she described her lonely visit to Martha Taylor's grave, her wanderings around the streets of Brussels and her impulsive determination to make her confession to a Catholic priest in the church of Sainte-Gudule. The priest agreed to listen to her confession only in the hope that it might be her first step in the 'true Church'.[28] For Charlotte, this was unthinkable, but the whole episode, both as recounted in the letter to Emily and even more in *Villette*, reveals her tormenting desire to confess or confide, to unburden her guilty conscience of the secret knowledge that she was passionately in love with a married man.

For her, this was a sin against every instilled tenet of her real, though not her Angrian, life, as was the act of confessing to a Roman Catholic priest, which she knew to be valueless without renunciation. For even though she guessed what misery awaited her, conscious though she was of doing wrong, at that time Charlotte Brontë was quite incapable of denying to herself all that M. Heger had grown to mean, and going home.

For many years, in her Angrian stories, Charlotte had been vividly imagining and portraying the passion of love, but it was the reality of her feeling for M. Heger which enabled her to create Mr Rochester, who was married, and the unforgettable Paul Emanuel who, unlike M. Heger, was not.

Charlotte endured her mortifying and inevitable ordeal until she was at last forced to return home. She brought with her a volume of French poetry, which she was to inscribe 'Given to me by Monsieur Heger on 1st January 1844', and a promise of future friendship and correspondence. M. Heger was sincerely interested in his protégée's future and had in mind recommending pupils when the sisters finally opened their long-projected school. But the nature of Charlotte's letters, which were read by Mme. Heger either before or after her husband had torn them up, and which she carefully stitched together and preserved, effectively brought the correspondence to an end.

It seems likely that Charlotte was never to realize the effect on her readers of the strongly passionate and underlyingly erotic quality of much of her writing, but this was plain to Mme. Heger, and if her husband had failed to perceive it, she soon pointed it out. Even now the letters, pathetically begging for affection, are painful to read and, under the circumstances, perhaps his eventually simply failing to reply was the kindest action M. Heger could have taken, unbearably cruel though it seemed to Charlotte. In her last letter, written in November 1845, to which the answer was silence, she wrote:

To forbid me to write to you, to refuse to answer me would be to tear from me my only joy on earth, to deprive me of my last privilege – a privilege I never shall consent willingly to surrender. Believe me, *mon maître,* in writing to me it is a good deed that you will do. So long as I believe that you are pleased with me, so long as I have hope of receiving news from you, I can be at rest and not too sad. But when a prolonged and gloomy silence seems to threaten me with the estrangement of my master – when day by day I await a letter and when day by day disappointment comes to fling me back into overwhelming sorrow, and the sweet delight of seeing your handwriting and reading your counsel escapes me as a vision that is vain, then fever claims me – I lose appetite and sleep – I pine away.[29]

Poetically, at last, Charlotte came to recognize that this chapter of her life had been firmly closed forever.

He was mute as is the grave, he stood stirless as a tower;
  At last I looked up, and saw I prayed to stone:
I asked help of that which to help had no power,
  I sought love where love was utterly unknown.[30]

Whether Charlotte confided the cause of her anguish to Emily can never be known, but it must have been clear to the younger sister how much she was suffering. In fact, Charlotte's long crisis coincided with Emily's great period of mystical experience and its poetic recreation, as Charlotte was later to discover.

Now Charlotte was home again, and there was the future to consider on a more humdrum level, which meant starting their school. With no Aunt Branwell there to keep an eye on him, the girls were reluctant to leave their father, especially as his failing sight was beginning to trouble him, and Charlotte decided that there was no reason, after all, to seek new fields as their school could perfectly well be established at Haworth parsonage.

Somewhat misleadingly, as anyone who has seen it will know, she wrote to M. Heger, 'Our parsonage is rather a large house – with a few alterations there will be room for five or six boarders. If I could find this number of children of good family I should devote myself to their education. Emily does not care much for teaching but she would look after the housekeeping and, although something of a recluse, she is too

goodhearted not to do all she could for the well-being of the children.'[31]
The alterations to extend the accommodation would have been both
practical and possible, as can be seen from the expanded parsonage of
today, but they would have to have been substantial rather than 'few'.
Otherwise it seems difficult indeed to imagine where the five or six
boarders would have been fitted, or squeezed, in.

A prospectus was hopefully drafted and circulars were sent out, but no
pupils were offered. Few parents would have been attracted to send their
daughters to such a remote spot, with its bad record of health. Since the
maximum sum the sisters could have made from their venture would
have been some £245 a year, less the costs of lodging and feeding the
girls, and all the consequent loss of privacy and upheaval, this was
probably just as well. Although the lack of response was disappointing, it
must have been accompanied by a certain amount of relief.

As Charlotte and Emily settled down at home together again, their
routine was punctuated twice a year by the holiday visits of Branwell and
Anne on leave from the Robinsons. They were at home, soon to depart,
when Charlotte came back from Brussels and reported to Ellen, 'Anne
and Branwell are wondrously valued in their situation. They have just left
us to return to York.'[32]

8. The Mystery of Thorp Green Hall: the Bell Brothers' Poems, 1844–6

Whatever really happened subsequently at the Robinsons, Anne must always have wished thereafter that she had left her post at Thorp Green when she had first intended, and even more fervently that she had never introduced her brother into the household. The events that occurred between the summers of 1844 and 1845 were to have a permanent effect not only on the two of them but on all the family. Certainly they hastened Branwell's disintegration and death, and probably the deaths of his two younger sisters. After they left the Robinsons, neither Branwell nor Anne was ever fit for employment again.

In her biography of Charlotte, Mrs Gaskell boldly embarked on her description of the episode, with no doubts. Her version of the story is simple and dramatic and until comparatively recently was accepted without further investigation by most biographers and their readers. She begins with a heavily weighted paragraph: 'The story must be told. If I could, I would have avoided it; but not merely is it so well-known to many living as to be, in a manner, public property, but it is possible that, by revealing the misery, the gnawing life-long misery, the degrading habits, the early death of her partner in guilt – the acute and long-enduring agony of his family – to the wretched woman, who not only survives but passes about in the gay circles of London society, as a vivacious, well-dressed, flourishing widow, there may be awakened in her some feelings of repentance.'[1]

Far from awakening repentance in 'the wretched woman', it aroused an immediate denial from her solicitors, who convinced her to keep the obvious libel case out of court but insisted on a retraction in *The Times* and the *Athenaeum* and the deletion of the offending paragraphs from the forthcoming third edition of Charlotte's *Life*. Mrs Gaskell firmly believed she had written the truth, which, as she had been given to understand it, she undoubtedly had. It seems strange that the shrewd and experienced George Smith risked publishing this part of her Brontë story. The paragraphs and the story they contained were later reinstated, as many will think, misleadingly.

According to her version, Branwell took the fancy of the 'bold and hardened'[2] Mrs Robinson, who was soon making loving advances towards him, even in the presence of her children. Swiftly infatuated, Branwell's behaviour on his returns to Haworth Parsonage distressed them all – 'at one time in the highest spirits, at another, in the deepest depression – accusing himself of blackest guilt and treachery, without specifying what they were; and altogether evincing an irritability of disposition bordering on insanity'.[3]

Mrs Gaskell describes how, on 17 July 1845, when the blow of his dismissal fell, Branwell had

> ... received a letter from Mr ————, sternly dismissing him, intimating that his proceedings were discovered, characterising them as bad beyond expression, and charging him, on pain of exposure, to break off immediately, and for ever, all communication with every member of the family ...
>
> All the disgraceful details came out. Branwell was in no state to conceal his agony of remorse, or strange to say, his agony of guilty love, from any dread of shame ...
>
> The pitiable part, as far as he was concerned, was the yearning love he still bore to the woman who had got so strong a hold upon him. It is true, that she professed equal love ... The case presents the reverse of the usual features; the man became the victim; the man's life was blighted, and crushed out of him by suffering, and guilt entailed by guilt; the man's family were stung by keenest shame.[4]

Mrs Gaskell goes on to tell of the death of the husband of Branwell's 'paramour':

> Strange as it seems, the young man still loved her passionately, and now he imagined the time was come when they might look forwards to being married and might live together without reproach or blame. She had offered to elope with him; she had written to him perpetually; she had sent him money – £20 at a time; he remembered the criminal advances she

had made; she had braved shame and her children's menaced disclosures, for his sake; he thought she must love him; he knew little how bad a depraved woman can be. Her husband had made a will, in which what property he left her was bequeathed solely on the condition that she should never see Branwell Brontë again. At the very time when the will was read, she did not know but that he might be on his way to her, having heard of her husband's death. She despatched a servant in hot haste to Haworth. He stopped at the Black Bull, and a messenger was sent up to the parsonage for Branwell. He came down to the little inn and was shut up with the man for some time. Then the groom came out, paid his bill, mounted his horse and was off. Branwell remained in the room alone. More than an hour elapsed before sign or sound was heard; then, those outside heard a noise like the bleating of a calf and, on opening the door, he was found in a kind of fit, succeeding to the stupor of grief which he had fallen into on hearing that he was forbidden by his paramour ever to see her again, as, if he did, she would forfeit her fortune. Let her live and flourish! He died, his pockets filled with her letters, which he had carried perpetually about his person, in order that he might read them as often as he wished. He lies dead; and his doom is only known to God's mercy. When I think of him I change my cry to heaven. Let her live and repent! That same mercy is infinite.[5]

These are strong words, and it is small wonder that the former Mrs Lydia Robinson thought she had a good case for libel. When she employed the mousy Miss Brontë and her brother, nothing could have been further from her thoughts than that they belonged to what was to become one of the world's most famous literary families. In view of this and the extremely prestigious Mrs Gaskell's outspoken biography, although no names had been mentioned, there was soon no secret about her identity.

Mrs Gaskell's defence would have been hard to substantiate in court. The only person, apart from Lydia and her children, with any first-hand knowledge of the situation had been Anne, whom Mrs Gaskell never met. Branwell's own account, related to his family and written to his friends, all dealt in a highly emotional, even hysterical, way with events that had mainly by then taken place in the past. Her principal informants, Mr Brontë and Charlotte had apparently accepted his version of the affair without question and in good faith, in spite of his previous record, but could hardly have been considered impartial. Charlotte, in addition, suffered guilt and remorse about her treatment of the brother who had for so long been her second self.

Certainly, if Lydia Robinson had written the many letters which it is claimed Branwell preserved, none of which has ever come to light, in accordance with her well-known behaviour, Charlotte would have had no doubts about prudently destroying them. But it seems unlikely that Lydia would even have considered bringing a case had she any reason to fear the faintest possibility that such an indiscreet and dangerous correspondence might still be in existence. Most damaging of all, facts which have now emerged, and which were in Lydia's possession at the time, show many discrepancies in Branwell's story. Moreover, Branwell's glib facility in concocting fictions to put a favourable – or less favourable – gloss on the truth had already been displayed after his flight from London and his dismissal from the Postlethwaites.

Without doubt, at that time, Lydia's solicitors were correct in assuming that such a case, in itself sensational and bound to receive untold additional publicity because of the then sensational quality of much of the Brontë sisters' published writings, could only cause her and her family less satisfaction than further distress.

As has been seen, all appeared well when the 'wondrously valued' Branwell and Anne returned to York in January 1844. Much of Anne's routine in the household can be gleaned from her account in *Agnes Grey*. In her book, the Murray family included two sons, and it is possible that Branwell's pupil Edmund had some of the attributes of both these fictional boys. Certainly, from an account of a later tutor, as well as from Anne's own testimony, Edmund Robinson must have had a low intelligence quotient. He was never sufficiently prepared to enter public school, so there was no reason why Branwell, had all continued to go well, should not have been responsible for the remainder of his education.

In 1850, when Edmund was being removed from his care, his then tutor, Theophilus Williams, wrote, more in sorrow than in anger, to the agent, Mr Seaton:

> Mr Robinson took his departure the week before last accompanied by my fervent wishes for his future welfare. Few young men I think have passed the critical period of life at which he has arrived with more purity and innocence. His moral conduct has been exemplary; and that his mental acquirements are so very inferior is his infelicity rather than his fault.

For my part I have laboured patiently and assiduously to impart information and can with truth affirm that the preparation of my pupil Mr Hammond for his brilliant career at Hayleybury (only one competitor above him last July) cost me far less stress of thought and continued attention. I have now only to hope that his transfer to another tutor may conduce to his advantage. It is a great satisfaction to be assured by Dr Thorp that had *his* voice been potential the change would not have been made and that the removal has his *unwilling* acquiescence.[6]

The letter almost makes one wonder if Branwell's final crime was that of losing his temper with the dull boy and giving him an immoderate thrashing. In *Agnes Grey*, Anne writes that John

> ... was about eleven when I came: A fine, stout, healthy boy, frank and good-natured in the main, and might have been a decent lad had he been properly educated; but now he was as rough as a young bear, boisterous, unruly, unprincipled, untaught, unteachable ... Master Charles was his mother's peculiar darling ... He was little more than a year younger than John, but much smaller, paler, and less active and robust; a pettish, cowardly caprious, selfish little fellow, only active in doing mischief, and only clever in inventing falsehoods: not simply to hide his faults, but, in mere malicious wantonness, to bring odium upon others.[7]

Introducing her sons to their new governess, Mrs Murray observes,

> But at all events, Miss Grey ... I hope you will keep your temper, and be mild and patient throughout; especially with dear little Charles: he is so extremely nervous and susceptible, and so utterly unaccustomed to anything but the tenderest treatment. You will excuse my naming these things to you; for the fact is, I have hitherto found all the governesses, even the very best of them, faulty in this particular. They want that meek and quiet spirit, which St Matthew, or some of them, says, is better than the putting on of apparel – you will know the passage to which I allude, for you are a clergyman's daughter. And remember on all occasions, when any of the young people do anything improper, if persuasion and gentle remonstrance will not do, let one of the others come and tell me; for I can speak to them more plainly than it would be proper for you to do ...[8]

It is easy enough again to believe that this passage is more or less a piece of direct reporting burned resentfully into Anne's memory.

In considering their lives at Thorp Green, an important aspect is the totally different portrayal of Lydia by Branwell, her self-declared lover, and by the dryly critical Anne. The following observations clearly apply just as much to the Mrs Robinson of real life as to the Mrs Murray of fiction:

> I observed that while Mrs Murray was so extremely solicitous for the comfort and happiness of her children, and continually talking about it, she never once mentioned mine; though they were at home surrounded by friends, and I an alien among strangers; and I did not yet know enough of the world not to be considerably surprised at this anomaly ...[9]
>
> For the girls she seemed anxious only to render them as superficially attractive and showily accomplished as they could possibly be made, without present trouble or discomfort to themselves; and I was to act accordingly – to study and strive to amuse and oblige, instruct, refine, and polish, with the least possible exertion on their part, and no exercise of authority on mine.[10]

Before the marriage of her daughter Rosalie: 'It seemed a horrible thing to hurry on the inauspicious match, and not to give the poor creature time to think and reason on the irrevocable step she was about to take. I made no pretention to 'a mother's watchful, anxious care,' but I was amazed and horrified at Mrs Murray's heartlessness, or want of thought for the real good of her child; ...'[11]

Here is her mistress offering the governess some good advice:

> 'The young lady's proficiency and elegance is of more consequence to the governess than her own, as well as to the world. If she wishes to prosper in her vocation she must devote all her energies to her business: all her ideas and all her ambitions will tend to the accomplishment of that one object ... if they begin to yield to indolence or self-indolence they are speedily distanced by wiser competitors: there is little to choose between a person that ruins her pupils by neglect, and one that corrupts them by her example. You will excuse my dropping these little hints; you know it is all for your own good. Many ladies would speak to you more strongly; and many would not trouble themselves to speak at all, but quietly look out for a substitute. That, of course, would be the easiest plan: but I know the advantages of a place like this to a person in your situation; and I have no desire to part with you, as I am sure you will do very well if you will only think of these things and try to exert yourself a *little* more: then, I am

convinced, you would *soon* acquire that delicate tact which alone is wanting to give you a proper influence over the mind of your pupil.'

I was about to give the lady some idea of the fallacy of her expectations; but she sailed away as soon as she had concluded her speech. Having said what she wished, it was no part of her plan to await my answer: it was my business to hear, and not to speak.[12]

When Agnes has bad news from home of her father's final illness, Mrs Murray reacts in much the same way as, it seems, Mrs Robinson received Anne's request to go home when Aunt Branwell lay dying: 'Then, immediately, I sought permission to anticipate the vacation, and go without delay. Mrs Murray stared, and wondered at the unwonted energy and boldness with which I urged the request, and thought there was no occasion to hurry; but finally gave me leave: stating, however, that there was "no need to be in such agitation about the matter – it might prove a false alarm after all; and if not – why, it was only common course of nature: we must all die sometime: and I was not to suppose myself the only afflicted person in the world." '[13]

All this is much more in line with what is known of Lydia Robinson's subsequent conduct than when Branwell was to write of his 'admiration of her mental and personal attractions, my knowledge of her unselfish sincerity, her sweet temper, and unwearied care for others, with but unrequited return where most should have been given ...'[14]

The first warning note that all was not well was sounded by Charlotte in a letter written to Ellen during the Christmas holidays of 1844–5: 'Branwell has been quieter and less irritable on the whole than he was in the summer ...'[15] But nothing in Branwell's behaviour had prepared the family for the blow that was to fall.

Life had certainly not been easy for Anne, having to cope with the younger Lydia, who shared many of the characteristics of Rosalie, her fictional counterpart, and the horse-mad Bessy, on whom Matilda was based. But Lydia was by now sharing many social occasions with her mother, and her thoughts and talk were all of balls, flirtations and young men, while Bessy was interested only in riding and sneaking off to enjoy the company of the grooms and stable-lads. Both girls were to all intents and purposes off Anne's hands so that she was more able to devote her attentions to her favourite, Mary, the most affectionate and rewarding of her pupils.

Whether Anne realized that during her last half year at Thorp Green serious trouble was brewing up for Branwell, or whether, along the lines of the conversation above, Mrs Robinson had been dissatisfied with Anne's failure to control Bessy's progress, hinting that she might be looking around for someone else, for some reason she made up her mind and gave in her notice of her intention to resign her post when she left, accompanied by Branwell, for her summer holidays. Since no other governess was appointed for Mary, it seems very likely that, remembering her unfair dismissal from Blake Hall, Anne decided to forestall a second such humiliation.

Charlotte and Emily were delighted at Anne's decision, as they had long urged her to leave an atmosphere so uncongenial to her sensitive character. Feeling she could go off with a clear conscience, leaving Emily and Anne happily reunited, Charlotte departed almost immediately on a long-planned visit to Ellen Nussey.

While she was away, Emily and Anne enjoyed a two-day visit to York Minster and Keighley, an occasion Emily described in her birthday paper written on 30 July. 'Anne and I,' she wrote, 'went on our first long journey by ourselves together, leaving home on the 30th June, Monday, sleeping at York, returning to Keighley Tuesday evening, sleeping there and walking home on Wednesday morning. Though the weather was broken we enjoyed ourselves very much, except during a few hours at Bradford.' The few tedious hours at Bradford were probably spent paying duty calls, and shopping.

During the excursion, the girls enacted various scenes from the lives of their imaginary characters, and Emily commented, 'The Gondals still flourish as bright as ever ... We intend sticking firmly by the rascals as long as they delight us which I am glad to say they do at present.'[16]

When Anne resigned her post at Thorp Green, there was every indication that Branwell intended and was expected to stay, his being the only pupil seriously in need of further education. He had returned home with Anne for a week, going back to the Robinsons on 25 June. On 5 July the Robinsons went off to Scarborough for their holiday as usual, leaving Edmund and Branwell alone together at Thorp Green. Apparently Branwell was not expected at Scarborough and, no doubt after some coaching, twelve days later Edmund joined his family and Branwell returned home with his quarters' wages, which were not due until 21 July.

When Charlotte arrived home on Saturday the 19th, refreshed and cheerful after her holiday, it was to find Branwell there, drunk. Since this was already by no means unusual, she was not at first unduly upset, ' ... but when Anne informed me of the immediate cause of his present illness I was greatly shocked. He had last Thursday received a note from Mr Robinson sternly dismissing him, intimating that he had discovered his proceedings, which he characterised as bad beyond expression and charging him on pain of exposure to break off instantly and for ever all communication with every member of his family. We have had sad work with Branwell since. He thought of nothing but stunning or drowning his distress of mind. No one in the house could have rest.'[17]

For poor Branwell, it was the beginning of the end.

As usual, he lost no time in giving his own explanation for this unexpected dismissal, which is substantially the version published by Mrs Gaskell. It is perhaps best described in his letter to his friend Francis Grundy, written just a few months later, in October 1845.

In a letter begun in the spring and never finished, owing to incessant attacks of illness, I tried to tell you that I was tutor to the son of a wealthy gentleman whose wife is the sister to the wife of — MP for the county of — and the cousin of Lord — ... This lady (though her husband detested me) showed me a degree of kindness which, when I was deeply grieved one day at her husband's conduct, ripened into declarations of more than ordinary feeling ... although she is seventeen years my senior, all combined to an attachment on my part, and led to reciprocations which I had little looked for. During nearly three years I had daily 'troubled pleasure soon chastised by fear'. Three months since, I received a furious letter from my employer, threatening to shoot me if I returned from my vacation, which I was passing at home; and letters from her lady's-maid and physician informed me of the outbreak, only checked by her firm courage and resolution that whatever harm came to her, none should come to me ... Eleven continuous nights of sleepless horror reduced me to almost blindness and taken into Wales to recover, the sweet scenery, the sea, the sound of music caused me fits of unspeakable distress ...[18]

Whether the unspeakable distress was caused by his dismissal or by the potent means Branwell had taken to soften the blow is debatable. Charlotte's account certainly suggests that she was by no means surprised to find him 'ill': 'He is often owing to his own fault.'[19] When Charlotte wrote 'ill' in such a context, Ellen knew that her discreet friend meant drunk – and it is important to note that even, as far as she first knew, still employed and at the very beginning of his holidays, Charlotte was not surprised to find him in this condition.

Having found him almost impossible to deal with, Mr Brontë had decided to send his son on a trip to Liverpool and Wales in the care of his old friend John Brown. To a certain extent, this had the calming effect on Branwell that his father had hoped for. Although very far from fully recovered, he returned home able to concentrate on some poetry and at least to think about seeking new employment.

He wrote to Joseph Leyland: ' ... I returned yesterday from a week's journey to Liverpool and North Wales, but I found during my absence that wherever I went a certain woman robed in black, and calling herself "MISERY" walked by my side, and leant on my arm as affectionately as if she were my legal wife. Like some other husbands I could have been spared her presence ...'[20]

The beauty of the scenery in North Wales inspired the poem 'Penmaenmawr':

These winds, these clouds, this chill November storm
Bring back again thy tempest-beaten form
To eyes that look upon yon dreary sky
As late they looked on thy sublimity:
When I, more troubled than thy restless sea,
Found in its waves, companionship with thee.

I had an ear which could on accents dwell
That might as well say 'perish!' as 'farewell!'
An eye, which saw, far off, a tender form,
Beaten, unsheltered, by afflictions storm;
An arm – a lip – that trembled to embrace
My Angel's gentle breast and sorrowing face,
A mind that clung to Ouse's fertile side
While tossing – objectless – on Menai's tide! ...

Let me, like it, arise o'er mortal care,
All woes sustain, yet never know despair;
Unshrinking face the grief I now deplore,
And stand through sun and shine, like moveless
     PENMAENMAWR[21]

It has been claimed that the period of subsequent calm was due to Branwell's inner conviction that he was secure in his love and that it was only a matter of time before the woman he adored was released from the chains of marriage to her sick husband, when they would be reunited, not as tutor and mistress but as husband and wife. But apart from, the puzzling aspects of Branwell's dismissal, Mrs Robinson's subsequent actions reveal that this was far removed from her own view of the situation.

The fact that Mr Robinson's totally unexpected letter of dismissal was evidently written in a white heat of anger, when his son joined the family at Scarborough, certainly suggests that he was reacting on the spur of the moment to something that Edmund had told him on arrival, something that rendered Branwell Brontë, as a tutor to his son, utterly abhorrent. This might simply have been an account of Branwell's drug-taking or drunkenness, while they were alone together, perhaps leading to a particularly reprehensible dereliction of duty, such as an emotional report of a homosexual approach or a confession of an emotional relationship. From the timing of the events alone, although it cannot be discounted, the least likely possibility seems to be the son's report of his mother's adultery or indiscretion with his tutor.

Mr Robinson's chief threat to Branwell in his letter appears to have been 'pain of exposure' of his proceedings 'bad beyond expression'. If this threat had related to the tutor's love for Lydia, it would have been empty indeed, since Branwell did nothing but reveal and elaborate on this theme for the rest of his life, certainly without any suggestions of shame.

It has sometimes been said that, following his letter of dismissal to Branwell, Edmund Robinson 'showered' his wife with gifts. Quite apart from the fact that this would have been a strange reaction from a husband on separating his wife from her lover, this does not appear to be the case from his account book, now preserved in the Brontë parsonage museum. The items listed may not even be gifts at all but perfectly normal expenditures requested by a wife from her husband on her summer holiday: 'Lydia £3. Brooch jet 7s 6d. Lydia £3. Lydia's dog', are mentioned after the dismissal. Before, there are a few items, 'brooches Lydia £1.8s, Lydia's shawl £1.17s, Lydia's scarf 7s 6d.'[22] Even bearing in mind the great depreciation of the value of money, for a man in Edmund's comfortable financial position, these little expenditures hardly account to a shower of gifts.

In Anne's birthday paper, she writes of her own stay at Thorp Green: 'I have had some very unpleasant and undreamt-of experiences of human nature.'[23] Anyone who has even dipped into the Gondal sagas or read *The Tenant of Wildfell Hall* must know that acts of adultery were maybe unpleasant but far from undreamt of by Anne. Her extreme reaction seems almost certainly to have been caused by circumstances much more complex and distressing.

On 20 October there occurred another event which may have underlain Anne's decision to leave the Robinson family. Lydia, the eldest daughter, for whom Mrs Robinson had no doubt been expecting to negotiate an advantageous match, eloped to Gretna Green with an actor.

By the time she left the family, Anne had certainly established an affectionate relationship with the girls, and sometimes they confided in her, just as Rosalie and Matilda did in Miss Grey:

'I know you think me a shocking, conceited, frivolous girl: but then, you know, I don't attribute it *all* to my personal attractions: I give some praise to the hairdresser, and some to my exquisitely lovely dress – you must see it tomorrow – white gauze over pink satin – and so *sweetly* made! and a necklace and bracelet of beautiful, large pearls!'

'I've no doubt you looked very charming: but should that delight you so very much?'

'Oh, no! not that alone! but then, I was so much admired; and I made so *many* conquests in that one night – you'd be astonished to hear' –

'But what good will they do you?'

'What good! Think of any woman asking that!'

'Well, I should think one conquest would be enough; and too much, unless the subjugation were mutual.'

'Oh, but you know I never agree with you on those points. Now, wait a bit, and I'll tell you my principal admirers – those who made themselves very conspicuous that night and after: for I've been to two parties since ... Lord F—, who hates his wife, was evidently much struck with me. He asked me to dance with him twice – he is a charming dancer, by-the bye, and so am I, you can't think how well I did – I was astonished at myself. My lord was very complimentary too – rather too much so in fact – and I thought proper to be a little haughty and repellant; but I had the pleasure of seeing his nasty, cross wife ready to perish with spite and vexation.'[24]

Among the many entertainments offered to holiday-makers at

Scarborough in those days were the plays presented at the Theatre Royal. Owned by Samuel Roxby, a member of an extremely talented theatrical family, the theatre was close by the Cliff lodgings where the Robinsons always stayed. The Roxby family home at Huntriss Row was in the same area.

During their summer visits, the Robinsons seem to have gone quite frequently to the theatre and, like many a young lady before and since, Lydia fell in love with the handsome and talented leading man, Henry Roxby, who acted under the name of Henry Beverley. Lydia was an extremely pretty girl, opportunities for meetings must have presented themselves and were eagerly pursued. Although Anne did not go on the family holiday in 1845, it is extremely likely that she heard that the flirtation had commenced in the previous summer. Fears about its continuation and results may well have been why she decided to forego that last holiday at Scarborough with the family, which she had always enjoyed so much.

When their much-prized eldest daughter eloped with Henry Roxby, the Reverend and Mrs Robinson were appalled. She was immediately 'cut off with a shilling'.[25] Mrs Robinson, who might have been expected to relent, given the sweetness of nature with which Branwell credited her, did no more than help out with an occasional small sum, speaking as though she had only two daughters, excluding Lydia from her own will and finally settling on her a 30 shillings a week allowance, which was far from generous. Was Lydia happier with her actor than Rosalie proved to be with Sir Thomas Ashby? Anne apparently feared this was unlikely.

Neither Branwell nor Anne was to learn of Lydia's elopement, in fact, until the following summer, and during the autumn of 1845, erratic though his behaviour undoubtedly was, Branwell was trying to pull himself together. He made tentative attempts to rejoin the railway, wrote some poetry and began what he intended to be a three-volume novel, *And the Weary are at Rest*. Isolated though he was from his sisters now by his sense of failure and distress, he was, in fact, pursuing much the same course as they in hoping that successful publication might free him from the need of seeking further employment.

In her birthday paper Anne mentioned, 'I have begun the third volume of *Passages in the Life of an Individual*', later to be re-entitled *Agnes Grey*.[26] Charlotte was busy with *The Professor*, in which she relived much of her life in Brussels, and Emily must have been secretly writing her great

Wuthering Heights, alongside her current work on the First Wars of the Gondals.

Anne, in particular, must have been pleased by one of her brother's activities at this time. Always generously anxious to do all in his power to help his friends, Branwell had obtained for Joseph Leyland the commission for the memorial tablet raised by subscription to William Weightman. He was able to write to his friend. 'The Tablet has fully satisfied all who have seen it.'[27] Its presence must have made Anne's visits to the church all the more poignant, when she could raise her eyes and read, 'In Memory of the Late WILLIAM WEIGHTMAN Who died September 6th, 1842, aged 26 years ... greatly respected For his orthodox principles, active zeal, moral habits, learning, mildness and affability.'

By now, there was a new curate at Haworth, Arthur Bell Nicholls, from Ireland, like Mr Brontë, although from a decidedly more comfortable family background. Little can he have realized the commitment he was undertaking when he took up this post, although from the first Mr Brontë's failing eyesight placed extra responsibilities upon him, and all too soon he was to become aware of the problems presented by Branwell.

Shortly after his arrival, Charlotte was writing to Ellen that curates seemed to her

> a self-seeking vain, empty race. At this blessed moment we have no less than three of them in Haworth parish, and God Knows, there is not one to mend another. The other day, they all three ... dropped, or rather rushed, in unexpectedly to tea. It was Monday (baking day) and I was hot and tired; still, if they had behaved quietly and decently I would have served them out their tea in peace; but they began glorifying themselves and abusing Dissenters in such a manner, that my temper lost its balance, and I pronounced a few sentences sharply and rapidly, which struck them all dumb. Papa was greatly horrified also. I don't regret it.[28]

She was to draw on her memories of these curates later, when she came to write *Shirley,* and perhaps it was from this somewhat striking moment that Arthur Bell Nicholls began to take a particulat interest in the fiery little Charlotte.

But the main event of the autumn of 1845, was Charlotte's discovery of one of her sister Emily's notebooks. 'I looked it over, and something

George Richmond's no doubt somewhat idealized portrait of Charlotte, after she had achieved success

Constantin Heger, the great love of Charlotte's life

Sir Edward Dolman Scott, the second husband of Branwell's Lydia. Although he was to die only a few years after their marriage, he was far from the elderly dotard he has often been described as being

Branwell's Lydia Robinson, at the time of her second marriage, when she
became Lady Scott – clearly a woman of determined character

P B Brontë.

Inset: Joseph Leyland's medallion of Branwell

Branwell's sketch of his lodgings at Thorp Green Hall

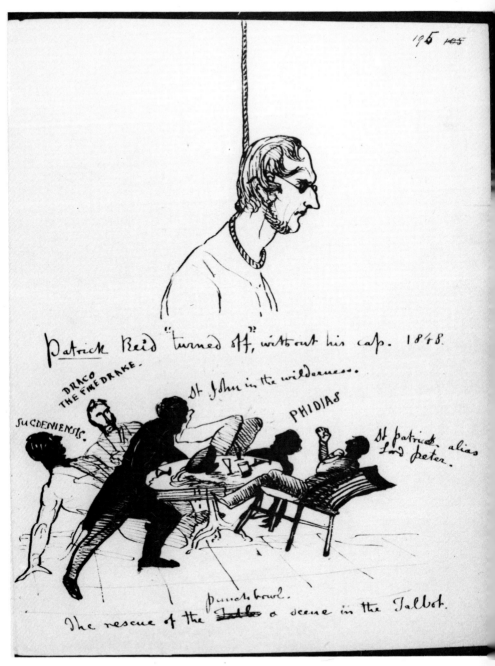

A curious self-portrait of Branwell included in a letter to Joseph Leyland

John Brown, perhaps
not always his best
friend, painted
most probably by
Branwell

Anne's beautiful
resting place
in Scarborough

Arthur Bell Nicholls, her father's curate, whom Charlotte grew to love, and married in 1854. Although she was to die so soon, their marriage was extremely happy, and Mr Nicholls remained a tower of strength to the ageing Mr Brontë, the only one of his family left

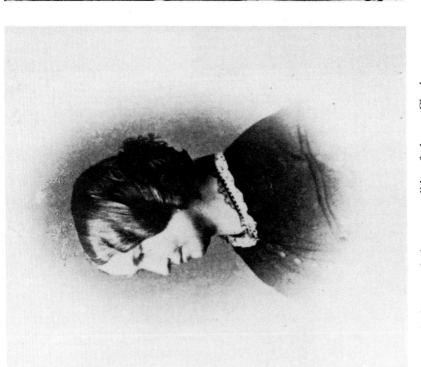

A photograph that may well be of a happy Charlotte on her honeymoon journey, recently discovered in the National Portrait Gallery

more than surprise seized me, – a deep conviction that these were not common effusions, nor at all like the poetry women generally write. I thought them condensed and terse, vigorous and genuine. To my ear, they had also a peculiar music – wild, melancholy, and elevating.'[29] It is to Charlotte's eternal credit that she immediately perceived the soaring genius of her sister's poetry. The possibility of publication came immediately to her mind, for Emily's poems and some of her own too.

Emily's fury when she found that her sister had invaded her privacy in this way must have been terrible. Five years later, in the knowledge that her own obstinate perseverance had overcome her sister's secretive pride, toning down the outburst, Charlotte wrote: 'My sister Emily was not a person of demonstrative character, nor one on the recesses of whose mind and feelings even those nearest and dearest to her could, with impunity, intrude unlicensed; it took hours to reconcile her to the discovery I had made, and days to persuade her that such poems merited publication. I knew, however, that a mind like hers could not be without some latent spark of honourable ambition, and refused to be discouraged in my attempts to fan that spark to flame.'[30]

Charlotte was aided in this determination by Anne's bringing out some of her own poems, probably in the midst of this fierce family turmoil, trying to pour oil on troubled waters. No doubt Anne's persuasion weighed in the balance with Emily, and Charlotte pushed ahead determinedly with her plans, which resulted in the publication at their own expense in May 1846 by Messrs. Aylott & Jones of a small, dark green volume with gilt lettering entitled *Poems by Currer, Ellis and Acton Bell*. The girls had decided to publish under what we might now call 'unisex' pseudonyms, which had probably been insisted upon by Emily, retaining their own initials and borrowing the easy-to-remember name of their father's new curate.

The selection of poems was uneven in quality, containing some of the finest poems of all three sisters and some of their least successful, with Emily's mastery apparent in many of the twenty-one poems she contributed, such as 'Cold in the Earth' and 'He comes with Western Wings'. The book did not sell more than a few copies but was kindly reviewed in the *Critic* and the *Athenaeum* and was of inestimable value as a forerunner.

Although Mr Brontë knew that his daughters, whose principal entertainment for most of their lives had been writing, were seeking

publication, in his usual detached and private manner, he held aloof and
made no attempt to influence their enterprise. He read their works only
when they appeared in print, and then with immense, if under-stated,
pride, and took a keen interest in their reviews.

It has been asserted that Branwell Brontë was never to know anything
about his sisters's publication of their works. This seems hard to believe.
He was an intelligent young man, not, at this time, sunk into the final
stages of his drugged and drunken oblivion, and there could have been
few secrets in such a small community as Haworth. Moreover, there can
be no doubt that, as far as the villagers were concerned, he was by far the
most popular member of the Brontë family. The ordinary folk liked him,
with all his faults.

Had he known, he must have been unbearably hurt at his exclusion
from the enterprise. The four of them had existed for so long as a quartet
embracing two partnerships, and certainly he could have provided a
contribution whch would in no way have reduced the quality of the
collection or lessened its impact. Whether he knew or not, it is hard to
understand why Charlotte did not tell him about it and ask him to join in.
At that time, when he was in any case seeking publication for his poetry
in the *Halifax Guardian,* it must have offered him a lifeline. But from the
moment of his dismissal from the Robinson family, Charlotte seems to
have turned her face against the brother she had once admired and loved
so much.

It has been conjectured that it was Mr Robinson's death that signalled
Branwell's final descent into hopelessness, but in March 1846 Charlotte
wrote to Ellen

> I went into the room where Branwell was, to speak to him, about an hour
> after I got home; it was very forced work to address him. I might have
> spared myself the trouble, as he took no notice and made no reply; he was
> stupified. My fears were not in vain. Emily tells me that he got a sovereign
> from papa while I have been away, under pretence of paying a pressing
> debt – he went immediately and changed it at a public house, and had
> employed it as was to be expected – she concluded her account by saying
> he was a hopeless being: 'it is too true – in his present state it is scarcely
> possible to stay in the room where he is.'[31]

It is all too probable that his sisters' shutting him out of what had been
a vital part of their joint lives, understandable though this was under the

circumstances, also played an important part in the last phase of Branwell's tragic life.

Mr Robinson's death can have come as no surprise to his wife. He had been a sick man while the Brontës were living at Thorp Green, and the course of his illness had accelerated since they had left. Doctors Crosby and Simpson had been in regular attendance for several months before he died.

The end came on 26 May 1846. Edmund Robinson was only forty-six, and the *Yorkshireman* reported, 'He died as he had lived, in firm and humble trust in his Saviour.' Clearly, distressed though she may have been, Lydia Robinson accepted calmly her husband's early, if expected death. Her account book continues in good order, noting payments for bitter beer and to the old servants ('for my angel'); details of interest paid, presumably on money held in trust to their family servant, Anne Marshall, and, on her decease, her mother, Ellen, in her clear and businesslike hand. On 10 July she notes an entry for proving the will and probate, and on 28 August there is an entry for £2. 5. 0. 'My locket for *My* Edmund's hair'. One gains an impression of a coolly affectionate, well-balanced woman.[32]

Charlotte's account of Branwell's reception of the news is much more dry and terse than Mrs Gaskell's more dramatic account written ten years later: 'The death of Mr Robinson which occurred about 3 weeks or a month ago, served Branwell for a pretext to throw all about him into hubbub and confusion with his emotions, etc, etc.... Shortly after, came news from all hands that Mr Robinson had altered his will before he died and effectually prevented all chance of a marriage between his widow and Branwell, by stipulating that she should not have a shilling if she ever ventured to reopen any communication with him.'[33]

Branwell himself, writing to Leyland, recreates some of the emotional hubbub and confusion:

Mr Robinson of Thorp Green is dead, and he has left his widow in a dreadful state of health. She sent the coachman over to me yesterday, and the account which he gave of her sufferings was enough to burst my heart.

Through the will she is left quite powerless, and her eldest daughter who married imprudently is cut off with a shilling.

The Executing Trustees detest me, and one declares that if he sees me he will shoot me.

These things I do not care about, but I do care for the life of the one who suffers even more than I do. Her Coachman said that it was a pity to see her, for she was only able to kneel in her bedroom in bitter tears and prayers. She has worn herself out in attendance on him, and his conduct during the few days before his death was exceedingly mild and repentant, but that only distressed her doubly ...

What I shall do I know not – I am too hard to die, and too wretched to live. My wretchedness is not about castles in the air, but about stern realities; my hardihood lies in bodily vigour; but, dear Sir, my mind sees only a dreary future which I as little wish to enter on as could a martyr to be bound to the stake.[34]

A few days later, apparently having heard from the family physician, Dr Crosby, he reported,

He knows me *well*, and he pities my case most sincerely for he declares that though used to the rough ups and downs of this weary world, he shed tears from his heart when he saw the state of that lady and knew what I should feel.

When he mentioned my name – she stared at him and fainted. When she recovered she in turns dwelt on her inextinguishable love for me – her horror at having been the first to delude me into wretchedness, and her agony at having been the cause of the death of her husband, who, in his last hours, bitterly repented his treatment of her.

Her sensitive mind was totally wrecked. She wandered into talking of entering a nunnery; and the Doctor fairly debars me from hope in the future.[35]

From all that can be gleaned about Mrs Lydia Robinson, it is surely impossible to believe that she ever considered marrying Branwell Brontë, let alone entering a nunnery. She appears to have been a socially conscious lady well entrenched in her own moneyed upper middle class. Her shocked reaction to her daughter's runaway match makes it perfectly clear that she herself would never even have contemplated marrying a small, short-sighted, red-haired Irish tutor, no matter how charming and cultivated, seventeen years her junior and penniless.

But the fiction of this passionate, reciprocated love affair had sustained Branwell's waning pride since his dismissal. When Mr Robinson died, apparently removing any impediment to the union of the desperate lovers, it became urgently necessary for Branwell to invent another story.

It has been suggested that the reported change of Mr Robinson's will was invented by his widow. But there seems no reason why Lydia Robinson should have made up such a tale, and every reason why Branwell might. However great he swore was their mutual love, he had to admit that he could never support a wife in his present circumstances, and without her fortune to aid them, he claimed, his only honourable course was to renounce her.

From earlier drafts of his will, long before the advent of Branwell Brontë into their lives, Edmund Robinson's intentions had always been quite clear in regard to his wife. Should she remarry after his decease, her interest in his own estate and her son's inheritance would come to an end, and she would retain only her personal dowry of some £7,000, and the annual £600 interest this paid. She would also cease to be one of her son's trustees. In fact, Lydia did lose certain rights on her remarriage after her husband's death, but these were totally unrelated to Branwell. Certainly it could not have been to her material benefit to enter a second marriage with any but a wealthy man. The only substantial revision of Edmund's will was to exclude his eldest daughter, now Lydia Roxby, from any inheritance – a change continued by his wife in her own will, which is framed as though only her two younger daughters still survived.[36] It is good to know her brother reinstated her in his will.

There are other weak points in Branwell's letter. Lydia could have had no reason for 'agony at having been the cause of the death of her husband'. Mr Robinson had suffered poor health increasingly for some years, and his illness certainly originated from some while before Branwell's arrival in the household. Neither was there any reason why he should have 'bitterly repented of his treatment' of his wife. As has been seen, he appears to have been an attentive husband, referred to by Lydia in her cashbook as 'my angel'. Far from her 'sensitive mind' being 'totally wrecked' and her 'talking of entering a nunnery', at this particular time Lydia was dealing efficiently with family affairs, corresponding with her agent and organizing the usual family seaside holiday. No doubt due to Lydia and Henry Roxby's embarrassing presence there, Scarborough this year gave place to Whitby, Hartlepool and Redcar.

Shortly after this, Lydia Robinson made arrangements for Edmund to go to his new tutor, Theophilus Williams, at Charlton Mackrel in Somerset, and for her daughters to stay with their uncles' families in

Derbyshire and with their paternal grandmother in York and Scarborough. An interesting point revealed in the Robinson papers is that, though the estate was a wealthy one, Lydia Robinson was left short of ready cash. She arranged a sale of timber for £800 to pay outstanding debts and tide her over and kept a watchful eye on the expenditure of her daughters. Bessy, in particular, seems to have been wayward and extravagant, although her mother wrote, 'Bessy *means* no harm and I have *written strongly* to her. Mary is a *good* girl and my boy *very kind* to me.'[37]

She herself let Thorp Green Hall and went to stay with relatives, Sir Edward and Lady Scott, at Great Barr Hall in Staffordshire. In his fifties, Sir Edward was a long-standing acquaintance; he had been Member of Parliament for Lichfield from 1831 to 1837; his wife, Lydia's cousin, was already suffering from her fatal illness. The correspondence between Lydia Robinson and her agent, Mr Seaton, indicates that her children were soon taking second place to affairs at Great Barr Hall, and it seems likely that the possibility of becoming the second Lady Scott might have had some influence on her attentive nursing. In any case, she was glad of the shelter of their home and to be of help in the household.

Having briskly and capably tidied up the past, she resolutely turned her face towards the future, which included looking around for suitable matches for her two girls. While her son's former tutor was professing to be pining to death on her account, it appears that she was far too busy and occupied to spare a thought for Branwell Brontë.

But puzzling aspects of the story remain. Gooch the coachman certainly seems to have travelled over to Haworth with the news of Mr Robinson's death – one wonders why? And why he went to the Black Bull instead of Haworth parsonage. In their letters, both Branwell and Charlotte hint at the go-between role of Dr Crosby in relation to letters and sums of money. But the records shown only the payment to Crosby of medical fees for the Robinsons and for Anne Marshall, which sound like perfectly genuine entries. The cash might, of course, have come from Dr Crosby himself, spurred by compassion for a fellow Mason.

Branwell also seems to have been in touch at times with Anne Marshall, Mrs Robinson's lady's-maid, a sad and shadowy figure, who appears to have 'banked' with Mr Robinson a sum of £520, which is in startling contrast to her annual salary of £12. This may, of course, have been some kind of legacy which she was never to enjoy and which, after her death at the age of thirty-eight, was paid to her mother, Ellen, in 1847. Some suggestion has been made that this sum of money implies a special relationship between Anne Marshall and Edmund Robinson, but in view of the way Lydia Robinson was to deal with the matter later, this seems unlikely. A memorial gravestone to poor Anne's memory described her as for many years a much respected servant of the Reverend Edmund Robinson of Thorp Green.

Branwell had declared, 'The Executing Trustees detest me, and one declares that if he sees me he will shoot me.' At this time the trustees were the Reverend Charles Thorp, the Reverend Charles Atmore Ogilvie, William and Thomas Evans, the solicitor Henry Newton and, of course, Lydia herself. None of them seems a likely candidate for an assassin.

Whether or not these trustees ever considered Branwell at all can never be known, but they certainly did not make life easy for Lydia Robinson, and to some extent it was probably a relief to her when she ceased to be one.

Apart from making clear her uneasy relationship with the other trustees, the following letter, cautiously worded as it is, although its intention was clearly quite plain to the recipient (presumably her agent Mr Seaton), is now open to interpretation.

> I return Dr Thorp's letter – and hope he will pursue his present pacific plan of acting and give us no unnecessary trouble and expense. I have certainly most strong opposition to the idea of Chancery – and Mr Evans was *most strongly* opposed to it also, and said the expense (if persisted in) would fall upon Dr Thorp.... I hope Dr T. may be less unguarded in questioning Edmund than he *used* to be for (tho to show my good feeling, I willingly let him go to the Dr) I am well aware of things he has said to me concerning Thorp Green – and all *our* management of it – which had better not have been said. And I am very glad you talked to my son upon it.[38]

In view of her comment, 'I have had some very unpleasant and undreamt of experiences of human nature', it has also to be considered whether some of Anne Brontë's brutally realistic descriptions in *The Tenant of Wildfell Hall* derived from scenes she might have witnessed or heard of at Thorp Green Hall.

The possibility that there may have been a homosexual connection, even if only of a sentimental and emotional kind, between Branwell and his pupil can reasonably be suggested: the lack of any known relationships with women in Branwell's life; his apparent rejection of the suitable and attractive Mary Taylor; Mr Robinson's 'threat of exposure' and its timing: Anne's aversion and horror at experiences at Thorp Green Hall; and the fact that the extremely eligible (at least, in worldly terms) Edmund was still unmarried when he died tragically in a drowning accident at the age of thirty-seven, leaving a considerable (for the time) annuity of £52. 10s. to his stud groom. Moreover, this need not exclude the possibility that there may also have existed a mother-and-son, older-sister-and-brother or simply idealistic young man and romantic older woman type of attachment between Branwell and his employer's wife, an attachment on which he was to build the passionate fiction with which he tried to justify the final waste of his own life.

What does seem certain is that there never existed the situation which Branwell described – or, perhaps it should be said, invented, very much on the lines of his Angrian fiction. It is also perhaps worth noting that three of the Odes of Horace which Branwell translated were addressed to Lydia, a circumstance quite sufficient to fire his romantic imagination.

'For four years (including one year of absence) a lady intensely loved me as I did her, and each sacrificed to that love all we had to sacrifice, and held out to each other HOPE for our guide to the future. She was all I could wish for in a woman, and she loved me even better than I did her.'[39]

Not only does Lydia Robinson's known behaviour totally belie these words but so does Branwell's, who never from the day of his dismissal until his death made the least attempt to go and see her.

So what did happen at Thorp Green Hall?

The facts and some probabilities have been presented, but the events remain impossible to define. Perhaps even now, one day some clinching piece of evidence will come to light. But there can be no doubt that the Brontë family and Mrs Gaskell were unfair in representing to the world that Lydia Robinson was responsible for Branwell's final tragic decline, for he was already well on the way to it before he entered her employ.

Nevertheless, the crucial importance of the episode to the whole family is beyond doubt, and from the time of Edmund Robinson's death, for Branwell Brontë it was downhill all the way.

9. And the Weary are at Rest, 1846–8

Isolated by failure, disapproval and his drug- and drink-imposed haze, for a while Branwell struggled on with *And the Weary are at Rest* and what were to be some of his last poems. He was never to complete 'Morley Hall,' which he evidently intended as a grateful memorial to the Leyland family, and 'Percy Hall', his last poem, also remained unfinished. Although he was looking back to the fate of his beloved sisters, Elizabeth and Maria, the poem strikes a sadly prophetic note:

> Too clear the proofs that in her face abounded
> Of swift Consumption's power! Although each day
> He'd seen her airy lightness fail away,
> And gleams unnatural glisten in her eye:
> He had not dared to dream that she could die,
> But only fancied his a causeless fear
> Of losing something which he held so dear – [1]

Another aspect of their brother's life which caused his father and his older and youngest sister much distress was his apparent rejection of religion. This had been expressed several years before in his poem 'Azreal,' but almost until the last days of his life, his attitude of unbelief persisted.

> Believe that he can rule above
>   When you shall see Him rule below;
> Believe that he's the God of love
>   When he shall end His children's woe ...
>
> There is no God – I know there's none!

137

Neither of spirit nor of stone;
No Holy Hill nor Idol Shrine
Has ever held a Power Divine;
Nor heaven above *nor hell* below
Can minister to wail or woe! –
I feel that when the Body dies
   Its memories and feelings die;
That they from earth shall never rise ...[2]

By now, Anne's *Agnes Grey*, Charlotte's *The Professor*, and Emily's *Wuthering Heights* were all completed. Having overcome Emily's objection to the publication of her poems, apparently Charlotte had no further difficulty in persuading her to submit her novel. No doubt, by framing her great work in the novel form, Emily had admitted the possibility of writing as a means of earning a living.

In July 1846 the manuscripts of the first three Brontë novels, still attributed to Currer, Ellis and Acton Bell, started their long round of the publishers. So inexperienced and unworldly were the girls that after each rejection they ruled out the name and address of the previously solicited publisher before sending their increasingly tatty package on to the next.

Apart from being disappointed, recovering and sending their manuscripts on their way once more, the sisters were mainly preoccupied by the state of their father's eyes. By now he was virtually blind. The elderly gentleman's disability and distress were sufficiently worrying, but, as has already been noted in connection with Branwell, this was a family matter of the utmost importance. If Mr Brontë could no longer perform his duties, they would lose their home at Haworth parsonage, and their lives would become extremely precarious. He bravely continued to preach, and Mrs Gaskell gives a powerful picture of him: 'I have heard that he was led up into the pulpit, and that his sermons were never so effective as when he stood there, a grey sightless old man, his blind eyes looking straight before him, while the words that came from his lips had all the vigour and force of his best days.'[3]

During these difficult times, Arthur Bell Nicholls began to prove himself a proverbial tower of strength, and Mr Brontë grew increasingly to rely on him.

On the advice of their doctor, Charlotte and Emily travelled to the Manchester Institution for Curing the Diseases of the Eye, where they were fortunate enough to see William James Wilson, the surgeon largely responsible for the setting up of the institution. He urged them to bring their father along to see him as soon as possible, even kindly recommending to Charlotte some nearby suitable lodgings.

Charlotte and her father arrived in Manchester on 19 August, and it was decided that his eyes were quite ready for the operation, which was to take place the following week.

Having been understandably nervous about it in advance, Mr Brontë faced his ordeal with courage and patience. The operation was carried out successfully, but great care had to be taken afterwards, and although she had the help of a nurse, Charlotte spent most of her five weeks in Manchester quietly tending her father. She was worried about catering, as they were boarding themselves, and anxious about Anne and Emily, left at home to cope with Branwell. At that stage, she could not be sure what eventual improvement there would be in her father's sight; she herself was suffering from agonies of toothache, and on the very day of the operation, her novel *The Professor* had been forwarded to her with an outright rejection.

All this would have sunk most people into a despondent lethargy, but it had the effect of arousing Charlotte's determined spirit. Possibly the very sight of the book she had created, even though it had been rejected, made her realize once again that writing was a feasible profession for her. She sent *The Professor* off to another publisher and, drawing on her childhood experiences and imaginative creations, plunged without restraint or difficulty into her second novel. This was to be *Jane Eyre*. By the time she and her father returned home at the end of September, by her profiting from the enforced long hours of quiet and solitude, the new book was well under way.

As Charlotte had feared, Branwell's dissolute life had continued while she and her father were away, and soon after their return there was a frightening incident when Anne discovered him insensible with the curtains of his bed in flames. As usual, it was the practical Emily who dealt with the crisis, rushing to the kitchen for water, hauling Branwell out of bed and putting out the flames.

Although it is recorded that Emily said, 'Don't tell Papa', Mr Brontë soon got to hear about it. In a village where keeping fires going was necessary for home workers in the wool trade, he was particularly conscious of the dangers of fire and had tried to ensure there were minimal risks in his own house. His concern can be readily appreciated from the following passage of a letter he addressed to the *Leeds Mercury* in March 1844:

> You know, and those less knowing than you are must be conscious that all garments of linen, or cotton, are particularly inflammable, and that clothes of woollen, or silk, are much less so, and cannot be ignited at all without the most careless and wanton neglect ... I have been at Haworth for more than twenty years, and during that long interval of time, as far as I can remember, I have performed the funeral service over ninety or a hundred children, who were burnt to death in consequence of their clothes having taken fire, and on inquiry in every case I have found that the poor sufferers had been clothed in either cotton or linen.

Small wonder that, realizing he was beginning to endanger not only himself but the whole household, Mr Brontë now insisted on his son's sharing his own bedroom.

Much of the time Branwell stayed at home was, in fact, spent in bed, often sleeping off his excesses. It was Emily who helped him when he staggered back home, often going out at night to guide him back from the Black Bull. Anne remained her own kind self but had not the physical strength to deal with Branwell as Emily could. Moreover, the difficulties should be borne in mind of dealing with such a patient in the days before running hot and cold water, and when the one and only household lavatory was situated outside the parsonage. Disgusted and disappointed beyond expression, Charlotte made no attempt to conceal her contempt and could hardly bring herself to speak to her once adored brother.

Added to all this, Branwell had left debts at Halifax, and the family had the ignominy of 'the arrival of a Sheriff's Officer on a visit to Branwell – inviting him either to pay his debts or to take a trip to York'. The trip to York would have meant a stay in prison, so his debts were paid. 'It is not agreeable to lose money time after time in this way but it is ten times worse to witness the shabbiness of his behaviour on such occasions,' Charlotte commented bitterly.[4]

While Charlotte was immersed in *Jane Eyre*, Anne was busy with her own second novel, the uneven, powerful and always interesting *The Tenant of Wildfell Hall*. It might also be conjectured that Emily was also writing her second novel which, among other papers, perhaps Charlotte later destroyed. She always regretted the writing and the publication of

The Tenant of Wildfell Hall, considering it an almost wilful perversion of Anne's talents. She recognized its genius but was fearful about *Wuthering Heights*, and Emily's second novel would doubtless have been similarly trenchant, original and challengingly individual – if not more so. Defensive about her sisters, Charlotte seemed unable to perceive the erotic quality which sustained her own two greatest novels.

At this time of disappointment, the one bright relief was that Mr Brontë had regained strength, his sight was restored, and he was able to resume his duties. There was no longer the immediate fear that they might lose their home. Six years later, to encourage a friend, Charlotte wrote, 'Tell your papa my father was seventy at the time he underwent an operation; he was most reluctant to try the experiment – could not believe that at his age and with his want of robust health it would succeed ... He has never since ... regretted the step, or a day seldom passes that he does not express gratitude and pleasure at the restoration of that inestimable privilege of vision whose loss he once knew.'[5]

In March 1847 Charlotte reported to her friend Ellen Nussey the somewhat incredible news that, 'The Misses Robinson, who had entirely ceased their correspondence with Anne for half a year after their father's death, have lately recommenced it. For a fortnight they sent her a letter almost every day ... They speak with great affection of their mother and never make any allusion intimating acquaintance with her errors. We take special care that Branwell does not know of their writing to Anne.'[6]

From then onwards, the girls continued to write to Anne until after Branwell's death. Once again, it is difficult to believe that Branwell did not learn of this during his many visits to the Black Bull.

Apart from the reviews they attracted, there can have been few more disappointing results in the history of publishing than that of the *Poems by Currer, Ellis and Acton Bell*. In a whole year, in spite of additional advertising, only two copies were sold. Choosing some of their heroes, Wordsworth, Hartley Coleridge, De Quincey, Lockhart and Tennyson, Charlotte sent off presentation copies with a charming and honest little note, 'Before transferring the edition to the trunkmakers, we have decided on distributing as presents a few copies of what we cannot sell: and beg to offer you one in acknowledgement of the pleasure and profit we have often and long derived from your works.'[7]

Not even Charlotte, who might have had an inkling, could have imagined what priceless first editions these 'copies we cannot sell' were to become in the next century.

Disappointingly, the three novels kept winging their way back like homing pigeons. But when the sisters had almost begun to despair, in the summer of 1847, there arrived a letter from a publisher called Thomas Cautley Newby of 72 Mortimer Street, offering terms for the publication of *Wuthering Heights* and *Agnes Grey* but rejecting *The Professor*. It is not difficult to see why Newby rejected Charlotte's bleak and grey first novel which, but for her subsequent fame and in spite of its merits, would probably never have seen the light of day. His terms were far from generous, since he asked for £50 – a great deal of money in those days and made possible only by Aunt Branwell's thrift – towards the printing of an edition of 350 copies.

It can well be imagined what a lift it gave to their spirits and prospects to know that at least two of their novels were to go before the public, even if Emily's aversion to publication was still not fully overcome. Then, in August, Charlotte's much travelled *Professor* returned from a firm of publishers called Smith, Elder & Co. with an extremely encouraging letter. 'It declined, indeed, to publish that tale for business reasons, but it discussed its merits and demerits so courteously, so considerately, in a spirit so rational, with a discrimination so enlightened, that this very refusal cheered the author better than a vulgarly expressed acceptance would have done. It was added that a work in three volumes would meet with careful attention.'[8]

No doubt it cheered the author even more particularly because, with perfect timing, *Jane Eyre* was almost completed. One cannot help regretting that Emily and Anne had not waited for Smith, Elder. While their books were being printed and Newby was being dilatory, Charlotte finished *Jane Eyre* without delay and sent it to Smith, Elder. Its fate was, of course, the direct opposite to that of the poems, and one of the most dramatic events in the history of publishing.

The manuscript was first read by the recently appointed William Smith Williams, who had served his apprenticeship with Keats's publishers and had in fact waved farewell to the young poet when he embarked on his fatal journey to Rome. A reader of experience and excellent judgement, he was immediately excited by the book's compelling quality and lost no time in recommending it to his director, Mr George Smith.

At this time George Murray Smith, an extremely personable young man, was only twenty-three years of age but, due to the retirement of Mr

Elder and his father's recent death, he had been forced to undertake responsibility for the publishing company which supported not only himself but his widowed mother, three sisters and young brother. The firm's prosperity in the past had been based largely on an annual publication entitled *Friendship's Offering*: other successes had been a series of art albums, and another on scientific voyages, which had included, in 1839, Darwin's account of *The Voyage of the Beagle*.

So far, the firm of Smith, Elder had not been renowned for its novelists, but almost overnight Charlotte Brontë was to change that. Impressed by his assistant's enthusiasm, George Smith began the book early on a Sunday morning and, like so many readers since, found himself unable to go to bed until he had finished it.

By 19 October Charlotte, in her guise of Currer Bell, was writing, 'The six copies of "Jane Eyre" reached me this morning. You have given the work every advantage which good paper, clear type, and a seemly outside can supply; if it fails the fault will lie with the author; you are exempt.'[9]

Far from failing, of course, it was an immediate sensation. It is still a gripping experience to read *Jane Eyre* for the first time, but probably it is impossible for present-day readers, for whom sensationalism is an everyday affair, to imagine quite the effect the novel had at the time. Its until then unique combination of realism and underlyingly erotic romance, written by a woman as William Makepeace Thackeray, in spite of the pseudonym, immediately spotted introduced a new strain into English literature which has been endlessly attempted ever since and has never failed to win an audience. The reviewers seized upon the novel with almost unanimous praise, the sales were brisk, and speculation about the author's identity was rife. No one ever really whole-heartedly believed in the myth of the brothers Bell, and many people besides Thackeray guessed from the first that *Jane Eyre* must have been written by a woman.

Anne and Emily had to wait another few weeks before their books were published, and they were to be disappointed, above all, by Newby's failure to carry out the corrections they had made on their proofs. No doubt this was because he suddenly made haste to cash in on the success of the third mysterious Bell. 'The books are not well got up – they abound in errors of the press,' Charlotte reported to Mr Williams, with whom she was now corresponding in a frank and friendly manner.[10] But in spite of this it can be imagined with what pleasure the younger sisters received and handled the two volumes of *Wuthering Heights* and the one of *Agnes Grey* bound in deep red cloth, with their titles in gold.

All three sisters were now published novelists.

The public and critics had been puzzled before, but the puzzlement was even greater now that there were three very striking and very different Bell novels on the literary scene.

Both Ellis and Acton received encouraging notices, but the enormous interest aroused by *Jane Eyre* tended to make the mystery of authorship considered more than the intrinsic worth of the novels under review. *Agnes Grey* was generally regarded as the more pleasing, and *Wuthering Heights* the more powerful. In fact, most critics simply did not know how to assess *Wuthering Heights*, never having come across anything remotely like it before and, unfortunately, no true appreciation of Emily Brontë's brilliant achievement was published until after her death.

Writing in the *Palladium* in September 1850, Sydney Dobell recognized then that much of the novel had the quality of a poetic masterpiece and that nowhere in recent prose had he found "such wealth and economy, such apparent ease, such instinctive art".[11] Even so, he attributed the novel to the author of *Jane Eyre*.

It seems strange that such a perceptive critic failed to hear two quite different voices in these novels. While 'wealth and economy' – loading 'every rift with ore' – are among the great virtues of *Wuthering Heights* (a taut, terse narrative with scarcely a superflous word) it must be admitted that many passages of *Jane Eyre* are over-long and diffuse, particularly in the section dealing with Jane's stay in the Rivers family. From the very start, the emotional tone and the vocabulary of all three novels are entirely individual and characteristic of their authors.

Neither Emily nor Anne, for example, could possibly have written the following passage: 'I stood motionless under my hierophant touch. My refusals were forgotten – my wrestlings paralyzed. The Impossible – i.e. my marriage with St John – was fast becoming the Possible. All was changing utterly, with a sudden sweep. Religion called – Angels Beckoned – God commanded – life rolled together like a scroll – death gate's opening, showed eternity beyond it; it seemed, that for safety and bliss there, all here might be sacrificed in a second. The dim room was full of visions.'[12]

Perhaps because she was so upset and dismayed by some of the reactions to *Wuthering Heights*, Charlotte gave Mrs Gaskell the impression that Emily suffered pangs of terrible disappointment as she read the reviews of her novel. But it is hard to believe that Emily's artistic and mystical self-knowledge and confidence were so vulnerable to the ephemeral reactions of the critics of the day.

By the time the reviews were read, most probably all three sisters were engaged on new writing. Charlotte, in particular, must have been conscious of the pressure that assails all novelists setting about their second novel when their first has been a runaway and critical success. She chose her next subject with care and began researching the newspapers for themes and facts in the preparation of *Shirley*, a novel to be set in the times of the Luddites, a subject to which she had no doubt been drawn by listening to her father's vivid accounts of those days.

Anne had already been wrestling for some time with the difficult novel she felt compelled to 'burn through', *The Tenant of Wildfell Hall*.

At this time, if only because of Emily's extreme dislike of any invasion of her privacy, there was every intention that the Bell pseudonyms should be maintained. But in June 1848 Anne's second novel appeared and proved immediately successful. By then her publisher had heard of the great run *Jane Eyre* had been enjoying in America, and when he began devising means of cashing in on it, in his usual far from scrupulous way, a crisis arose.

In good faith, Smith, Elder had offered the sheets of Currer Bell's next novel to Harper Brothers of New York, only to find that they had already received a similar offer from Newby, who had asserted his belief that all the Bell novels were written by the author of *Jane Eyre*. George Smith, who knew a lot about Newby to his discredit, did not accept the story, but he wrote to Currer Bell to say that he would, understandably, 'be glad to be in a position to contradict the statement'.[13]

Clinging to Newby, when they might so easily have moved across to the reputable firm of Smith, Elder, now treating their sister so favourably, seems to have been foolish obstinacy on the part of both Emily and Anne, but at the same time it was also perhaps a natural assertion of independence. However, George Smith's letter and all the complications of ensuing publication made it plain that the Bell brothers would have to reveal their precarious secret. It would have been a simple matter to write, but Charlotte, no doubt wanting to see for herself just what sort of men were Mr Smith and Mr Williams, immediately resolved that a personal visit would be the best way of putting the record straight.

Always reluctant to leave her home, Emily, with no book at present in question, had no need to go, and in any case she was the most competent person to stay at the parsonage with her father and Branwell. So, bravely, on the very day that Charlotte received George Smith's letter, she and Anne walked the four miles through a heavy rainstorm to Keighley and caught the night train to London.

Charlotte had travelled to London and Brussels but Anne's most extensive journeys had been to Thorp Green, York and Scarborough, so the trip must have been far more momentous and exciting to her than to her sister.

They arrived at Euston on 8 July 1848 early in the morning. Drawing on her previous experience, Charlotte hailed a cab to take them to the kindly and familiar Chapter Coffee House, where she and Emily had stayed with their father and where lady guests were in the nature of a novelty. Impatient to begin their mission, they soon set off to walk to the offices of Smith, Elder. Already bedraggled from their difficult journey, they were even more so when they arrived after a fascinating hour-long walk through the city to find their destination.

In a letter to Mary Taylor, Charlotte wrote, 'We found 65 Cornhill to be a large bookseller's shop, in a street almost as bustling as the Strand. We went in, walked up to the counter ... There were a great many young lads here and there; I said to the first I could accost: "May I see Mr Smith?" He hesitated, looked a little surprised.'[14] But he was scarcely as surprised as George Smith himself, who, in the course of an extremely busy Saturday morning, understandably enough hesitated about granting an interview without appointment to two unknown ladies. But his natural kindness ensured that they were shown in.

As he described, he saw, 'two rather quaintly dressed little ladies, pale faced and anxious looking'.

'We have both come that you might have ocular proof that there are at least two of us.'[15]

Certainly George Smith must have strongly suspected that Currer Bell might be a woman, and Thackeray, who had written an enthusiastic letter to him, had scarcely a doubt of it, but it is unlikely that either of them could have imagined that such a strong work as *Jane Eyre* could have been written by the tiny, inexperienced, provincial woman who, at first sight, Charlotte Brontë seemed to be. If Smith had finally decided Currer Bell was a woman, he must have had a very different, more bold and dramatic creature in mind. Equally, Anne hardly appeared a likely author of the somewhat scandalous *The Tenant of Wildfell Hall*.

Charlotte found Mr Smith loquacious and attractive, and she was later to model her Dr John Bretton on him in *Villette*; Mr Williams, who had corresponded with her so sympathetically, she found 'a pale, mild stooping man of fifty'.[16]

George Smith's observations on both sisters are invaluable. Charlotte, he said, 'had fine eyes, but her face was marred by the shape of her mouth and by the complexion. There was but little feminine charm about her; and of this fact she was herself uneasily and perpetually conscious ... I believe she would have given all her genius and all her fame to have been beautiful.'[17] This was written with hindsight, and there can be no doubt that, had Charlotte Brontë been blessed with nothing but beauty, she would have craved genius and fame. Moreover, there was a time when Mrs Smith, George's powerful mother, was beginning to be quite alarmed about the relationship between her son and this strange lady writer, and Charlotte, with or without beauty, certainly inspired attraction and then passion in her father's curate, Arthur Bell Nicholls.

Charlotte took the lead in this encounter, and it is not surprising that George Smith found Anne 'a gentle, quiet, rather subdued person, by no means pretty, yet of a pleasing appearance. Her manner was curiously expressive of a wish for protection and encouragement, a kind of constant appeal, which invited sympathy.'[18] Most observers found Anne the prettiest of the Brontë sisters, with her pinker complexion, violet blue eyes and lighter hair, so it must be remembered that George Smith was a man about London town, used to seeing the beauties of the day in the height of fashion. If Anne had enjoyed their advantages, she might have made a very different impression.

Astounded by what he heard, Mr Smith immediately invited the sisters to stay at his family home while they were in London. This was not possible, as they had come prepared only for a brief trip, not a visit, and both were acutely aware of the problems they had left at home. But Mr Smith did insist that they should, at least, join him and his sisters at the opera to which they were going that night.

They returned to the Chapter House aglow, but Charlotte's excitement soon gave way to a thundering headache and to the mortifying realization that, although they had both brought a change from their travelling dresses, these simple garments were hardly suitable for a visit to the Opera House at Covent Garden. Her fears were realized: 'The gentlemen were in evening costume, white gloves, etc. and the ladies – two elegant young ladies, were in full dress .... They must have thought us queer, quizzical-looking beings, especially me with my spectacles.'

But still, in spite of her sick headache, she was able to feel pleasantly excited, while Anne, suitably partnered by Mr Williams, seemed as usual 'calm and gentle'. For her, the fashionable occasion and her own humble appearance were of much less importance than the chance of hearing *The Barber of Seville* beautifully performed.[19]

On Sunday Mr Williams came to escort the sisters to church at St Stephen, Walbrook, and in the afternoon Mr Smith and his mother arrived in a carriage to take them to their home at 4 Westbourne Place, Bayswater. They were warmly welcomed to this rather grand setting, with no additional guests outside the family, but, even so, Charlotte and Anne found the occasion somewhat overpowering. 'We had a fine dinner, which neither Anne nor I had appetite to eat, and were very glad when it was over.'[20]

On Monday they went to the Royal Academy Exhibition and to the National Gallery, dined again at Mr Smith's and took tea with Mr Williams. They did some shopping and, 'On Tuesday morning we left London laden with books which Mr Smith had given us, and got safely home. A more jaded wretch than I looked when I returned it would be difficult to conceive,' wrote Charlotte. It had been a crowded, exciting, nerve-racking time but extremely satisfactory. Almost as an after-thought, Charlotte observes, 'We saw Newby', which had been one of the important reasons for the visit, 'but of him more another time ...'[21] Unfortunately, nothing more about their encounter appears to have been recorded.

Various factors marred their home-coming. Anne, who had had several attacks of illness since Christmas, had caught a severe cold on the rainy walk to Keighley. Branwell was 'the same in conduct as ever. His constitution seems much shattered. Papa and sometimes all of us have sad nights with him. He sleeps most of the day, and consequently will lie awake at night.'[22] Then Emily, who had listened with delight to all that her sisters had to tell of their adventures in London, burst into a truly terrifying fury when she discovered that her identity had been revealed along with her sisters'. In a way, this was unreasonable, as once two of the authors had revealed their authorship, it must have been well nigh impossible to conceal that Ellis Bell was, in fact, a third sister. But Emily's fierce anger forced Charlotte to write a difficult letter to Mr Williams: 'Permit me to caution you not to speak of my sisters when you write to me. I mean, do not use the word in the plural. Ellis Bell will not endure to be alluded to under any other appellation that the 'nom de plume'. I committed a grand error in betraying his identity to you and Mr Smith ... the words 'we are three sisters' escaped me before I was aware. I regretted the avowal the moment I had made it; I regret it bitterly now, for I find it is against every feeling and intention of Ellis Bell.'[23]

For Anne, her first task on arriving home was to write a preface for the second edition of *The Tenant of Wildfell Hall*. Not just because of all the authorship speculation, but on its own merits as a boldly told and powerful story, Anne's second novel was to sell, at the time, better than any of the other Brontë novels, except *Jane Eyre*. Even with Newby's disreputable way of doing business, she was earning some very useful money. It must certainly have confirmed Anne in the belief that her future fulfilment and means of livelihood could be much better secured by her writing than by the drudgery of being a governess.

Even so, she had been shocked and hurt by many of the harsh criticisms and notices her book had received, which seemed to have misunderstood completely her purpose in writing it, which was preceptive not sensational. Not least among these critics, it must be said, was her sister Charlotte, who always disapproved of the book and regretted the effort it had cost her sister to write it. In her preface to the new edition, Anne spoke, as she always did, honestly and from her heart. Perhaps she hoped that, as much as anyone else, it would help Charlotte to understand. But it did not.

As the story of *Agnes Grey* was accused of extravagant over-colouring in those very parts that were carefully copied from life, with a most scrupulous avoidance of all exaggeration, so, in the present work, I find myself censured for depicting con amore, with a 'morbid love of the coarse, if not the brutal' those scenes which, I will venture to say, have not been more painful for the most fastidious of my critics to read than they were for me to describe ...

I would not be understood to suppose that the proceedings of the unhappy scapegrace, with his few profligate companions I have here introduced, are a specimen of the common practices of society – the case is an extreme one, as I trusted none would fail to perceive: but I know that such characters do exist, and if I have warned one rash youth from following in their steps, or prevented one thoughtless girl from falling into the very natural error of my heroine, the book has not been written in vain ... when I feel it my duty to speak an unpalatable truth, with the help of God, I will speak it, though it be to the prejudice of my name and to the detriment of my reader's immediate pleasure as well as my own ...

The preface ends with a reaffirmation of the separate identities of the three Bell brothers and a declaration from Anne that would be equally relevant today: '... I am satisfied that if a book is a good one, it is so whatever the sex of the author may be. All novels are, or should be written for both men and women to read, and I am at loss to conceive how a man should permit himself to write anything that would be really disgraceful to a woman, or why a woman should be censured for writing anything that would be proper and becoming for a man.'[24]

At the time, this was a startling statement. Even now, the scenes of degradation depicted in Arthur Huntingdon's decline, and his wife's terrible disillusion, are upsetting and unpleasant. Although not so strongly autobiographical as *Agnes Grey*, much of the book is clearly drawn from Anne's life. Helen's conversations with her aunt, for example, about her proposed marriage, must have mirrored some of Anne's conversations about salvation and the after-life with Aunt Branwell. Her censure of the different upbringings then considered appropriate for boys and girls, and all the elements of compensating moral laxity, were drawn from her observations of her pupils, as well of from her own brother's life. One wonders how much her descriptions of the bacchanalian indulgences of Arthur and his friends resulted not only from her experiences of Branwell but from what she might have seen or heard at Thorp Green Hall. It is certainly difficult to believe that such a scene as the following sprang solely from Anne's imagination.

'Now, Huntingdon!' exclaimed his irascible friend, 'I will not have you sitting there and laughing like an idiot!'

'Oh, Hattersley!' cried he, wiping his swimming eyes – 'you'll be the death of me.'

'Yes, I will, but not as you suppose: I'll have the heart out of your body, man, if you irritate me with any more of that imbecile laughter! – What! – are you at it yet? There! see if that'll settle you!' cried Hattersley, snatching up a footstool and hurling it at the head of his host; but he missed his aim, and the latter still sat collapsed and quaking with feeble laughter, with the tears running down his face; a deplorable spectacle indeed.

Hattersley tried cursing and swearing, but it would not do; he then took a number of books from the table beside him, and threw them, one by one, at the object of his wrath, but Arthur only laughed the more; and, finally, Hattersley rushed upon him in a frenzy, and, seizing him by the shoulders, gave him a violent shaking, under which he laughed and shrieked alarmingly. But I saw no more: I thought I had witnessed enough of my husband's degradation ...

At last he came slowly, and stumblingly, ascending the stairs, supported by Grimsby and Hattersley, who neither of them walked quite steadily themselves, but were both laughing and joking at him, and making noise enough for all the servants to hear. He himself was no longer laughing now, but sick and stupid ...[25]

By now, Branwell's own degradation was almost complete. Amazingly, in view of his state of health at the time, he had been able to make his way into Halifax and run up unpaid bills at his favourite hostelries. One of the publicans had written to Mr Brontë threatening to sue, and rather pathetically the old man had handed his son 10 shillings to settle the account, without realizing not only that this was inadequate but that the bill was one of many. Branwell wrote off immediately to Joseph Leyland to help him out of this new difficulty, assuring him that his 'receipt of money, on asking, through Dr Crosby, is morally certain'.[26] (Whether this was fact or fantasy cannot be proved but certainly Branwell was getting sums of money from somewhere.) But by now the generous and talented Leyland was himself in a very bad way. Beset by creditors, he was eventually arrested as bankrupt for a trivial sum and tragically died in Manor Gaol in January 1851. He was in no position to help Branwell Brontë.

On 4 August 1848, although Branwell was never to know the significance of this event, Lady Scott died, leaving the field clear for the vigilant and attentive Lydia Robinson to succeed her, which she did, marrying Sir Edward Dolman Scott just three months later on 8 November. It is hard to believe that Lydia Robinson, the new Lady Scott, ever spared a thought to Branwell Brontë, not in his illness, nor in his death, not, in fact until the unfortunate (from her point of view) publication of Mrs Gaskell's biography of his sister. A portrait of the new

Lady Scott shows a handsome, vivacious, confidant, middle-aged woman, evidently pleased with her new role in life.

As the following note shows, by now Branwell's world had dwindled to where the next drink was coming from. He could rely on some help in getting supplies from his father's sexton, his own lifelong friend, John Brown:

> Dear John
>   I shall feel very much obliged to you if you can contrive to give me Five Pence worth of Gin in a proper measure.
>   Should it be speedily got I could perhaps take it from you or Billy at the lane top, or, what would be quite as will, sent out for, to you.
>   I anxiously ask the favour because I know the good it will do me.
>   *Punctually* at Half-past Nine in the morning you will be paid the 5d. out of a shilling given to me then.
>   Yours P.B.B.[27]

The letter suggests that Branwell had an ally in the household, but it would be interesting to know whom he might have sent out to collect his gin and who was to give him that precious shilling.

Mrs Gaskell, whether or not she accepted too readily Branwell's myth or his very elaborately distorted fragment of truth about his relations with Lydia Robinson, had certainly talked about his last months with Mr Brontë and Charlotte and had spoken to and questioned the villagers when she was researching her book. She paints a terrible and vivid picture.

> He took opium, because it made him forget for a time more effectually than drink; and, besides, it was more portable. In procuring it he showed all the cunning of the opium-eater. He would steal out while the family were at church – to which he professed himself too ill to go – and managed to cajole the village druggist out of a lump; or, it might be, the carrier had unsuspiciously brought him some in a packet from a distance. For some time before his death he had attacks of delirium tremens of the most frightful character; he slept in his father's room, and he would sometimes declare that either he or his father should be dead before morning. The trembling sisters, sick with fright, would implore their father not to expose himself to this danger; but Mr Brontë is no timid man, and perhaps he felt he could possibly influence his son to some self-restraint, more by showing

trust in him than by showing fear ... In the morning young Brontë would saunter out, saying with a drunkard's incontinence of speech, 'The poor old man and I have had a terrible night of it; he does his best – the poor old man! but it's all over with me.' ...[28]

One September evening, Branwell's friend Grundy from his railway days journeyed out to Haworth to see him. He ordered up dinner for two at the Black Bull and sent a messenger to the parsonage to ask Branwell to join him. Instead of Branwell, Mr Brontë came to say that his son was in bed and had been unwell for a few days, when the message arrived, but was getting up and would join him shortly. Before leaving, Mr Brontë spoke of his son affectionately but with an air of hopelessness.

Thirty years later, in his *Pictures of the Past*, Grundy described, no doubt with some customary exaggeration, the vivid impression his last meeting with Branwell had left upon him:

Presently the door opened cautiously and a head appeared. It was a mass of red unkempt uncut hair, wildly floating round a great gaunt forehead; the cheeks yellow and hollow, the mouth fallen, the thin lips not trembling but shaking, the sunken eyes, once small now glaring with the light of madness – I hastened to my friend, greeted him with my gayest manner, as I knew he liked best, drew him quickly into the room and forced upon him a stiff glass of hot brandy ... Another glass of brandy and returning warmth gradually brought him back to something like the Brontë of old. He even ate some dinner, a thing which he said he had not done for long; I never knew his intellect clearer. He described himself as waiting anxiously for death – indeed longing for it ...[29]

Branwell did not have long to wait. Neither his family nor his doctor suspected the end was so close. He was in the village two days before he died, virtually wasted away, and entirely confined to his bed for only a single day. Charlotte wrote, 'He died, after twenty minutes struggle, on Sunday morning, September 24th. He was perfectly conscious till the last agony came on. His mind had undergone the peculiar change which frequently precedes death, two days previously; the calm of better feelings filled it; a return of natural affection marked his last moments ...'

When Branwell's last agony came upon him unexpectedly, his good old friend John Brown, who in some ways knew him better than anyone, was sitting with him. Grasping his hand, Branwell cried, 'Oh, John, I'm dying!'[30] There was time for John to call the family. As his father said the last prayers, to the joy of all who heard him, Branwell struggled to say 'Amen' before he died clasped in his father's arms.

Mr Brontë was acutely distressed, and in their different ways so were his sisters. Yet Branwell's release from a life that had travelled beyond redemption must have been a relief to them all.

Branwell was buried four days later. The funeral service was conducted by William Morgan, his father's old and loyal friend. It was a chilly day, and at her brother's burial Emily caught a cold.

10. With Those that I have Loved and Lost, 1848–9

Immediately after Branwell's death, Emily's nasty cold took second place to Charlotte's illness.

'It was my fate to sink at the crisis, when I should have collected my strength. Headache and sickness came on first on the Sunday; I could not regain my appetite. Then internal pain attacked me. I became at once much reduced. It was impossible to touch a morsel. I was confined to bed a week, – a dreary week. But, thank God! health seems now returning.'[1]

Besides her grief at the loss of the brother with whom she had shared so much and with whom in many ways she had been more in tune than she was with her almost twin-like sisters, Charlotte must have suffered from regret and remorse that she had not tried harder to help him. This can only have been reinforced by that glimpse of the old optimistic golden Branwell of his youth they had all seen just before the end.

Luckily, there arrived at this time to distract her the reprint by Smith, Elder of the *Poems*. Emily refused to take any interest in the second appearance of the book, which was perhaps just as well, since once again, to Charlotte's incomprehension and dismay, the reviewers failed to recognize the outstanding contribution made to the collection by 'Ellis'. But there were sales, and at last the neglected *Poems* began to make a little money.

Charlotte recovered and began to pick up the threads of her third novel, *Shirley*, in which to a certain extent she was to depict her two sisters. But Anne continued poorly while, as autumn turned into the early days of winter, it became clear that from being merely unwell Emily was becoming seriously ill. She behaved with her usual stoicism, and since she had always been the strong and healthy member of the family, living up to her nickname 'the Major', at first none of the rest of them was unduly alarmed. But as November wore on and Emily grew thin and weaker, her harsh cough ever worse, her breathing more an effort, so that it was quite impossible for her to go out even briefly to exercise the dogs, Charlotte grew frightened. She had long faced the prospect of an early death for Anne, but losing the strong sister on whom they had all so much relied was a possibility she had never contemplated.

The crisis was made worse by Emily's obdurate refusal to admit how ill she was, to take any of the medicines she knew were proving useless in Anne's case, or to see a doctor. Charlotte did her best to persuade her, even seeking advice on homoeopathic remedies, not that they or any current treatment could have proved effective at this stage, when the latent tubercular condition had emerged with terrifying speed and violence. Horrified at seeing Emily literally dying on her feet, her loving family could only stand by helplessly, praying that she would allow them to seek medical relief before it was too late.

At this time of intolerable anxiety, as if to bring the story of Thorp Green to an end as far as Anne was concerned, Mary and Elizabeth (Bessy), her two former pupils, came to see her. By now Mary was Mrs Henry Clapham, settled only four miles away at Keighley, and her sister, under pressure from her mother, soon to wed herself, was staying with her. It was a good opportunity for the two girls to drive over and see their former governess, with whom apparently they were still corresponding.

It seems that Lydia Robinson, in her haste to get her daughters off her hands before her own second marriage, had unwisely entangled Elizabeth with a certain Mr Milner, who threatened a breach of promise case and in a most ungentlemanly manner to publish the correspondence between them in the *Halifax Guardian*. This horrible possibility was averted and that case settled, at some cost, out of court. Bessy (Elizabeth Lydia) was later to marry a Mr Jessop and to bear him five surviving children, three boys and two girls. Mary's first husband died suddenly, leaving her with one little girl. She was married again to the Reverend George Pocock but was to have no more children.[2]

Whether or not Anne knew already, before their visit, of Lydia Robinson's remarriage and gratifying translation into Lady Scott, certainly the girls were full of the information now. She had been married on 8 November 1848 and had easily adapted to her agreeable new life, as is shown by a note to her agent, 'We are at Southampton seeing to the fitting out of Sir Edward's Yacht which is going to meet us at Marseilles.

Next Monday I shall be for a time at 45 Bryanston Square, London, previous to leaving England as we want to get into warmer quarters for the winter on the coast of the Mediterranean.'[3] Although this second marriage was to last only three years, through it the new Lady Scott had clearly augmented her social position, demonstrating anew a character in complete contradiction to the Lydia Branwell had constantly depicted.

Reporting the Robinson visitors to Ellen, Charlotte wrote: 'They are attractive and stylish looking girls. They seemed overjoyed to see Anne: when I went into the room, they were clinging round her like two children – she, meantime, looking perfectly quiet and passive ...'[4] As far as is known, this was the last contact Anne was to have with the Robinson family, and she must have been pleased to see them, especially Mary, for whom she had a special affection. Yet there must have been sadness too in the reminder of the hopes she had entertained for Branwell when she had first introduced him, and nothing could have held much joy for her now, when she was daily fearing a second experience of losing the one she loved most.

Frustrated by Emily's resistance, in every way she tried to help, Charlotte witnessed her suffering with 'an anguish of wonder and love'.[5] One evening, while Anne, suffering in her own more tranquil way sat sewing by the fireside, and Emily tried to make herself comfortable, leaning back in her chair to aid her breathing, Charlotte attempted to interest them in an article that had appeared in the *North American Review*, which Mr Williams had sent her: 'I studied the two ferocious authors,' she told him, 'Ellis the "man of uncommon parts, but dogged, brutal, and morose" ... looking, alas! piteously pale and wasted ... smiled half amused and half in scorn as he listened. Acton ... no emotion ever stirs him to loquacity ... only smiled too, dropping at the same time a single word of calm amazement to hear his character so darkly portrayed.'[6]

Charlotte also read to her sisters from the parcels of books Mr Smith sent down to entertain them, sometimes managing to give them a little pleasure. For all three of them, writing was impossible, and *Shirley*, once again, had to be put aside.

Mrs Gaskell's description of Emily's death cannot be paraphrased:

I remember Miss Brontë's shiver at recalling the pangs she felt when, after having searched in the little hollows and sheltered crevices of the moors for a lingering spray of heather – just one spray, however withered – to take in to Emily, she saw that the flower was not recognised by the dim and indifferent eyes ... One Tuesday morning, in December, she arose and dressed herself as usual, making many a pause, but doing everything for herself, and even endeavouring to take up her employment of sewing: the servants looked on, and knew what the catching, rattling breath, and the glazing of the eye too surely foretold; but she kept at her work; and Charlotte and Anne, though full of unspeakable dread, had still the faintest spark of hope ...

The morning drew on to noon. Emily was worse: she could only whisper in gasps. Now, when it was too late, she said to Charlotte, 'If you will send for a doctor, I will see him now.' About two o'clock she died.[7]

Emily died on 10 December 1848 at the age of thirty. Naturally enough, she did not leave a large body of work, but a group of some of the finest mystical poems in the English language, and her unique novel, which, although written in prose, is a poetic masterpiece that can be compared with the great tragic plays of Shakespeare.

Emily was reserved and enigmatic in her life to a degree that has baffled her biographers. It has been said that her refusal to seek medical aid was part of a death-wish, although it could equally well have been (in view of medical practices of the time and considering the case of John Keats) a desire for self-preservation. It has also been suggested that the circumstances of her life had stemmed the flow of her writing, but since it is known that Charlotte destroyed many of her papers, this can never be proved.

Undoubtedly, like all inspired mystics, Emily had known moments when she had gone beyond the physical limitations of her earthbound body. Her spiritual experiences certainly took her beyond the religious restrictions of her own time. Emily Brontë's inner and outward awareness could accept no restraint.

In one of the best known of her poems, she had written:

Then dawns the Invisible, the Unseen its truth reveals;
My outward sense is gone, my inner essence feels –
Its wings are almost free, its home, its harbour found;
Measuring the gulf it stoops and dares the final bound!

Oh dreadful is the check – intense the agony
When the ear begins to hear and the eye begins to see;
When the pulse begins to throb, the brain to think again,
The soul to feel the flesh and the flesh to feel the chain!

But this time for Emily there was no painful coming back, and she could remain where:

> Mute music soothes my breast – unuttered harmony
> That I could never dream till earth was lost to me.[8]

Keeper, the great dog Emily had fiercely chastised into love and obedience, howled outside her door for weeks after her death, and her simple funeral was made even more memorable by his presence. Mr Brontë led him at the head of the little procession into the family box pew, with Charlotte and Anne, the limping old Tabby and Martha Brown. Arthur Bell Nicholls, who had helped the family so much after the last unhappy months, took the service.

'We are very calm at present. Why should we be otherwise. The anguish of seeing her suffer is over; the spectacle of the pains of death is gone by; the funeral day is past. We feel she is at peace. No need to tremble for the hard frost and the keen wind. Emily does not feel them.'[9]

Emily could no longer feel them, but Anne did. Unlike her sister, she wanted to live, to go on and do more in the world, and she was what would be described as a good patient, ready to submit to examinations, painful treatments and nasty medicines.

Soon after Christmas, when, mercifully for Charlotte, Ellen Nussey was staying with them, Mr Brontë was so alarmed by Anne's state, especially in view of Emily's tragic death, that he called in Dr Teale, a lung specialist from Leeds. Ellen recalled that the patient was looking sweetly pretty and flushed, a heightened state so often present with fever. Dr Teale's examination revealed advanced consumption in both lungs, and that Anne could have only a brief while to live. She was already beyond any hope of recovery.

Mr Brontë came to sit beside his youngest daughter on the black horsehair sofa where Emily had at last consented to rest before she died. 'My *dear* little Anne!', he said, drawing her close. Quietly, Anne accepted this death sentence, which for her held the consolation and firm belief that she would be rejoining Emily and William Weightman in a better world.[10]

But as she was to write so honestly in her last poem, she was young, and she was frightened of the challenge inevitably lying soon ahead.

A dreadful darkness closes in
   On my bewildered mind;
Oh, let me suffer and not sin,
   Be tortured yet resigned ...

Thus let me serve Thee from my heart,
   Whate'er may be my written fate:
Whether thus early to depart,
   Or yet a while to wait.

If thou shouldst bring me back to life,
   More humbled I should be;
More wise, more strengthened for the strife
   More apt to lean on Thee.

Should Death be standing at the gate,
   Thus should I keep my vow;
But, Lord, whate'er my future fate,
   So, let me serve Thee now![11]

No doubt with much painful effort, this poem was finished on 28 January 1849, and it was probably the very last of Anne's creative writing.

It is only too easy to imagine what a distressing time this must have been for Charlotte. Far from recovered from the deaths of her brother and Emily, she now had to watch the slow and inexorable progress of Anne's illness in the terrible knowledge that nothing could save her. Somehow she found the courage to care for her sister with strength and tenderness.

> I can scarcely say that Anne is worse, nor can I say she is better. She varies often in the course of a day, yet each day is passed pretty much the same. The morning is usually the best time; the afternoon and evening the most feverish. Her cough is the most troublesome at night, but it is rarely violent. The pain in her arm still disturbs her. She takes the cod-liver oil and carbonate of iron regularly; she finds them both nauseous, but especially the oil. Her appetite is small indeed ... the days pass in a slow, dark march; the nights are the test; the sudden wakings from restless sleep, the revived knowledge that one lies in her grave and another not at my side but in a separate and sick bed.[12]

Dr Teale had forbidden the sisters to share a bed but had agreed to their using single beds in the same room, a compromise that was clearly unwise and dangerous for Charlotte.

The question had now become not whether Anne would die but how long she could live, and Charlotte could only pin her hopes on the end of the wintry cold and cutting winds and the coming of some sunny spring weather, when perhaps Anne might be able to venture out of the chilly and draughty house.

Since Anne was so apparently calm and resigned and giving as little trouble as was possible, Charlotte was able at least to make a fair copy of what she had written of *Shirley*, and both girls and their father welcomed the parcels of books which Mr Williams continued to send.

In March Ellen Nussey kindly wrote to ask Anne to Brookroyd for a visit, thinking that a change of air and some cosseting might help her. Anne was grateful for the suggestion but could not accept to be a burden on her friends. Yet she yearned to get away from the parsonage and all its memories, and her thoughts flew to Scarborough and the sea. She was loth to take Charlotte away from their father, but perhaps it might be possible for Ellen to accompany her. For once in her life, Anne was in possession of a little capital, recently augmented by a legacy from her godmother, Fanny Outhwaite, and could comfortably pay both their expenses for the journey and the lodgings she had enjoyed with the Robinsons at Mr Wood's establishment on St Nicholas Cliff.

The kindly Ellen was clearly ready to go, but her family put various obstacles in her way, and she spoke of delaying the trip until later in the summer. This Anne, knowing that time was not on her side, was reluctant to do.

You say May is a trying month and so say others. The earlier part is often cold enough I acknowledge, but according to my experience, we are almost certain of some fine warm days in the latter half when the laburnums and lilacs are in bloom; whereas June is often cold and July generally wet. But I have a more serious reason than this for my impatience of delay; the doctors say that change of air or removal to a better climate would hardly ever fail of success in consumptive cases if the remedy were taken in *time* but the reason why there are so many disappointments is, that it is generally deferred till it is too late. Now I would not commit this error … I think there is no time to be lost. I have no horror of death; if I thought it inevitable I think I could resign myself to the prospect, in the hope that you, dear Miss Nussey would give as much of your company as you possibly could to Charlotte and be a sister to her in my stead. But I wish it would please God to spare me not only for Papa's and Charlotte's sakes, but because I long to do some good in the world before I leave it. I have many schemes in my head for future practise – humble and limited indeed – but still I should not like them to come to nothing, and myself to have lived to so little purpose. But God's will be done ...[13]

Probably it was Mr Brontë who insisted that Charlotte as well as Ellen should accompany Anne. He knew that Tabby and Martha would care for him, Mr Nicholls was increasingly of assistance, and above all he hoped that Charlotte, who had been under such great strain, would also benefit from the change.

The journey was to be complicated because Anne wanted so much to see York Minster and, at this stage, Charlotte felt she could deny her nothing. They were due to set off on 23 May and to meet Ellen at Leeds. Waiting for them there, Ellen was full of foreboding when they failed to arrive. Sensibly she returned home and set off the next day for Haworth. It is easy to forget how difficult arrangements were to make and cancel before the days of telegrams and telephones.

Ellen arrived at the parsonage just in time to join the sisters. Anne had been too ill to travel the day before, and even though Ellen had been warned of her frailty and emaciation, she must have been shocked by the sight of her and felt she was still far too ill to travel. Bidding farewell to her father, Tabby and Martha and her faithful dog, Flossie, Anne was helped into the gig which was to take them to the station. Throughout the journey, they received the utmost kindness and consideration, and Anne's pitiful fortitude awoke the sympathies of all who saw her.

In spite of all their fears about the uncertainty of the weather, late May that year proved warm and sunny, just as Anne had hoped.

When they arrived at York and had settled into the George Hotel, Anne's first wish was to see her beloved Minster, no doubt for the spiritual help she had always found there amid its glorious splendour, but also for the most precious memories of her visit there alone with Emily. She was heard to whisper as she gazed at the beauty around her, 'If finite power can do this, what is the ...'[14] Then, fearing too much emotional excitement might weaken her, her kind companions led her away.

But probably not even York Minster, which gave her that glimpse of the possibilities of infinite power, compared with Anne's joy at once more beholding the sea. They arrived at their Scarborough lodgings on Friday 25 May, finding them comfortable and with beautiful sea views.

Although so much more tractable a patient than Emily, Anne was equally determined to carry on as normally as possible. The next morning she went to the Baths and walked back to the lodgings alone, getting back so exhausted that she fell down at the gate. In the afternoon she hired a donkey cart for a drive on the sands, insisting that Charlotte and Ellen should go off on their own, anxious that they should enjoy their holiday. They arrived back to find her characteristically chastising the donkey boy for not treating his animal with sufficient kindness.

On Sunday morning, Anne very much wanted to go to church and could not understand why both Charlotte and Ellen opposed it. However, as usual, she complied with their wishes. But they helped her walk out in the beautiful afternoon, and she sat in a sheltered seat in the sunshine while Charlotte and Ellen explored the various spots she so much wanted them to see.

Ellen recorded for Mrs Gaskell that the evening 'closed in with the most glorious sunset ever witnessed. The castle on the cliff stood out in proud glory gilded by the rays of the declining sun. The distant ships glittered like burnished gold ... The view was grand beyond description. Anne was drawn in her easy chair to the window, to enjoy the scene with us. Her face became illumined almost as much as the glorious scene she gazed upon.'[15]

Having passed a reasonably quiet night, Anne was up and dressed by seven o'clock on the Monday morning. The courageous strength of will displayed by both Anne and Emily in their last hours is sadly illustrated by the fact that they were both to die fully clad to meet the business of the day.

At eleven o'clock Anne felt a change. Sensing the presence of death, she did not know what to do for the best. On the one hand it might cause distress and embarrassment to die in the lodgings; yet on the other, was there time for her to get home? As usual, she thought nothing of her own peace of mind and comfort, only for the others.

Calmly she agreed that a physician should be sent for. With perfect composure, 'She begged him to say "How long he thought she might live; – not to fear speaking the truth, for she was not afraid to die." The doctor admitted that the angel of death was already arrived, and that life was ebbing fast. She thanked him for his truthfulness, and he departed to come again very soon. She still occupied her easychair, looking so serene, so reliant ...'[16] In fact, Anne's thoughts were all for Charlotte, and again she implored Ellen to give her as much of her company as she could, thanking them both for their kindness and attention.

Becoming restless, she was moved to the sofa, saying, ' " ... soon all will be well, through the merits of our Redeemer." Shortly after this, seeing that her sister could hardly restrain her grief, she said, "Take courage Charlotte; take courage." Her faith never failed, and her eye never dimmed till about two o'clock, when she calmly and without a sigh passed from the temporal to the eternal.'[17] Charlotte must have been struck sadly by the recollection that Emily had also died at two in the afteroon.

The kindly doctor who, in such unusual circumstances, had done all he could to help the distressed young women, was amazed at Anne's 'fixed tranquillity of spirit and settled longing to be gone. He said in all his experience he had seen no such deathbed, and that it gave evidence of no common mind.'[18]

Wanting to spare her elderly father the long journey and the pain of a third family funeral in so short a time, and knowing that Anne had been happy in the thought of being buried at Scarborough, the place where perhaps in her imagination, like Agnes Grey and Edward Weston, she had found love with William Weightman, Charlotte hurried on the arrangements.

Anne was buried on 30 May 1849 in St Mary's churchyard. Her age is given on the tombstone as twenty-eight but she was in fact twenty-nine. She must have often admired the beautiful view from that spot and would have been glad to think of her earthly remains resting there in sight of the sea.

Anne's quiet, gentle, brave, strong and unselfish character was exemplified by the dignity of her death.

The year before, with an echo of Spenser's 'Sleep after toil, port after stormy seas' and an anticipation of Tennyson's 'For tho' from out our bourne of Time and Place The flood may bear me far, I hope to see my Pilot face to face, When I have crost the bar', she had written:

However wild this rolling sea,
However wide my passage be,
How e'er my bark be tempest-tossed,
    May it but reach that haven fair,
    May I but land and wander there,
With those that I have loved and lost.[19]

11. Gone like Dreams, 1849–55

Now only Charlotte and her father were left: 'A year ago,' she wrote to Mr Williams, 'had a prophet warned me how I should stand in June 1849 ... I should have thought – this can never be endured. It is over. Branwell – Emily – Anne are gone like dreams – gone as Maria and Elizabeth went twenty years ago.'[1]

Probably Charlotte's salvation at this time was that she had a commitment with her publisher to produce *Shirley*. She was well on with it, but it needed a tremendous effort of will to take up the threads again. There was only one person nearby to help her at this desolate time – her father's curate, Arthur Bell Nicholls. But from a distance Mr Williams, Mr Smith and then Mr James Taylor, also of the publishing firm, constantly wrote to encourage her. James Taylor's interest in Charlotte went almost to the point of his wanting to make her his wife. But although Charlotte enjoyed his letters, his presence failed to captivate her, and when he went off to serve his firm in India, he went alone. It would have been impossible for Charlotte to go with him – even more impossible than the marriage that, from being out of the question, finally became a probability.

When Mr Brontë realized that his curate's kindliness towards his daughter had turned into first an affectionate and then a passionate attachment, he was appalled. It is easy to see why. Charlotte was his only remaining child, and he was justifiably proud of the fame her writing had achieved and the fact that she was beginning to be a figure in the literary world. Above all, as it proved correctly, he judged that the tiny, frail Charlotte, advancing into her late thirties, was not strong enough for marriage and the risk of bearing a child. Perhaps also feeling that, now the two of them were left alone, they should be all in all to each other, he could not understand how much his daughter had always yearned for the fulfilment of romantic love.

Shirley was published on 26 October 1849. By now Ellen had long been admitted into the authorship secret, which she had always suspected, and it would have been impossible for Charlotte to maintain it after the publication of *Shirley*, with its local setting and recognizable portraits of various familiar characters. Her identity revealed, she was to find that in her role of the author of *Jane Eyre*, considered by many an exceedingly daring and outspoken book, she received a distinctly mixed reception. Her godmother, Mrs Atkinson, cut her acquaintance; Miss Wooler, her old headmistress, generously agreed to overlook it; the broad-minded Taylors, who appeared in *Shirley* as the Yorke family, were excited and delighted.

'Jane Eyre, it appears,' she wrote to Mr Williams, 'has been read all over the district ... I met sometimes with new deference, with augmented kindness: old schoolfellows and old teachers, too, greeted me with generous warmth. And, again, ecclesiastical brows lowered thunder at me.'[2]

In many ways a fine achievement, *Shirley*, naturally enough, considering the usual difficulties of following a brilliantly successful début in addition to the grievously distressing period in which it was written, lacks the compulsive narrative drive, the underlying element of passion, and the total involvement with her leading characters which give *Jane Eyre* and *Villette* their particular vibrancy and radiance. By comparison with those exciting novels, it must be admitted that, though finely written, with some excellent scenes and characterization, including in Shirley and Caroline portraits of Emily and Anne, and, above all, a deeply felt statement of the position of women in her time, *Shirley* is dull.

None the less, although she was very sensitive about them, on the whole the reviews were favourable, and Charlotte received warm letters from Mrs Gaskell and Harriet Martineau, with both of whom she was to become friendly.

In late November Charlotte accepted George Smith's invitation, enthusiastically seconded by his mother, to stay with them in London. The two highspots of this busy visit, which included seeing Macready in *Othello* and *Macbeth* and an exhibition of the paintings of Turner, were her meetings with her hero Thackeray and the most distinguished woman writer of the day, Harriet Martineau.

Thackeray recorded, 'I remember the trembling little frame, the little hand, the great honest eyes. An impetuous honesty seemed to characterise the woman.'³ As for Miss Martineau, although she had guessed Currer Bell to be a female writer, she was astonished by the little creature she behold. 'When she was seated by me on the sofa, she cast up such a look, – so loving, so appealing, – that, in connexion with her deep mourning dress, and the knowledge that she was the sole survivor of her family, I could with the utmost difficulty return her smile, or keep my composure. I should have been heartily glad to cry.'⁴ It seems evident that Charlotte's greatest charm lay in her eloquent eyes.

She was not always easy to entertain. 'My mother and sisters found her a somewhat difficult guest,' George Smith was to write later, 'and I am afraid she was not always perfectly at her ease with them. She was very quiet and self-absorbed, and gave the impression that she was always engaged in observing and analysing the people she met.'⁵

Writing to Ellen on her return, Charlotte was conscious of this defect: 'I explained to him [George Smith] over and over again that my occasional silence was only failure of the power to talk, never of the will, but still he always seemed to fear there was another cause underneath.'⁶ One wonders whether the silences were so occasional.

As Charlotte's fame grew, so did the invitations: to visit Sir James and Lady Shuttleworth at Gawthorpe, and another visit to the Smiths in London in the beautiful weather of June 1850, during which her likeness was taken by George Richmond and she had further meetings with Thackeray. Thackeray's daughter Anne, later Lady Ritchie, Virginia Woolf's Aunt Annie, remembered vividly Charlotte's visit to their house: 'a tiny, delicate, serious, little lady, pale, with fair straight hair, and steady eyes. She may be a little over thirty; she is dressed in a little barége dress with a pattern of faint green moss. She enters in mittens, in silence, in seriousness; our hearts are beating with a wild excitement.'⁷ In fact, on this occasion Charlotte's reticence proved so formidable that after dinner Thackeray with ungallant cowardice deserted his guests and escaped to his club.

In July 1850 she enjoyed a brief and happy trip to Scotland with the Smiths. This was followed in August by a visit to the Kay-Shuttleworths, who had taken a holiday home at Windermere. It was here, at Briery Close, that she was to meet Mrs Gaskell. Charlotte had admired Mrs Gaskell's *Mary Barton* very much more than she could admit to any liking for the novels of Jane Austen. The two very different women became friends. When she wrote about her new friend, Mrs Gaskell did not mince words: 'She is ... more than ½ a head shorter than I, soft brown hair not so dark as mine; eyes (very good and expressive looking straight and open at you) of the same colour, a reddish face; large mouth and many teeth gone; altogether *plain*, the forehead square, broad, and *rather* overhanging. She has a very sweet voice, rather hesitates in choosing her expressions, but when chosen they seem without an effort, *admirable* and *just* befitting the occasion.'[8]

Soon after she arrived back at Haworth Parsonage, Charlotte received a suggestion from Smith, Elder that both pleased and grieved her. This was that they reprint her sisters' literary *Remains* and that she should reintroduce them to the public with a preface. She was delighted to think her sisters' works would be published under a respectable imprint, but greatly though she admired and recognized the quality of Emily's verse and to a lesser extent some of Anne's, and though she could enjoy and appreciate the truthfulness, especially on the life of a governess of *Agnes Grey,* she had considerable misgivings and reservations about *Wuthering Heights* and *The Tenant of Wildfell Hall.* To a certain extent, she could not help sharing in some of the criticisms that had been made concerning the books' violence and brutality. In particular, she felt that Anne had aggravated her illness by obstinately and painfully persevering in what was meant to be a cautionary tale but which was received in the wrong spirit as a shocking and sensational novel. Probably she even thought of it in those terms herself.

Mr Williams had hoped there might be some additional unpublished material that could be included, and it is not possible to say what was destroyed, but Charlotte certainly withheld a good number of both sisters's poems and removed the Gondal titles, sometimes making them difficult to understand out of context. She may have feared that revealing Gondal might have lead to the discovery of Angria. Worst of all, she took it upon herself to edit the poems, changing and cutting where she thought fit. Beyond all this, going through their works again, poring over their thoughts and handwriting, looking back on their brief lives, revived for Charlotte all the anguish and suffering and increased her own sense of loneliness and loss.

Charlotte may never have fully understood either of her sisters in the way they understood each other, but her memoirs of Emily and Anne published as introductions to the 1850 edition of *Wuthering Heights* and

Agnes Grey, with selections from their poems (*The Tenant of Wildfell Hall* was not reprinted at this time), speak eloquently of her love for them.

'My sister Emily loved the moors. Flowers brighter than the rose bloomed in the blackest of the heath for her; out of a sullen hollow in a livid hill-side her mind could make an Eden. She found in the bleak solitude many and dear delights: and not the least and best loved was – liberty.'

Charlotte had found the religious struggles Anne had described in her poems very saddening, 'as if her whole innocent life had been passed under the martyrdom of an unconfessed physical pain'. But she was consoled by Anne's unclouded hour of dying, when she had rested on the sure and steadfast conviction of salvation 'by which she was enabled to bear what was to be borne – patiently – serenely –victoriously'.

December 1850 saw Charlotte enjoying a most congenial week with Harriet Martineau at the Knoll at Ambleside, the beautiful home Harriet was justly proud of having paid for entirely by her writing. She seems to have been an admirable hostess. 'Her visitors enjoyed the most perfect liberty; what she claims for herself she allows them. I rise at my own hour, breakfast alone (she is up at five, and takes a cold bath, and a walk by starlight, and has finished breakfast and got to her work at 7 o'clock). I pass the morning in the drawing-room, she in her study.'[9]

In the afternoons and evenings, the two writers spent a more sociable time, getting to like and admire each other, and no doubt enjoying their arguments about religion. Harriet was a declared atheist, while Charlotte remained a convinced believer, totally rejecting what she described as 'a hopeless blank'.[10] Similar discussions between Harriet and Emily might have been even more interesting could Emily have been prevailed upon to speak.

Still finding herself unable to make a good start on her next novel, in May 1851, Charlotte went to stay with the Smith family in London again. She attended Thackeray's lecture on the English Humorists, where, to her dismay and embarrassment, he caused her to be recognized; she went to the Crystal Palace; she watched the great Rachel acting; she saw Cardinal Wiseman and heard him speak. Her prejudice against Roman Catholics remained unabated: 'He has a very large mouth with oily lips, and looks as if he would relish a good dinner with a bottle of wine after it.

He came swimming into the room smiling, simpering and bowing like a fat old lady, and sat down very demure in his chair, and looked the picture of a sleepy hypocrite.'[11]

On her way home from this London visit, Charlotte paid the first of her visits to the comfortable and well-run home of Mrs Gaskell and her family in Victoria Park, Manchester. The two novelists met again in cordial friendship and complete harmony. Apart from her sisters, Mary Taylor and Ellen Nussey, Elizabeth Gaskell was to prove the most congenial woman Charlotte was ever to meet. Different though they were in appearance, life and background, they immediately became close friends. To find a married woman friend with children, who had suffered the loss of a child, to whom she could confide the problems of her life and work (now that she had lost her sisters; in the absence of Mary Taylor, so impossibly far away; on her own intellectual level in a way that Ellen Nussey, dear though she was, never could be) was a wonderful boon to Charlotte at this desolate time, when she had begun to feel she might never write again.

Charlotte was to enjoy sharing Mrs Gaskell's family life again on two other visits, in March 1853 and May 1854. In September 1853 Mrs Gaskell visited Haworth. When she left, Charlotte wrote: 'The house felt very much as if the shutters had been suddenly closed and the blinds let down. One was sensible during the remainder of the day of a depressing silence, shadow, loss, want. However if the going away was sad, the stay was very pleasant and did permanent good. Papa, I am sure, derived real benefit from your visit; he has been better ever since.'[12]

It seems very likely that this friendship with the generous and warm-hearted Mrs Gaskell, who was also a professional writer Charlotte very much respected, helped her to gather courage and begin work on *Villette*, when she was once again able to tell her story with that vivid passion which had made such a success of *Jane Eyre*. Much of Charlotte's own life history again went into *Villette*. George Smith and his mother were the models, only too clearly recognizable, for Graham Bretton and his. Lucy Snowe was Charlotte herself, while that splendid *tour de force* of a character, Paul Emanuel, was an idealized version of M. Heger.

Villette, in fact, proved not much easier to write than *Shirley* had been, largely because it was interrupted so often by its author's ill health, yet it proved far more successful. The book was probably started some time in 1851; on 5 January 1853 Charlotte went to London to help see it through the press. She stayed there nearly a month, and *Villette* was published on 28 January 1853. It was an immediate success, as it deserved to be. Even the sensitive Charlotte could not complain of her reviews: 'I think I ought to be and feel I *am*, very thankful ... that in the Literary Gazette is as good as any author can look for.'[13]

Unfortunately, Harriet Martineau's review in the *Daily News* was to bring her friendship with Charlotte to an abrupt end. Harriet, who gave the book much praise, disliked her handling and the predominance of the love interest. Charlotte bridled: 'If man or woman should be ashamed of feeling such love, then there is nothing right, noble, faithful, truthful, in this earth ... To differ from you gives me keen pain.'[14]

Although Charlotte was luckily never to know this, Thackeray felt much the same: 'I can read a great deal of her life as I fancy in her book, and see that rather than have fame, rather than any earthly good or mayhap heavenly one she wants some Tomkins or another to love her and be in love with. But you see she is a little bit of a creature without a penny worth of good looks, thirty years old I should think, buried in the country, and eating up her own heart there, and no Tomkins will come.'[15]

In fact, Charlotte was so annoyed with Harriet because to a certain extent she had gone to the heart of the matter. But what neither Harriet nor Thackeray could know was that for a long while a very respectable Tomkins had been waiting in the wings.

Although Mr Nicholls had long admired and been falling in love with Charlotte, probably she took little notice of him, not having a great opinion of curates in general, until he revealed he had enjoyed *Jane Eyre* and, better still, when the book was under fire, had very much appreciated *Shirley*, much to her surprise, finding her descriptions of the curates hilariously amusing. A man who could laugh uproariously, as his landlady reported, at a caricature of himself, must have humour and generosity of spirit. From his photographs, he seems to have been a somewhat heavy-looking but handsome and distinguished man. Mrs Gaskell, who, of course, met him, described him as 'a grave, reserved, conscientious man, with a deep sense of religion, and of his duties as one of its ministers'.[16]

He finally summoned up courage to propose on 13 December 1852. 'He stopped in the passage: he tapped: like lightning it flashed upon me what was coming ... Shaking from head to foot, looking deadly pale, speaking low, vehemently yet with difficulty – he made me for the first time feel what it costs a man to declare affection where he doubts response.'[17]

No doubt equally shaken herself, Charlotte promised to give him an answer the next day. Clearly, however much she pitied him, if she had not felt tempted, Charlotte must have said a firm 'No' straight away. She could have had little doubt what her father's response to the suggestion would be, even if its violence shocked her so much that she agreed to write her refusal to Mr Nicholls the very next day. All her small circle admitted to the secret seemed equally opposed to the match. No doubt the fierceness of the opposition and a sense of its unfairness, as is so often the case, finally strengthened Charlotte's resolve.

At first the rejected Mr Nicholls proposed rushing off to do good deeds in Australia. He got as far as handing in his resignation to Mr Brontë, and he left Haworth at the end of May for a new post at Kirk Smeaton, not so very far away. His tearful farewell to the parishioners on the Whit Sunday and his final leavetaking show him to be emotionally very much akin to the woman with whom he had fallen in love: 'Remembering his long grief, I took courage and went out trembling and miserable. I found him leaning against the garden door in a paroxysm of anguish, sobbing as women never sob. Of course I went straight to him. Very few words were interchanged, those few barely articulate.'[18] From that moment Mr Nicholls' cause was won. It was then only a question of perseverance and time.

Tremulously and with many fears and reservations, Charlotte Brontë married Arthur Bell Nicholls on Thursday 29 June 1854. Much of Mr Brontë's opposition to his new son-in-law had been eroded by his dislike of the curate who had succeeded him and made his life a misery. Though he was reluctant to admit it, it was a great relief that the curate who had served him so faithfully for eight years was coming back, now as his son-in-law. Even so, he could not bear to give his only remaining daughter away, and finding there was no bar to it, her old headmistress, Miss Wooler, performed this office.

As a bride, Charlotte looked like a snowdrop, it was said, in her white muslin dress bordered with green ivy leaves, with its pretty matching bonnet which can still be seen in the Brontë parsonage museum. Arthur Bell Nicholls took her off proudly on their honeymoon journey to his own country – which was, in a way, hers. Like many hesitant brides, Charlotte fell deeply in love with her husband after her marriage, and their honeymoon was a loving and happy voyage of discovery. For some reason, Mr Brontë had felt that his now famous daughter was marrying beneath her, but Charlotte was to find that the Nicholls family was both respected and professional, a far cry indeed from her father's Irish origins.

If only Charlotte's health might have been strengthened and maintained, there is no reason to believe that she would not have enjoyed an exceptionally happy married life, combined with her career as a writer. That she was very far from written out is demonstrated by the intriguing fragment of her last, unfinished novel *Emma*. Perhaps, now that she was purged of autobiographical experience, she might have gone on to create the different style of novel that *Emma* seems to suggest. But, as Mr Brontë had rightly feared, Charlotte quickly became pregnant and most probably fell a victim to hyperemesis gravidarum, an exaggerated condition of the nausea and sickness which many women suffer in early pregnancy and which Charlotte, particularly at her age, did not have the stamina and constitution to overcome.[19]

In her brief married life Charlotte suffered the loss of two old friends. Before Christmas Anne's beloved Flossy 'drooped for a single day, and died quietly in the night without pain'. After a cosseted life, Flossy went to join Emily's Keeper, who had gone before, in the garden. As Charlotte wrote to Ellen, describing the severing of this last link with Anne: 'Perhaps no dog ever had a happier life or an easier death.'[20]

Happily, old Tabby Aykroyd was spared the great sadness of her mistress's death. By this time Charlotte could no longer have the responsibility of caring for her, and she died at her sister's home, on 17 February 1855, after a lifetime of faithful service with the Brontë family.

In spite of her husband's care and tenderness and her own great desire to live on and enjoy her marriage, for poor Charlotte there was nothing to be done. In hope and courage, she endured a terrible period of sickness and suffering, until weakness, and no doubt the underlying family curse of consumption defeated her. Wakening to the sight of her kind and devoted husband praying by her side one day made her realize the danger of her condition, 'Oh!' she whispered forth, 'I am not going to die, am I? He will not separate us, we have been so happy.'

As Mrs Gaskell wrote, 'Early on Saturday morning, March 31st, the solemn tolling of Haworth churchbell spoke forth the fact of her death to the villagers who had known her from a child, and whose hearts shivered within them as they thought of the two sitting desolate and alone in the old grey house.'[21]

Mr Brontë had known the bitter sorrow of losing his wife and all his six gifted children, and yet, in a curious way, at the end he had been blessed. He was to survive his daughter by six more years, and during this time he was loyally served by her husband, the man he had been so reluctant to take as his son-in-law. Bitterly though Patrick Brontë had opposed her marriage, Charlotte's husband was all that remained of his family, her last gift to him. When this father-in-law, died, at the age of eight-four, at last Arthur Bell Nicholls was free to go home to his own country, where he left the Church to become a gentleman farmer, and after more than forty years there was no longer a Brontë at Haworth parsonage.

It speaks well of them both to learn that Mr Nicholls and the faithful Martha Brown remained friends, and after his return to Banagher she often paid long visits there.

More than ten years after his wife's death, Mr Nicholls married his cousin, Mary Anne Bell, whom Charlotte had met on her honeymoon and who was was always to understand and honour her husband's loving memories of his first brief marriage. They were to be happy together for forty years, for Mr Nicholls was to survive into the twentieth century, dying in 1906, his death ending any living link with the tragic and triumphant Brontës.

12. Peaceful Resolution

All the children of Patrick and Maria Brontë were unusually gifted. Mr Brontë was always to believe that, had she lived, his eldest daughter, Branwell's beloved Maria, might have proved the greatest genius of them all. As their lives happened, it is Emily who is now universally accorded that accolade. She was the exceptional member of her exceptional family, although her reputation was surpassed in their own time by that of her sister Charlotte.

The two great Brontë sisters have their established places in the history of English literature. Emily as poet and mystic, and poetic novelist. Charlotte as the first, and still supreme, exponent of the romantic novel.

Whether Anne and Branwell would have continued to receive any attention without the fame of their sisters is debatable, but undoubtedly they both have claims to be studied in their own right.

As 'Benjamin Wiggins', Branwell described his youngest sister as 'nothing, absolutely nothing ... next door to an idiot.'[1] She was, in fact, a much stronger character than either he or Charlotte ever recognized. Emily was not deceived, and she and Anne formed the most permanent partnership in the family, which was only weakened towards the end of Emily's life, when their work had gone before the public and Anne could no longer follow her sister in her increasing isolation and mysticism. Her own belief, through her sufferings and doubtings, had become simplified into the Christian conviction that every sinner would find salvation in the life to come.

Many of her poems were written to fit into the Gondal saga; some of them may have been lost. Emily in her finest poems, was a great poet, but many will feel that Anne's because of their unselfconscious simplicity and utter lack of pretentiousness, are more to be admired than Charlotte's or even Branwell's.

She wrote a good deal on religious themes, almost as if in these she was discovering her own position, arguing with herself. Although she was sometimes full of sadness and near despair, many of the poems speak of her joy in her natural surroundings and compassion for animal life. Perhaps alone of the sisters, she was able to express in her own characteristic way, her real-life experience of true and enduring human love, and one that might well have been reciprocated and requited, had only William Weightman lived.

The temptations to quote from her poetry are endless, but the following extracts have been chosen to illustrate these points. This is the concluding verse from the long poem of twenty-seven eight-line stanzas called 'The Three Guides', written in 1847, in which Anne describes the Spirit of Earth, the Spirit of Pride, in which it has been considered she reflects many of Emily's attitudes and characteristics, and the Spirit of Faith:

> Spirit of Faith, I'll go with thee!
>   Thou, if I hold thee fast,
> Wilt guide, defend, and strengthen me,
>   And bear me home at last:
> By thy help all things I can do,
>   In thy strength all things bear, –
> Teach me, for thou art just and true;
>   Smile on me, thou are fair![2]

The following verse recalls the scene in *Agnes Grey* when the governess is forced to kill the fledgling birds to save their suffering:

> But I would rather be the hare
> That, crouching in its sheltered lair,
>   Must start at every sound:
> That forced from cornfields waving wide
> Is driven to seek the bare hillside,
> Or in the tangled copse wood hide,
>   Than be the hunter's hound![3]

Anne's poem 'Severed and Gone' very likely had its place in the Gondal saga. In its more gentle way, it is also reminiscent of the spirit of *Wuthering Heights* and influenced by memories of her own dream of love:

Severed and gone, so many years,
　　And thou art still so dear to me,
That throbbing heart and burning tears
　　Can witness how I clung to thee?

I know that in the narrow tomb
　　The form I loved was buried deep,
And left in silence and in gloom
　　To slumber out its dreamless sleep ...

A few cold words on yonder stone,
　　A corpse as cold as they can be;
Vain words and mouldering dust alone, –
　　Can this be all that's left of thee?

Oh, no! thy spirit lingers still
　　Where'er thy sunny smile was seen;
There's less of darkness, less of chill
　　On earth, than if thou hadst not been.

Thou breathest in my bosom yet,
　　And dwellest in my beating heart;
And while I cannot quite forget,
　　Thou, darling, canst not quite depart.[4]

These are lines that can always be echoed by anyone who has suffered a
deeply felt bereavement.

But it is happier to quote Anne Brontë, the poet, in a very different
mood, in a very different rhythm from the pale grey creature she is so
often depicted as having been and which she was so very far from being.
These 'Lines Composed in a Wood on a Windy Day' in the Long
Plantation at Thorp Green, on 30 December 1842, show her in the
vigorous form her spirit would surely have dictated more often if only she
had enjoyed a happier life and more robust health:

My soul is awakened, my spirit is soaring
And carried aloft on the wings of the breeze;
For above and around me the wild wind is roaring,
Arousing to rapture the earth and the seas.

The long withered grass in the sunshine is glancing,
The bare trees are tossing their branches on high;
The dead leaves, beneath them, are merrily dancing,
The white clouds are scudding across the blue sky.

I wish I could see how the ocean is lashing
The foam of its billows to whirlpools of spray;
I wish I could see how its proud waves are dashing,
And hear the wild roar of their thunder today![5]

Once publication had been decided upon, the three Brontë sisters soon proved that, artistic considerations apart, novel writing offered them their best hope of earning their own livings. In the way they loved best, they could become financially independent, eventually even affluent. There was no longer any need for them to struggle along in uncongenial employment.

Brief though it is, Anne's first novel, *Agnes Grey,* is unforgettable.

No doubt George Moore exaggerated when he described it as 'the most perfect prose narrative in English literature ... in which style, characters and subject are in perfect keeping'. But most readers of this truthful piece of fictionalized autobiography will agree with him that it is 'as simple and beautiful as a muslin dress.'[6]

Anne set her heroine, Agnes Grey, in a home very different from her own, but her two posts as governess are faithfully described. Suffering so silently from the loss of the man she loved, Anne, the novelist, permitted herself the happiness of uniting Agnes with the worthy Edward Weston.

> Edward, by his strenuous exertions, has worked surprising reforms in his parish, and is esteemed and loved by its inhabitants as he deserves; for whatever his faults may be as a man (and no one is entirely without) I defy anyone to blame him as a pastor, a husband, or a father.
>
> Our children, Edward, Agnes, and little Mary, promise well; their education, for the time being, is chiefly committed to me; and they shall want no good thing that a mother's care can give. Our modest income is amply sufficient for our requirements: and by practising the economy we learnt in harder times, and never attempting to imitate our richer neighbours, we manage not only to enjoy comfort and contentment

ourselves, but to have every year something to lay by for our children, and
something to give to those who need it.[7]

In this passage Anne described the very life she would have loved for
herself. That she wanted children is clear from her moving poem *Dreams,*
written in 1845:

> Then I may cherish at my breast
>   An infant's form beloved and fair;
> May smile and soothe it into rest,
>   With all a mother's fondest care.
>
> How sweet to feel its helpless form
>   Depending thus on me alone:
> And while I hold it safe and warm,
>   What bliss to think it is my own! ...
>
> To feel my hand so kindly prest,
>   To know myself beloved at last;
> To think my heart has found a rest,
>   My life of solitude is past.[8]

That she named one of her fictional children Mary supports the belief
that in Mary Robinson she had found one child she could love.

From her correspondence, it is well known that Charlotte Brontë had
not read any of the works of Jane Austen until, in a review of *Recent
Novels* including *Jane Eyre,* G.H. Lewes directed her attention to the
earlier author.

> Why do you like Miss Austen so very much? [she asked]. "I am puzzled on
> that point. What induced you to say that you would rather have written
> *Pride and Prejudice,* or *Tom Jones,* than any of the Waverley Novels?
>
> I had not seen *Pride and Prejudice* till I read that sentence of yours, and
> then I got the book. And what did I find? An accurate, daguerreotyped
> portrait of a commonplace face! A carefully-fenced, highly cultivated
> garden, with neat borders and delicate flowers; but no glance of a bright,
> vivid physiognomy, no open country, no fresh air, no blue hill, no bonny
> beck.[9]

It is easy to understand that Jane Austen's restraint was uncongenial to the passionate Charlotte, but lovers of Elizabeth Bennett must always feel that this particular criticism is unjust: 'Elizabeth continued her walk alone, crossing field after field at a quick pace, jumping over stiles and springing over puddles with impatient activity, and finding herself at last within view of the house, with weary ancles, dirty stockings, and a face glowing with the warmth of exercise.'[10]

The brilliant economy of the first brief chapter of *Pride and Prejudice* may not have appealed to Charlotte, but it certainly might have attracted Anne. There are several hints in her novels that she may have read the works of Jane Austen, possibly from the library to which Mrs Robinson subscribed.

With their love of Cowper, their clear-eyed view of children, their religious persuasion, their dry sense of humour, the two novelists, both from a parsonage, would have found much in common. For example, 'Soon after tea, Mary Ann went to bed, but Tom favoured us with his company and conversation till eight.'[11] The dreadful Tom's *favouring* them with his company, has a ring of Mary Bennett's *delighting* the company with her playing, long enough.

This description of Jane Wilson might almost be of Jane Fairfax from *Emma*: 'Their sister Jane was a young lady of some talents, and more ambition. She had, at her own desire, received a regular boarding school education superior to that any member of the family had obtained before. She had taken the polish well, acquired considerable elegance of manners, quite lost her provincial accent, and could boast of more accomplishments than the vicar's daughters. She was considered a beauty besides: but never for a moment could she number me among her admirers ...'[12]

Emma Woodhouse did not admire Jane Fairfax any more than Gilbert Markham, the hero of *The Tenant of Wildfell Hall*, cared for his neighbour's daughter, Jane Wilson.

It is not surprising that in their time both *Wuthering Heights* and *The Tenant of Wildfell Hall* were considered extremely violent books. Even today, many passages in both books still have a jarringly ugly ring, surprising at the time had they been written by men but shocking when it was discovered that their authors were sheltered young spinsters.

'Terror made me cruel; and, finding it useless to attempt shaking the creature off, I pulled its wrist on to the broken pane, and rubbed it to and fro till the blood ran down and soaked the bedclothes; ...'[13]

' "There's a tigress!" exclaimed Mrs Linton, setting her free, and shaking her hand with pain. "Begone, for God's sake, and hide your vixen face. How foolish to reveal those talons to *him*! Can't you fancy the conclusions he'll draw? Look, Heathcliff! they are instruments that will do execution – you must beware of your eyes." '

' "I'd wrench them off her fingers, if they ever menaced me," he answered brutally, when the door had closed after her.'[14]

Generations of readers have been puzzled by the practical details of Heathcliff's transformation from poor waif to sophisticated man.

In an article in the *Transaction of the Bronte Society*,[15] Joan Quarm makes two interesting suggestions. She speculates that after his flight from Wuthering Heights, Heathcliff's sudden acquisition of wealth may have been gained in the exceedingly lucrative opium trade, thriving at the time of which Emily was writing. Moreover, she suggests that Heathcliff's final and terrible dissolution may have been due to his becoming an addict himself. She had seen Branwell in the throes of opium addiction, as had Anne, and had first hand experience of the symptoms.

'Recollecting that opium addicts often die by asphyxiation because they simply stop breathing,' she points to Heathcliff's words, 'I have to remind myself to breath – almost to remind my heart to beat ... I have a single wish, and my whole being and faculties are yearning to attain it ... it has devoured my existence.'

Branwell's addictive habits certainly contributed to *Wuthering Heights* and *The Tenant of Wildfell Hall*. ' ... though he refused to drink like an honest Christian, it was well known to me that he kept a private bottle of laudanum about him, which he was continually soaking at – or rather, holding off and on with, abstaining one day, and exceeding the next – just like the spirits.'[16]

'In his desperate eagerness, he seized the bottle and sucked away, till he suddenly dropped from his chair, disappearing under the table amid a tempest of applause. The consequence of this imprudence was something like an apoplectic fit, followed by a rather severe brain fever.'[17]

The Tenant of Wildfell Hall, in spite of being a somewhat awkwardly constructed book, is still worthwhile reading. It is marred by the fact that its hero and part-narrator, Gilbert Markham, does not quite succeed as a character. The unhappy heroine, Helen Huntingdon, is far more effective, and in this book Anne Brontë speaks in a very advanced and liberated way for the time about education, the existing inequalities in marriage and the need for women to be able to earn their own living.

'You would have us encourage our sons to prove all things by their own experience, while our daughters must not even profit by the experience of others. Now I would have both so to benefit by the experience of others, and the precepts of a higher authority, that they should know beforehand to refuse the evil and choose the good, and require no experimental proofs to teach them the evil of transgression. I would not send a poor girl into the world, unarmed against her foes, and ignorant of the snares that beset her path; nor would I watch and guard her, till, deprived of self-respect and self-reliance, she lost the power of the will to watch and guard herself.'[18]

It has been said that the character of Arthur Huntingdon was drawn from the sad life of Branwell Brontë, but though it is certain that Branwell's drugged and drunken career helped Anne in her description of such scenes in her book, and that she perhaps portrayed in it the indulgent upbringing that had initiated Branwell's decline, Arthur Huntingdon, with his insidious influence on his friend, Lord Lowborough, his adulterous betrayal of his wife and friend, his steady progress from agreeable charmer to vicious dissolute, without any trace of humane or artistic aspirations, displays none of Branwell Brontë's redeeming attributes.

Forced to leave the husband she had once so much loved, Helen Huntingdon has the compassion to return to him when he lies, terrified, awaiting death.

'How could I endure to think that that poor trembling soul was hurried away to everlasting torment? It would drive me mad! But, thank God, I have hope – not only on a vague dependence on the possibility that penitence and pardon might have reached him at the last, but from the blessed confidence that, through whatever purging fires the erring spirit may be doomed to pass – whatever fate awaits it, still, it is not lost, and God, who hateth nothing that He hath made, will bless it in the end!'[19]

Anne concludes her turbulent tract happily with the union of Gilbert and Helen, blessed by Helen's aunt: 'I hope God will prosper your union, and make my dear girl happy at last. Could she have been contented to remain single, I own I should have been better satisfied; but if she must marry again, I know of no one, now living and of a suitable age, to whom I would more willingly resign her than yourself, or who would be more likely to appreciate her worth and make her truly happy, as far as I can tell.'[20]

'As for myself,' Gilbert says, 'I need not tell you how happily my Helen and I have lived together, and how blessed we still are in each other's society, and in the promising young scions that are growing up about us.'[21]

Just as *Wuthering Heights* ends in peaceful resolution, with the union of Catherine Heathcliff and Hareton Earnshaw and 'the sleepers in that quiet earth', so *The Tenant of Wildfell Hall* changes from a theme of degradation to one of hope. Unfortunately, Branwell Brontë's life had changed from a theme of hope to one of the utmost degradation.

Branwell suffered from being the only boy in the family. Had he been sent away to persevere with the rough and tumble of a school, he might have been better able to cope with life, but it is easy to understand why Mr Brontë decided that his frail only son was perhaps too sensitive for nineteenth-century schoolboy life.

Although Mr Brontë gave his son a good grounding in classical education at home, encouraged his interest in music and paid for expensive lessons in art, he failed to instil in the boy any sense of self-discipline. Yet Branwell produced in his short life a considerable volume of work. He was not lazy, but he was unable to cope with failure. As each of his various enterprises proved unsuccessful, so his fragile store of confidence and the will to start again deserted him. Largely because social life in Haworth began and ended at the Black Bull, he early acquired an addiction to stimulants. He was, above all, a brilliant talker, and his talents were displayed to their best in this ambience.

A close reading of his life suggests that he may have had homosexual tendencies. Apart from a brief flirtation with the forthright and attractive Mary Taylor, who might have been so good for him, and which was to end as soon as she gave a hint that his apparent interest was reciprocated, there is no mention of any woman in Branwell's life until his disastrous entry into the Robinson family. As has been seen, it is now possible only to conjecture what really took place there, but even if there was for a while some kind of sentimental attraction between Lydia Robinson and her son's versatile tutor, it is clear that there was never the passionate and tragic relationship between them which, after his dismissal, was the myth on which Branwell based the remnant of his life. Lydia Robinson's subsequent behaviour puts that beyond any doubt.

Branwell's problem was that he was gifted in too many directions. If only he had applied himself strictly and earnestly to develop one of his talents, he might have succeeded as a writer, an artist or a musician, but he dissipated his abilities, much as he did his life.

As has been said, some of his poetry reaches a level which enabled it to be mistaken for Emily's. His translations from Horace have been considered among the best English versions of the Latin poet. Here is another short and graceful example:

XXIII To Chloe

Why, whenever she can spy me,
Like a fawn will Chloe fly me?
Like a fawn its mother seeking
O'er the hills, through brambles breaking;
Frightened if the breezes move
But a leaflet in the grove;
Or a branch the Zephyr tosses;
Or its path a Lizard crosses;
Nothing can its fear dissemble
Heart and knees together tremble.
  Stop my love; Thou needst not fear me,
For I follow not to tear thee
Like the lion, prowling o'er
Far Letulia's savage shore:
Stop – Thy budding charms discover
Tis thy time to choose a lover.[22]

In translating from the Latin, Branwell was held down to a discipline. Unfortunately, unlike his sisters, when writing more freely he was not able to break away from the bad habits developed during his long sojourn in the dizzy, uninhibited world of Angria. He was a self-indulgent writer, not sufficiently critical of his own productions. Even so, it is possible to feel that if only Charlotte had drawn him into the family scheme for publishing, he might still have been able to redirect his life, find a new resolve and purpose, and some success. It is difficult to believe he was totally unaware of what was going on in this close-knit family in the intimacy of their small home and village and that he did not feel rejected, left out in the cold. Whether or not his health would have improved is another matter. Never robust, he had done his best to undermine his own constitution, and it was probably already too late for him to reform.

Quite near to the end of his life, he was still working on poems and trying to push ahead with his projected three-volume novel *And the Weary are at Rest,* of which the best thing seems to have been the title. He was not able to succeed, as each of his sisters did, in lifting his tale above one of his Angrian Chronicles, from a private fantasy into the reality of human experience.

Anyone who has read the fragment of the novel which remains is in a position to refute instantly the suggestion that Branwell might have had anything to do with the writing of *Wuthering Heights.* It is true that there is one point of similarity, the character of Emily's Joseph to Branwell's Bob: 'Naw, Maister, Aw tak the blessed book, or owd John Wesley's hymns, or ought else yaw like to witness that Aw wor there and then filling your hampers and feeding yaw're dogs. For me – me – me that's getten to age Aw hev getten to – to be called a follower o'woman is railley – nay it's beyond raison!'[23] But it is only too likely that Emily and Branwell based these two abrasive, scripture-invoking old rascals on a local character known to them both.

In *And the Weary are at Rest,* Branwell tried unsuccessfully to blend three elements: his old Angrian chronicles, a cynical comical skit on the Wesleyans, and a high-flown version of his story of his love for Lydia Robinson. For a reader unfamilar with this background, it can only be incoherent, tedious and virtually meaningless. No wonder Branwell gave it up in despair, being himself the best judge of its hopelessness. His narrative technique, dialogue and characterization give little promise that he could have succeeded with a full-length novel, but there are patches of attractive prose, and there is amusement to be gained from his description of the Special Extraordinary Meeting of the Wesleyan Society. Apart from his poetry, it seems he might have been better equipped in prose to handle short stories or humorous essays on topical themes. If he could have avoided the taverns, almost an occupational hazard with his likeable personality, he might have made a good journalist. He had retained an active interest in politics. This passage has an almost Shelleyan ring: 'Another clime which God has favoured – which he has blessed with small gratitude received in return – a clime that has seized the ruins and will direct the progress of earthly improvement. That clime, too, I must plead for. I plead for wealth changed to pride – power changed to tyranny – religion changed to hypocrisy – truth changed to falsehood – population changed to corruption – knowledge obtained only to work the deeds of darkness. I plead for Europe.'[24]

The work peters out on a more romantic note, with a prayer from Maria Thurston, who is adulterously in love with Alexander Percy – or, no doubt, in his imagination, Lydia Robinson suffering similarly for Branwell Brontë:

> My God, I cannot cast him aside. I should die if I promised it. I long to be his own, but I have, through my life longed to be Thine own. I cannot be both, and now I must try to long to be in my grave ...
>
> Forgive me if I pray for him this night when I shall not dare to pray for myself. Forgive me if my eyes turn from the daily repeated scene of sorrow to the seldom coming hour of joy. I ask Thee to forgive me, but I dare not hope it, so I must entirely trust myself to my darkening fate and to Thine own Almighty Power.'[25]

Like Emily and Anne, Branwell was gifted musically. He frequently played the organ at Haworth church, and there seems little doubt that, had he concentrated on music, he could have made a living, playing and teaching, even perhaps composing. There must have been some suitable openings in this direction on which this clearly likeable and engaging young man might have based a career.

But his most spectacular failure was, of course, the one which occurred at the outset and which, unfortunately, set the pattern for the rest of his unhappy life. That was his hopeful departure to enrol in the Royal Academy Schools, his failure to do so, his squandering of the funds that had been raised with much difficulty to send him there, and his panic-stricken invention of a fictitious excuse to justify his unworthy performance, a series of events which, in different forms, was to recur over and over again. There can be no doubt that he had a talent for painting, but it was never developed, never submitted to the necessary rigorous discipline, and although he tried again in Bradford, because of this early lack of training, he had doomed himself to failure.

His tragedy was not that he was the damned and wicked creature into which he had fictionalized himself by the end, but that his gifted, generous, warm-hearted character was flawed by an apparently irremediable lack of self-discipline, and the fatal weakness that led to his final and devastating dependence upon alcohol and drugs.

Anne and Branwell were linked by Aunt Branwell's preference for them, and by their shared experience in the Robinson family. Anne's spirit survives, perhaps not so much through her poems and novels, as in the few verses of hers that have been included to give consolation and comfort in the hymn books. Most people that sing and receive help from her simple truthful words may never know that they were written by Anne Brontë. But anyone who has studied her life must feel that this is the quiet and anonymous way in which she would have best liked her spirit to live on.

'Branwell is not only the most underestimated member of the Brontë family but also one of the most underrated of English poets,'[26] Dr Juliet Barker states in her recent selection of poems. This is understandable, since in the wealth of English literature there are so many underrated, even forgotten poets. Fortunately, the fame of Charlotte and Emily will always keep the memories of Anne and Branwell alive.

Yet, above all, he will be remembered for his portrait of Anne, Emily, and Charlotte, and the delicate profile of Emily that hangs beside it. Haunting paintings in sharp contrast to some of the bland representations of celebrities that surround them in the National Portrait Gallery. By so vividly depicting his sisters, who went on to become famous, Branwell Brontë undoubtedly achieved his own particular and enduring fame.

Principal Works Consulted

Alexander, Christine, *The Early Writings of Charlotte Brontë*, Blackwell, 1983

Allott, Miriam, ed. *Casebook, Charlotte Brontë, Jane Eyre & Villette*, Macmillan, 1973

Barker, Juliet, R.V., *The Brontës Selected Poems*, Dent, 1985

Bentley, Phyllis, ed. *The Professor, Tales from Angria, Emma: a fragment* by Charlotte Brontë, Collins, 1954

Bentley, Phyllis, *The Brontës and their World*, Thames & Hudson, 1969

Brontë, Emily Jane and Anne, *The Poems* of, The Shakespeare Head, ed. T.J. Wise & J.A. Symington, Basil Blackwell, Oxford, 1936

Brontë, Anne, *The Poems of, A new Text and Commentary* by Edward Chitham, Macmillan, 1979

Brontë, Anne, *Agnes Grey*, Introduction Anne Smith, Everyman Paperback, Dent, 1985

Brontë, Anne, *The Tenant of Wildfell Hall*, Introduction Margaret Lane, Everyman Paperback, 1982

Brontë, Charlotte and Patrick Branwell, *The Poems* of, The Shakespeare Head, ed. T.J. Wise & J.A. Symington, Basil Blackwell, Oxford, 1936

Brontë, P. Branwell, *History of Angria*, BPM

Brontë, P. Branwell, *The Odes of Horace*, Introduction by John Drinkwater, privately printed 1923

Brontë, Branwell, *The Poems*, ed. Tom Winnifrith, New York University Press, New York and London, 1983

Brontë, Branwell, *And the Weary are at Rest*, privately printed, 1924, BPM

Brontë, Charlotte, *The Poems*: A new annotated and enlarged edition of the Shakespeare Head Brontë, ed. Tom Winnifrith, Basil Blackwell, Oxford, 1985

Brontë, Charlotte, *Jane Eyre*, Introduction Margaret Lane, Everyman Paperback, Dent. 1980

Brontë, Charlotte, *Shirley*, Introduction Margaret Lane, Everyman Paperback, Dent, 1983

Brontë, Charlotte, *Villette*, Introduction Margaret Drabble, Everyman Paperback, Dent, 1983

Brontë, Charlotte, *The Professor and Emma, a fragment*, Introduction Anne Smith, Everyman Paperback, Dent, 1985

Brontë, Emily, *Wuthering Heights & Poems*, Introduction by Margaret Drabble, including Charlotte's Biographical Notice of Ellis and Acton Bell, 1850, Everyman Paperback, Dent, 1984

Brontës, The; Critical Heritage, Routledge & Kegan Paul, 1974

Chitham, Edward, *The Poems of Anne Brontë, A New Text and Commentary*, Macmillan, 1979

Chitham, Edward & Winnifrith, Tom, *Brontë Facts and Brontë Problems*, Macmillan, 1983

Craik, Wendy, *The Brontë Novels*, Methuen, 1972

Crompton, Margaret, *Passionate Search*, Cassell, 1955

Du Maurier, Daphne, *The Infernal World of Branwell Brontë*, Gollancz, 1960

Gaskell, Elizabeth Cleghorn, *The Life of Charlotte Brontë*, Everyman edition, 1908, constantly reprinted

Gaskell, Elizabeth Cleghorn, *Life and Letters*, ed. Chapple & Pollard, Manchester University, 1966.

Gérin, Winifred, *Anne Brontë*, Nelson, 1959

Gérin, Winifred, *Branwell Brontë*, Nelson, 1961

Gérin, Winifred, *Charlotte Brontë*, OUP, 1967

Gérin, Winifred, *Emily Brontë*, OUP, 1978

Graves, Richard Percival, *The Powys Brothers*, Routledge & Kegan Paul 1983

Grundy, Francis, *Pictures of the Past*, Griffiths & Farrar, 1878

Harrison, Ada, and Stansfield Derek, *Anne Brontë, Her Life and Work*, Methuen, 1959

Hatfield, C.J., ed. *The Complete Poems of Emily Jane Brontë*, Columbia University Press, 1941

Lane, Margaret, *The Brontë Story*, Heinemann, 1953

Leyland, Francis A., *The Brontë Family, with special reference to Patrick Branwell Brontë*, London, 1886

Lock, John & Dixon, W.T., *A Man of Sorrow*, Nelson, 1965

Moers, Ellen, *Literary Women*, W.H. Allen, 1977

Peters, Margot, *Charlotte Brontë: Style in the Novel*, Madison, University of Wisconsin Press, 1973

Peters, Margot, *Unquiet Soul*, Hodder & Stoughton, 1975

Pinion, F.B., *A Brontë Companion*, Macmillan, 1975

Ratchford, F.E., *The Brontës' Web of Childhood*, Columbia University Press, 1941.

Ratchford, F.W., *Gondal's Queen,* University of Texas Press, 1955

Reid Bankes, Lynne, *The Dark Quartet,* Weidenfeld and Nicolson, 1976

Scott, P.J.M., *Anne Brontë, A New Critical Assessment,* Vision and Barnes Noble, 1983

Sinclair, May, *The Three Brontës,* Hutchinson, 1912

Shorter, Clement, *The Brontës and their Circle,* Dent, 1914

Shorter, Clement, *The Brontës, Life and Letters,* 2 vols, Hodder, 1908

Taylor, Mary, *Letters from New Zealand and Elsewhere,* Auckland and Oxford University Press, 1972

Transactions of the Brontë Society, 1898 to present date

Wilks, Brian, *The Brontës,* Hamlyn, 1975

Winnifrith, Tom, *The Brontës and their Background,* Macmillan, 1973

Winnifrith, Tom and Chitham, Edward, *Brontë Facts and Brontë Problems,* Macmillan Press Ltd., 1983

Wise, T.J., and Symington, J.A., ed. *Miscellaneous and Unpublished Writings, Charlotte and P. Branwell Brontë,* The Shakespeare Head, Basil Blackwell, Oxford, 1936

Wise, T.J. and Symington, J.A., *The Poems of Charlotte Bronte and Patrick Branwell Brontë,* The Shakespeare Head, Basil Blackwell, Oxford, 1934

Wise, T.J. and Symington, J.A., *The Poems of Emily Jane and Anne Brontë,* Shakespeare Head, Basil Blackwell, Oxford, 1934

Wise, T.J. and Symington, J.A., *The Brontës, Their Lives, Friendships and Correspondence,* 4 vols, Shakespeare Head, Basil Blackwell, Oxford, 1932

Source Notes

Quotations from the novels have been taken from the Dent Everyman paperback edition, all six of which are currently in print. References have been abbreviated as follows: Anne Brontë, *Agnes Grey*, 1985 – AB, *AG*; Anne Brontë, *The Tenant of Wildfell Hall*, 1982 – AB, *TWH*; Charlotte Brontë, *Jane Eyre*, 1980 – CB, *JE*; Charlotte Brontë, *Shirley*, 1983 – CB, *S*; Charlotte Brontë, *Villette*, 1983 – CB, *V*; Emily Brontë, *Wuthering Heights*, EB, *WH*.

Other abbreviations in order of use: Gaskell, Elizabeth Cleghorn, *The Life of Charlotte Brontë*, Everyman edition, J. M. Dent & Sons Ltd., 1908 – Gaskell; *Brontë Society Transactions* – BST; Brontë Parsonage Museum, BPM; Gérin, Winifred, *Anne Brontë* – Gérin, *AB*; Gérin, Winifred, *Branwell Brontë* – Gérin, *BB*; Gérin, Winifred, *Charlotte Brontë* – Gérin, *CB*; Gérin Winifred, Emily Brontë – Gérin, *EB*; Shorter, Clement, *The Brontës: Life and Letters* – Shorter, *LL*; Shorter, Clement, *The Brontës and their Circle* – Shorter, *BC*; Leyland, F. A., *The Brontë Family with Special Reference to Patrick Branwell Brontë* – Leyland, *BF*; ed. T. J. Wise & J. A. Symington, *The Poems of Charlotte and Patrick Branwell Brontë* – W & S, *Poems CB & PBB*; ed. T. J. Wise & J. A. Symington, *The Poems of Emily Jane Brontë and Anne Brontë* – W & S, *Poems EJB & AB*; ed. Chitham, Edward, *The Poems of Anne Brontë* – Chitham, *AB*; ed. T. J. Wise & J. A. Symington, *The Brontës: their Lives, Friendships and Correspondence* – W & S, *Brontës*; Brontë, P. Branwell *The Odes of Horace* – BB, *Odes Horace*

1 : Origins: from Dewsbury to Cowan Bridge, 1812–24

1. Gaskell, p 25
2. Ibid, p 26
3. Lock & Dixon, *A Man of Sorrow*, p 238
4. Gaskell, p 3

5. Ibid, p 384

6. BST, Philip Rhodes, *A Medical Appraisal of the Brontës*, 1972

7. Lock & Dixon, *A Man of Sorrow*, p 237

8. Register, Clergy Daughters' School, Cowan Bridge, 1824, Casterton, Westmorland.

2: Only Four Left, 1824–31

1. BST, *Interview with Nancy Wainwright*, 1958

2. Shorter, *LL*, p 102

3. Gaskell, p 45

4. Gaskell, p 36

5. Brontë, P. B., *History of the Young Men*, 1830, BPM

6. Brontë, C., *History of the Year 1829*, BPM

7. Brontë, C., *Tales of the Islanders*, Gérin, p 31 (Christopher North – the pen name of John Wilson – & Co. were writers on *Blackwood's Magazine*)

8. Brontës early writings, see, Ratchford, F. E., *The Brontës' Web of Childhood*, and *Gondal's Queen*; Alexander, Christine, *The Early Writings of Charlotte Brontë*.

9. Graves, Richard Percival, *The Powys Brothers*, p 13

10. Shorter, *LL*, i, pp 304–5

11. Gérin, *BB*, p 27

12. Brontë, C., *History of the Year 1829*, BPM, Gaskell, p 55

13. Brontë, Emily, Diary Paper, November 24 1834, BPM

14. Gaskell, p 65

15. Ibid, pp 60–61

16. Ibid, p 66

17. Shorter, *LL*, i, p 84

18. Shorter, *BC*, p 111

3: Into the World, 1832–35

1. Leyland, *BF*, I, p 88

2. W & S, *Poems from CB & PBB*, p 257. For insights into the editorship of Wise and Symington, see Chitham, E. & Winnifrith, T., *Brontë Facts and Brontë Problems*, Chapter 11

3. BST, Edgerley, 1944

4. Shorter, *LL*, i, p 84

5. Shorter, *LL*, i, p 103

6. Ibid, i, p 103

7. Brontë, C., *My Angria and the Angrians*, 1834, BPM

8. Shorter, *LL*, i, p 131

9. Shorter, *LL*. ii, p 419

10. Brontë, C., *Biographical Notice*, 1850, EB, *WH*, xxxi

11. Brontë, P. B., *History of Angria*, BPM

12. W & S, *Poems, CB & PPB* p 306; among others, these lines appeared in *The Complete Works of Emily Brontë in 2 vols*. ed. Shorter, 1910

13. Brontë, P. B. to *Blackwood's Magazine*, December 1835
Oliphant, M., *Annals of a Publishing House*, 1897

14. W & S, *Poems, C & PBB*, p 293
    PBB to Wordsworth, 19 Jan. 1837

15. W & S, *Poems, C & PBB*, p 266

4: *Tension and Change, 1835–8*

1. Roehead Journal, Bonnell Collection (No. 98), BPM

2. Gaskell, p 92

3. Shorter, *BC*, p 164

4. BST, 1898, pp 26–27

5. W & S, *Poems, EJB & AB*, p 197; (Chitham, *AB*, p 60)

6. Ibid, *The North Wind*, p 200; (Chitham, *AB*, pp 63/4)

7. Gaskell, p 109

8. W & S, *Brontës*, p 110

9. EB., Diary Paper, 26 June 1837, BPM

10. W & S, *Poems, EJB & AB*, p 191

11. Convincing doubts have been expressed about the traditional dating of Emily's stay at Law Hill, and similar details. For a discussion of these and other interesting points, see Chitham, E. and Winnifrith, T., *Brontë Facts and Problems*. See also the diary of Caroline Walker, Halifax Public Library.

12. Gaskell, p 96

13. Gérin, *EB*, p 82

14. Brontë, P. Branwell, *Angrian Fragment*, BPM

15. Shorter, *LL*, i, p 340

16. Ibid, p 138

17. BPM

18. BST, 1895

19. W & S, The Brontës, p 167

5: Three Lost Posts, 1839–40

1. AB, *AG*, p 7
2. BST, Brooke, Susan, 1958
3. Shorter, *LL*, i, p 174
4. AB, *AG*, p 10
5. Ibid, p 12
6. Gaskell, p 113
7. AB, *AG*, p 13
8. Ibid, p 12, 13
9. Ibid, p 20
10. Ibid, p 39
11. Ibid, p 40
12. Ibid, p 41
13. Ibid, p 41
14. Shorter, *LL*, p 159
15. Ibid, p 163
16. Ibid, p 165
17. Ibid, p 175
18. Nussey, Ellen, *Reminiscences of CB*, Scribners Magazine, May 1871
19. Shorter, *LL*, i, p 171
20. Ibid, i, pp, 167/8
21. W & S, *Brontës*, i, pp 198–9
22. Ibid, p 198–9
23. PBB, *Odes Horace*, BPM
24. W & S, *Poems, CB & PBB*, p 372
25. Shorter, *LL*, i, p 181
26. PBB, *Odes Horace*, BPM

6: Wish for Wings, 1840–41

1. Leyland, *BF*, I, p 266
2. W & S, *Poems, CB & PBB*, p 382
3. W & S, *Poems, EJB & AB*, p 208; (Chitham, p 72)
4. Gaskell, p 132
5. W & S, *Poems, EJB & AB*, p 209; (Chitham, p 74)
6. Ibid, p 211

7. Gaskell, p 125
8. Shorter, *LL*, i, pp 206–7
9. AB, *AG*, p 46
10. Robinson Papers, BPM
11. AB, *AG*, p 50
12. Ibid, pp 50–51
13. W & S, *Poems, EJB & AB*, p 118
14. Shorter, *LL*, i, p 216
15. Ibid, p 218
16. Ibid, pp 219–21
17. Ibid, pp 223–4
19. AB, *AG*, p 82
19. Ibid, pp 154–5
20. W & S, *Poems, EJB & AB*, p 213

7: *Sorrows, Hopes and Fears, 1842–4*

1. Brontë, P. B., *Luddenden Foot Notebook*, BPM
2. Grundy, Francis, *Pictures of the Past*, p 75
3. Brontë, P. B., *Luddenden Foot Notebook*, BPM
   W & S, *Poems, CB & PBB*, p 389
4. Grundy, Francis, *Pictures of the Past*, p 85
5. W & S, *Brontës*, i, p 270
6. W & S, *Poems, CB & PBB*, p 391
7. Shorter, *LL*, p 227
8. AB, *AG*, p 137
9. Shorter, *LL*, p 239
10. Gaskell, p 151
11. Shorter, *LL*, ii, pp 237–8
12. Lock & Dixon, *A Man of Sorrow*, pp 308–310, BPM
13. W & S, *Poems, EJB & AB*, p 229; (Chitham, p 100–1)
14. Ibid
15. Grundy, Francis, *Pictures of the Past*, p 83
16. Shorter, *LL*, i, p 246
17. Ibid, p 243
18. Gaskell, p 90
19. AB, *AG*, pp 87–8
20. W & S, *Poems, EJB & AB*, p 216; (Chitham, p 84)

21. Ibid, p 220; (p 89)
22. AB, *TWH*, p 140
23. Shorter, *LL*, i, p 226
24. W & S, *Poems, CB & PBB*, p 180
25. Shorter, *LL*, i, p 265
26. Ibid, p 105
27. CB, *V*, Chapter 15
28. Shorter, *LL*, i, p 270
29. CB to Constantin Heger, 18 Nov. 1845, British Museum, Add. Mss. 38732, translated from the French by M. H. Spielmann
30. W & S, *Poems, CB & PBB*, p 240
31. CB to Constantin Heger, 24 July 1844, BM, Add. Mss. 38732, translated from the French by M. H. Spielmann
32. Shorter, *LL*, i, p 277

8 : *The Mystery of Thorp Green Hall: the Bell Brothers' Poems, 1844–6*

1. Gaskell, p 188
2. Ibid
3. Ibid
4. Ibid, pp 194–5
5. Ibid, pp 196–7
6. Robinson Papers, BPM
7. AB, *AG*, p 55
8. Ibid, pp 51–2
9. Ibid, p 52
10. Ibid, p 51
11. Ibid, p 116
12. Ibid, pp 126–7
13. Ibid, p 130
14. Grundy, Francis, *Pictures of the Past*, p 87
15. W & S, *The Brontës*, ii, p 21
16. Shorter, *LL*, i, pp 304–5
17. W & S, *The Brontës*, ii, pp 42–43
18. Grundy, Francis, *Pictures of the Past*, pp 87–88
19. W & S, *The Brontës*, ii, p 42
20. Leyland, Francis, *BF.* Vol II, p 76
21. W & S, *Poems, CB & PBB*, p 415

22. Robinson Papers, Account Book, BPM
23. Shorter, *LL*, i, p 306
24. AB, *AG*, p 64
25. Gérin, *AB*, p 204
26. Shorter, *LL*, i, p 306
27. W & S, *Brontës*, ii, p 59
28. Shorter, *LL*, i, p 301
29. CB, *Biographical Notice*, 1850 (in Everyman, Emily Brontë, *Wuthering Heights and Poems*, p xxxi)
30. Ibid, p xxxii
31. W & S, Brontës, ii, pp 83–4
32. The Robinson Papers, BPM
33. Shorter, *LL*, i, p 331
34. Leyland, *BF*, ii, p 144
35. Ibid, p 98
36. Robinson Papers, BPM
37. Ibid
38. Ibid
39. W & S, *Brontës*, ii, p 125

9: *And the Weary are at Rest, 1846–8*

1. W & S, *Poems, CB & PBB*, p 432
2. Ibid, pp 397–9
3. Gaskell, p 209
4. Shorter, *LL*, i, p 341
5. W & S, *Brontës*, iii, p 331
6. Shorter, *LL*, i, p 347
7. W & S, *Brontës*, ii, p 132
8. Gaskell, p 222
9. W & S, *Brontës*, ii, p 149
10. Ibid, p 162
11. BST, 1918
12. CB, *JE*, p 422
13. Smith, George, *Cornhill Magazine*, December 1900
14. W & S, *The Brontës*, ii, pp 250–4
15. Smith, *Cornhill Magazine*, December 1900
16. W & S, *The Brontës*, ii, pp 250–4

17. Smith, *Cornhill Magazine*, December 1900
18. Ibid
19. Shorter, *LL*, i. pp 437–8
20. Ibid, p 438
21. Ibid, p 439
22. W & S, *The Brontës*, ii, pp 239–40
23. Ibid, p 240–3
24. Brontë, Anne, Preface to second edition *TWH*
25. AB, *TWH*, pp 217–8
26. W & S, *The Brontës*, ii, p 223
27. W & S, *The Brontës*, ii, p 224
28. Gaskell, pp 197–8
29. Grundy, Francis, *Pictures of the Past*, p 91
30. W & S, *The Brontës*, ii, p 264

10: With Those that I have Loved and Lost, 1848–9

1. W & S, *The Brontës*, ii, p 264
2. Robinson Papers, BPM
3. Ibid
4. Shorter, *LL*, ii, p 12
5. CB, *Biographical Notice*, 1850, Everyman EB, *WH*, p xxxvi
6. Shorter, *LL*, i, p 464
7. Gaskell, pp 257–8
8. W & S, *Poems, EJB & AB*, p 14
9. W & S, *The Brontës*, ii, p 294
10. BST, 1932, 21–2
11. W & S, *Poems, EJB & AB*, p 295
12. W & S, *The Brontës*, ii, p 299
13. Gaskell, pp 194–5
14. Gaskell, p 271
15. Ibid, p 272
16. Ibid, pp 272–3
17. Ibid, p 273
18. W & S, *The Brontës*, ii, p 339
19. W & S, *Poems, EJB & AB*, p 292 (Chitham p 160)

11: Gone like Dreams, 1849–55

1. W & S, *The Brontës*, ii, p 339
2. Ibid, iii, p 29
3. Thackeray, *The Last Sketch*, Cornhill Magazine, April 1860
4. Martineau, H., *Autobiography*, ii, p 326
5. Smith, G., *Cornhill Magazine*, December, 1900
6. W & S, *The Brontës*, iii, p 60
7. Thackeray-Ritchie, Anne, *Chapters from some Memoirs*, pp 60–65
8. Gaskell, E., *Letters of*, to C. Winkworth, 25 August 1850, p 123
9. W & S, *The Brontës*, iii, p 189
10. Ibid, iii, p 208
11. Ibid, p 241
12. Ibid, iv, p 96
13. Ibid, p 44
14. Ibid, p 38
15. Thackeray, W. M., *Letters and Private Papers*, iii, 231-253
16. Gaskell, p 370
17. W & S, *The Brontës*, iv, pp 28–30
18. Ibid, p 65
19. BST, 1972
20. W & S, *The Brontës*, iv, p 164
21. Gaskell, p 400

12: Peaceful Resolution

1. CB, *My Angria and the Angrians*, BPM
2. W & S, *Poems, EJB & AB*, p 281, Chitham, p 36
3. Ibid, p 250, Chitham, p 121
4. W & S, *Poems, EJB & AB*, p 272
5. Ibid, p 219
6. Moore, George, *Conversations in Ebury Street*, p 219
7. AB, *AG*, p 164
8. W & S, *Poems, EJB & AB*, p 241, Chitham, p 113
9. Gaskell, p 240
10. Austen, Jane, *Pride and Prejudice*, Penguin, 1972, p 79
11. AB, *AG*, p 17

12. AB, *TWH*, p 11
13. EB, *WH*, p 22
14. Ibid, p 92`
15. *BST*, 17, 2, p 281
16. AB, *TWH*, p 153
17. Ibid
18. Ibid, pp 22/3
19. Ibid, p 356
20. Ibid, p 388
21. Ibid, p 389
22. Brontë, P. B., *Odes Horace*, BPM
23. Brontë, P. B., *And the Weary are at Rest*, BPM
24. Ibid
25. Ibid
26. Barker, Juliet R. V., ed., *Selected Poems*, p xxv

Index